THE ADVERSARIAL PROCESS AND THE VULNERABLE WITNESS

The Adversarial Process and the Vulnerable Witness

LOUISE ELLISON

OXFORD

UNIVERSITY PRESS

This book has been printed digitally and produced in a standard specification
in order to ensure its continuing availability

OXFORD
UNIVERSITY PRESS

Great Clarendon Street, Oxford OX2 6DP

Oxford University Press is a department of the University of Oxford.
It furthers the University's objective of excellence in research, scholarship,
and education by publishing worldwide in

Oxford New York

Auckland Cape Town Dar es Salaam Hong Kong Karachi
Kuala Lumpur Madrid Melbourne Mexico City Nairobi
New Delhi Shanghai Taipei Toronto
With offices in
Argentina Austria Brazil Chile Czech Republic France Greece
Guatemala Hungary Italy Japan South Korea Poland Portugal
Singapore Switzerland Thailand Turkey Ukraine Vietnam

ISBN 978-0-19-829909-7

Printed and bound in Great Britain by CPI Antony Rowe,
Chippenham and Eastbourne

Cover illustration: Priscilla Coleman

Acknowledgements

I am grateful to the Department of Law, University of Reading for the valuable support I received while completing this monograph. I also thank the Dutch legal practitioners whom I interviewed in the Netherlands for their unstinting co-operation.

General Editor's Preface

Recent years have seen increasing understanding of, and concern for, the plight of vulnerable and intimidated witnesses in the criminal justice system. In pragmatic terms, heavy reliance is necessarily placed on the evidence of these witnesses if the guilty are to be convicted. Yet even basic rights which should be protected — such as those under Articles 8, 5, and even 3 of the European Convention on Human Rights — have not always received recognition and respect. Now many legislatures are moving quickly to introduce new measures in an effort to improve the lot of such witnesses. In this detailed study, Dr Ellison subjects these measures, and the assumptions underlying them, to critical scrutiny. Relevant psychological research is reviewed, as are the ethical and cultural issues arising from the English approach to the cross-examination of witnesses. Questions are raised about the compatibility of the special measures with the structure of English evidence law, and with core tenets such as the principle of orality. The innovative protections for witnesses introduced by the Youth Justice and Criminal Evidence Act 1999 are examined critically, in the context of reforms introduced or recommended in other jurisdictions, and the author also draws on her comparative research in the Netherlands. The result is a searching re-assessment of this sensitive and increasingly important field of criminal justice policy.

Andrew Ashworth
October 2001

Contents

Table of Cases

Table of Statutes

I.

Introduction

Witnesses play a crucial part within the criminal justice system, as the successful prosecution of offenders will usually depend upon their co-operation from the initial stage of reporting to the trial itself. Until quite recently however it was commonplace to describe the witness as the 'forgotten man' of the criminal process.[1] Only relatively recently has research focused on witnesses and their experiences within the trial system. This belated research revealed a pattern of 'witness-blindness' and official neglect with witnesses receiving scant information and support and enduring considerable inconvenience, discomfort, and distress as a result.[2] At court, witnesses routinely experienced lengthy, unexplained delays and intimidation as they were forced to share limited accommodation and inadequate facilities with the defendant and his or her supporters.[3] More significantly, the process of testifying was itself found to be extremely stressful for many witnesses given, *inter alia*, the 'strange' court-room environment, the public nature of criminal trials and the aggressiveness of cross-examination. As Rock reports, witnesses arrive at court to find themselves vilified and shamed as they are questioned about matters that are painful and embarrassing by a examiner intent on destroying their credibility.[4] In sum, the experience of giving evidence was for many confusing, intimidating, and demeaning.

In recent years the needs and interests, and indeed rights of witnesses have gained some recognition. Key in bringing witness protection issues to the fore have been concerns regarding an increase in international and organized crime and the threat of intimidation. In 1997 the Council of Europe issued *Recommendation No. R (97) 13 on Intimidation of Witnesses and the Rights of the Defence*. It was unacceptable, the recommendation states, that the criminal justice system might fail to bring defendants to trial and obtain a judgment because witnesses were effectively discouraged from testifying freely and truthfully. The responsibility placed on witnesses gives rise, the document maintains, to a corresponding duty on the part of the criminal justice system to protect their interests through the adoption, where necessary, of appropriate legislative and practical measures. A further major development was the ruling of the European Court of Human Rights in the case of *Doorson v The Netherlands*.[5]

---

[1] Ash, M., 'On Witnesses: A Radical Critique of Criminal Court Procedures' (1972) 48 *Notre Dame Lawyer*, 159, 160.

[2] Raine, J. W. and Smith, R. E., *The Victim/Witness in Court Project: Report of the Research Programme* (1991, London: Victim Support).

[3] Shapland, J., Willmore, J. and Duff, P., *Victims in the Criminal Justice System* (1985, Aldershot: Gower).

[4] Rock, P., *The Social World of the English Crown Court* (1993, Oxford: Clarendon Press) 35.

[5] *Doorson v The Netherlands* (1996) 22 EHRR 330.

For the first time the Court recognized that witnesses had rights which were to be balanced, in line with principles of fairness, against those of defendants. In this case the right of an anonymous witness to privacy and protection from intimidation were weighed against the right of the defendant to challenge contrary evidence. It was decided that the compensatory procedures adopted by the national courts had allowed for the meeting of the former without undue infringement of the latter.[6] The ruling was to an extent foreshadowed by decisions of the European Commission of Human Rights in which the interests of sexual offence complainants were recognized as a legitimate consideration for national courts.[7]

At an international level, the establishment of international criminal tribunals for the former Yugoslavia and Rwanda to deal with gross violations of humanitarian law represents a landmark in the recognition of witnesses' rights. The tribunals' rules of procedure and evidence require, *inter alia*, that the safety of witnesses be balanced against the fair trial rights of accused persons. The rules provide for the protection of witnesses from harassment, publicity, and intimidation and in so doing provide valuable guiding principles for critiques of domestic laws.[8] The rules of evidence and procedure for the International Criminal Court are couched in similar terms.

In domestic fora political and academic interest has until now focused predominantly on 'victim-witnesses' or complainants as opposed to witnesses more generally.[9] The last two decades have seen a massive shift in thinking about victims of crime and their place within the trial system. Traditionally marginalized and regarded essentially as a 'professional tool at the disposal of lawyers, judges and court officials',[10] the victim of crime has now become a key player in the criminal justice process.[11] This revival of interest in victims is attributable to no single cause but to a diverse range of factors that can be given only cursory mention here. It is commonly accepted that the advent of both national and local victimization surveys played a key role by disclosing the long-term physical, emotional, and financial impact of

---

[6] See Chapter IV below.

[7] *Baegen v The Netherlands* (1995) Application 16696/90; *Finkensieper v The Netherlands* (1995) Application 19525/92.

[8] Dennis, I., 'Criminal Procedure: The Advancement of International Standards' in (eds.) Nijboer, J. F. and Reijntjes, J. M., *Proceedings of the first World Conference on New Trends in Criminal Investigation and Evidence*, The Hague, The Netherlands, 1–5 December 1995; World Conference on New Trends in Criminal Investigation and Evidence (1997, Netherlands: Koninklijke Vermande) 523.

[9] The *Charter for Court Users*, first published in 1992, did set out the standards of service witnesses could expect from the courts. Home Office, *Courts Charter* (1992, London: Home Office). This was followed by the *Statement of National Standards of Witness Care in the Criminal Justice System*, commissioned by the Trial Issues Group, which similarly sets national parameters for standards of service for witnesses in criminal cases.

[10] Pollard, C., 'Victims and the Criminal Justice System: A New Vision' [2000] *Criminal Law Review* 5.

[11] Zedner, L., 'Victims' in (eds.) Maguire, M., Morgan, R. and Reiner, R., *The Oxford Handbook of Criminology* 2nd edn. (1997, Oxford: Oxford University Press) 577.

victimization.[12] Studies found that crime victims suffered a wide range of deleterious effects including persistent and in some cases profound psychological consequences.[13] Psychologists have, for example, documented the devastating and long-term debilitating effects of offences such as rape[14] and prolonged physical abuse.[15] In disclosing the scale of misery wrought by crime, victimization surveys and psychological research fuelled demands for victims to be provided with support and assistance in their recovery.

The growth of the victim movement has also done a great deal to raise the profile of victims of crime and to promote their interests. In the 1970s the pioneering work of feminist campaigners in establishing refuges for victims of domestic violence and rape crisis centres secured unprecedented publicity for the plight of female victims of male violence as well as providing women with much needed practical assistance and support. In the UK organizations such as the Rape Crisis Federation, Women Against Rape ('WAR'), Support After Murder and Manslaughter ('SAMM'), MENCAP, Childline, the Zito Trust, and the NSPCC have all highlighted the plight of specific categories of victims. In recent years the national voluntary organization Victim Support has played a major campaigning role for the greater recognition of victims' rights within the criminal justice system.[16] While adopting an ostentatiously non-political stance, the organization has fostered close ties with successive governments to the extent that it has become the central organ of the victim movement in the UK.[17]

Other factors include the emergence of victimology as a sub-discipline of criminology. Criminological research was preoccupied with the aetiology of crime and naturally focused predominantly on the offender. However, with the publication of Hans Von Hentig's *The Criminal and his Victim* in 1948 the

---

[12] See Rock, P., *Victimology* (1994, Aldershot: Dartmouth) xiii; Lurigio, A. J., 'Are all Victims Alike? The Adverse, Generalised and Differential Impact of Crime' (1987) 33(4) *Crime and Delinquency*, 452.

[13] Shapland *et al.*, for example, interviewed nearly three hundred victims of physical and sexual assault and robbery about the effects that the offence had had on their lives. The researchers found that 75% of those interviewed were still reporting some negative effects two and a half years after the incident had taken place: Shapland *et al.*, n. 3 above. Maguire and Bennett's research into the effects of burglary on victims similarly reported evidence of lasting emotional effects ten weeks after the event: Maguire, M. and Bennett, T., *Burglary in a Dwelling* (1982, London: Heinemann) 125.

[14] Burgess, A.W. and Holmstrom, L. L., 'Rape Trauma Syndrome' (1974) 131 *American Journal of Psychiatry* 981; Resick, P., 'Psychological Effects of Victimization: Implications for the Criminal Justice System' (1987) 33(4) *Crime and Delinquency*, 468.

[15] Walker, L., *The Battered Woman* (1979, New York: Harper & Row).

[16] Victim Support, *The Rights of Victims of Crime: A Policy Paper* (1995, London: Victim Support). See also European Forum for Victim Services, *Statement of Victims' Rights in the Process of Criminal Justice* (1996, London: European Forum). The Forum has 17 member organizations in 15 countries.

[17] Today Victim Support offers help to over one million crime victims and witnesses each year and has 386 schemes covering England, Wales, and Ireland. For the history of Victim Support see Rock, P., *Helping Victims of Crime* (1990, Oxford: Clarendon Press).

victim of crime became a deliberate object of study.[18] The last three decades in particular have seen a proliferation of international victimological research. The Tenth International Symposium on Victimology, held in Montreal, is testament to both the diversity of the subject and to global interest in victim issues. In August 2000 over 1,000 representatives from over forty countries attended over 100 workshops devoted to topics as diverse as crime prevention, restorative justice, victims' rights, violence against women, victimization surveys, fear of crime, witness intimidation, victim compensation, and sentencing.[19]

Finally, the rise of the victim has been linked with a corresponding sense of disillusionment across political parties with the ability of the criminal justice system to 'do anything' about rising crime rates.[20] The relief of victims of crime is by contrast perceived as a feasible objective and one with strong political and personal appeal. As Koffman has remarked, a 'concern for victims provides the "softer face" of official policy at a financial cost which is relatively modest in comparison to the expenditure on the police and the penal system'.[21] Concern that negative experiences with legal authorities among victims may ultimately lead to diminished co-operation and reduced respect for the law is also said to have triggered instrumental policy changes to improve their treatment.[22]

In terms of victim policy, the publication of the first *Victim's Charter* in February 1990 represents the first attempt in England and Wales to mark out appropriate practice for the various agencies of the criminal justice system in their relationship with the victim of crime.[23] Following its publication commentators were quick to point out that, despite a reference to 'rights' in the subtitle, the Charter had no legal status, provided victims with no remedies for deficiency in provision, and therefore could not be said to furnish victims with 'rights' in any meaningful sense.[24] Nevertheless, the Charter can be seen as a major milestone in that it confirmed for the first time that there was a problem to be addressed. A substantially revised *Victim's Charter* was published by the Home Office in 1996. This statement was couched not in terms of 'rights' but in terms of twenty-seven standards of service which victims could expect from the police, the CPS, the Probation Service, and the

---

[18] Von Hentig, H., *The Criminal and his Victim* (1948, New Haven, Conn.: Yale University Press). The needs and interests of victims were not, however, the focus of early victimological research which was narrowly concerned with notions of victim precipitation and victim proneness. See Mendelsohn, B., 'The Origin of the Doctrine of Victimology' in (ed.) Rock, P., *Victimology* (1994, Aldershot: Dartmouth) 4.   [19] See http://www.victimology.nl.

[20] Zedner, n. 11 above, 598.

[21] Koffman, L., *Crime Surveys and Victims of Crime* (1996, Cardiff: University of Wales Press) 27.

[22] Wemmers, J. M., *Victims in the Criminal Justice System* (1996, Amsterdam: Kluger Publications) 215.

[23] Home Office, *Victim's Charter: A Statement of the Rights of Victims of Crime*, (1990, London: HMSO). The Charter's declared guiding principles were that victims deserve to be treated with both sympathy and respect and that any upset and hardship connected with the victim's involvement within the criminal justice system should be minimized.

[24] Fenwick, H., 'Rights of Victims in the Criminal Justice System: Rhetoric or Reality?' [1995] *Criminal Law Review* 843; Fenwick, H., 'Procedural "Rights" of Victims of Crime: Public or Private Ordering of the Criminal Justice Process?' (1997) 60 *Modern Law Review* 317.

Courts.[25] Unlike the original version, the 1996 Charter addressed itself to the victim rather than to service providers and included complaints procedures for individual agencies. In February 2001 the government announced its intention to introduce a new Victim's Charter that would take into account evolving practice and 'developments over the past five years both domestically and internationally, and . . . show the increasing commitment the Government is giving to helping victims and witnesses'.[26] At the same time the government raised the possibility of statutory rights for victims of crime and the appointment of a Victims' Ombudsman who would 'investigate complaints and champion victims' interests'.[27] The proposed 'bill of rights' would include the right to be kept informed, to be treated with respect, and to receive support and protection.[28] The government's announcement follows a series of high-profile victim-centred initiatives. These include the announced introduction of a national Victim Personal Statement scheme, the planned establishment of 'one stop shops' providing victims with a single police point of contact, the development of recommendations made in the Macpherson[29] and Glidewell[30] reports, and changes to the Criminal Injuries Compensation Scheme.

On the international stage, the *United Nations Declaration of Basic Principles of Justice for Victims of Crime and Abuse of Power* 1985 and accompanying *Handbook on Justice for Victims* have proved highly influential in the development of victim policy.[31] Both recommend measures to be taken on behalf of victims of crime internationally, regionally, and nationally to improve access to justice and fair treatment, restitution, compensation, and assistance. At the European level, the Portuguese Presidency of the Council of Ministers submitted a draft Framework Decision on the status of victims under criminal procedures in March 2000.[32] The draft forms part of the extension of the conclusions of the October 1999 Tampere European Council calling for the establishment of minimum standards for the protection of victims of crime. The draft decision, which remains subject to approval by EU member states, would for the first time provide outline rights for victims across the EU. The draft provides that rules

---

[25] Home Office, *The Victim's Charter: A Statement of the Service Standards for Victims of Crime* (1996, London: HMSO).

[26] Home Office, *A Review of the Victim's Charter* (2001, London: HMSO).

[27] 'The Ombudsman would be an arbiter of last resort should complainants remain unhappy with an agency's response. The Ombudsman would be unable to comment on or intervene in judicial or other legally based decisions, but would be able to investigate and comment on the way a case or an individual victim had been dealt with': ibid., 1.

[28] These same rights were called for in Victim Support's policy paper, *The Rights of Victims of Crime* (1995, London: Victim Support).

[29] Macpherson, W., *The Stephen Lawrence Inquiry: Report of an inquiry* (1999, London: HMSO).

[30] Glidewell, I., *The Review of the Crown Prosecution Service: A report* (1998, London: HMSO).

[31] United Nations, *Handbook On Justice For Victims: On the use and application of the United Nations Declaration of Basic Principles of Justice for Victims of Crime and Abuse of Power* (1999, New York: United Nations ODCCP).

[32] Initiative of the Portuguese Republic with a view to adopting a Council Framework Decision on the standing of victims in criminal proceedings, OJ 2000 C243/4.

and practices regarding the standing and main rights of victims need to be approximated, with particular regard to the right to be treated with respect for their dignity, the right to provide and receive information, the right to understand and to be understood, the right to be protected at the various stages of the procedure, and the right to compensation. In the same year, the European Parliament resolution on the Commission Communication to the Council, the European Parliament and the Economic and Social Committee on *Crime Victims in the European Union: Reflections on Standards and Action* was adopted. This resolution states that the rights of victims of crime must be the subject of more effective and fairer legislation by both member states and the European Union. Alleged victims of crime thus derive standing from their status as complainants and as witnesses more generally.

A. THE YOUTH JUSTICE AND CRIMINAL EVIDENCE ACT 1999

It is against this backdrop that the Labour Party included in its manifesto for the 1997 general election a pledge to provide greater protection for victims in rape and serious sexual offence trials and for those subject to intimidation, including witnesses. To take forward this manifesto commitment the Home Secretary, Jack Straw, established an interdepartmental working group to review current arrangements for assisting and protecting vulnerable and intimidated witnesses. The Group was charged with the task of identifying measures that would improve the treatment of such witnesses, encourage them to give evidence in criminal proceedings, and enable them to give their best evidence in court. At the same time, the group was required to have regard to the interests of justice and the need to balance the rights of the defendant to a fair trial against the needs of witnesses not to be traumatized or intimidated by the criminal justice process. The report of the working group, *Speaking Up for Justice*, was published by the Home Office in June 1998.[33] In total, the group made seventy-eight recommendations for improvements to the criminal justice system including measures to assist witnesses before, during, and after the trial. These recommendations have been largely implemented in Part II of the Youth Justice and Criminal Evidence Act 1999.

The Act represents a major piece of legislation that promises to change the face of criminal trials as far as vulnerable and intimidated witnesses are concerned. Through the issuing of 'special measures directions' eligible adult witnesses will for the first time be afforded the protection formerly reserved for child witnesses in cases of sexual and physical abuse. The available special measures will include the use of live television links and the admission of

---

[33] Home Office, *Speaking Up For Justice: Report of the Interdepartmental Working Group on the Treatment of Vulnerable or Intimidated Witnesses in the Criminal Justice System* (1998, London: Home Office).

video-recorded evidence in place of live testimony. For the first time provision is made for video-recorded pre-trial cross-examination. The established use of screens in court is placed on a statutory footing as are the practices of removing wigs and gowns and clearing the court of spectators. Among the measures to be made available to those with an intellectual or physical disability are intermediaries and communication aids. The former are to be charged with communicating and, where necessary, explaining both questions put to a witness and a witness's replies. In line with the government's pledge to improve the position of rape complainants, the 1999 Act also makes further inroads into the right of defendants to cross-examine witnesses in person and imposes new restrictions on the use of sexual history evidence in sexual offence cases.

The principal declared aim behind the 1999 Act is to improve the quality of evidence received by the courts. This represents a critical acceptance that in some cases traditional methods of proof-taking and testing may militate against receipt of the best evidence potentially available. It is moreover an acknowledgement that certain witnesses are caused unacceptable levels of stress when called upon to testify in accordance with conventional adversarial trial procedures and methods. The 1999 Act represents an attempt to modify orthodox trial arrangements so as to reduce stress and assist eligible vulnerable and intimidated witnesses to give more effective, reliable testimony in criminal proceedings. The approach which the Act embodies can be described as one of *accommodation* in that solutions have been primarily sought and crafted within the constraints of the established trial framework. For all the talk of fundamental change, the touchstones of adversarial trial procedure have been left largely intact. These include the principles of orality with its insistence upon direct oral evidence, and the use of cross-examination as a device for testing the credibility of witnesses. All in all, there has been little deviation from the adversarial model.

A central aim of this book is to demonstrate the significant limitations of an accommodation approach to the problems facing vulnerable and intimidated witnesses. By engaging in a systematic critique of the special measures provisions of the 1999 Act it identifies a basic conflict between the needs and interests of vulnerable witnesses and the assumptions and resultant evidentiary safeguards of the adversarial trial process, thus signalling the need for more radical solutions. At the heart of this conflict is the principle of orality which dictates that witnesses give live testimony in all but limited circumstances. The traditional attachment to orality is explained partly by the fact that proceedings are temporally condensed into a single continuous hearing and partly by the system of jury trial. It is also crucially assumed that testimony presented in open court is made more reliable by the testing conditions that operate therein. For example, public scrutiny, the presence of the accused, and the formality of the court-room itself are thought capable of exciting the conscience of a witness who may otherwise tender dishonest or unconsidered evidence. Live cross-examination conducted before the fact-finder is of course widely regarded within the common law tradition as the most effective means of testing witness credibility. Such is the commitment to orality that out-of-court statements are generally denied evidential status in the absence of any consideration of their probative force.

Chapter II reviews the results of psychological research that has in recent years provided substantial grounds for questioning the wholesale rejection of evidence tendered at the pre-trial stage of proceedings in favour of that elicited in court. Research on eye-witness memory suggests that accounts given at trial many months after a witnessed incident are inevitably affected by both the passage of time and contamination by what is termed 'post-event' information. The best evidence potentially available is thus most likely to be that gathered and recorded shortly after the incident in question. Stress associated with testifying in court has also been found to have a negative correlation with the ability of observers to give complete and accurate versions of witnessed events. A less formal recall environmental with key 'stressors' removed, including the physical presence of the defendant, has been found to be more conducive to reliable reporting. Naturally, the deleterious effects of delay and court-related stress are compounded when the witness is vulnerable by virtue of age, incapacity, or situational factors including the nature of the offence and the threat of intimidation. For these witnesses, who include children, the learning disabled, complainants in sexual offence cases, the elderly, and those with a severe physical or mental disorder, the adversarial process creates intractable difficulties resulting in unnecessary distress and fear in court, prolonged pre-trial stress, and diminished testimonial evidence.

In 1989 the Advisory Group on Video Evidence, chaired by Thomas Pigot QC, examined ways of improving the position of child witnesses within criminal proceedings. The Pigot committee concluded that children testifying in cases of sexual and physical abuse should be spared the ordeal of a courtroom appearance and radically recommended that video-recorded interviews made at preliminary hearings replace both examination in chief and cross-examination. Videotaping a child's evidence at an earlier stage in the process would, the committee concluded, capture a fresher and more reliable account and alleviate the emotional trauma associated with trial delay. The committee also considered the position of vulnerable adult witnesses within the criminal process, including those with learning disabilities and alleged adult victims of sexual offences. The existing circumstances under which such witnesses were required to give evidence were described as 'neither decent nor humane' and the committee recommended the extension of protective measures to these groups. To the disappointment of many, the then government elected to implement a considerably diluted version of the Pigot proposals. Video-recorded interviews with child witnesses were made admissible as an exception to the hearsay rule but this was dependent upon the child being available for cross-examination at trial. The plight of vulnerable adult witnesses was not addressed. Deviation from the orthodox adversarial model was thus effectively checked.

Most of the special measures contained in the Youth Justice and Criminal Evidence Act 1999 ('YJCEA') have been imported directly from the domain of child witnesses. The assumption was apparently made that the established regime was operating sufficiently well to warrant extension to a potentially much broader cohort of witnesses. Chapter III examines recent research which challenges this assumption. The deficiencies of what has become known as the 'half-Pigot' scheme were apparent to critics from the outset. The most obvious was that child witnesses were still required to provide *vive voce* testimony albeit by television link. Recent studies have identified further structural and procedural problems that call into question, *inter alia,* the evidential reliance placed on investigatory video-taped interviews. The YJCEA does, in line with the Pigot committee's original proposals, introduce the possibility of pre-trial cross-examination. It is however envisaged that this special measure will be preserved in the main for child sexual abuse complainants. The majority of vulnerable and intimidated witnesses who qualify for assistance under the Act will continue to testify at trial with the limited protection and questionable advantages that screens, television links, and video-taped interviews afford.

Having analysed the orality principle in terms of an evidentiary dimension, Chapter IV turns to due process concerns and claims that special protective procedures infringe the so-called confrontation rights of defendants. Opponents specifically maintain that the interposing of physical and technological barriers between witness and accused fails to comport with the notions of trial fairness embodied in Article 6(3)(d) of the European Convention on Human Rights. Close examination of recent jurisprudence of the European Court of Human Rights however reveals that the significance attached within adversarial theory to unmediated face-to-face confrontation finds no reflection in contemporary rulings. The right enshrined in Article 6(3)(d) is more accurately described as a right to *challenge*, protecting a defendant's legitimate interest in being able to contradict evidence meaningfully. Further claims that protective procedures imbue the testimony of witnesses with undeserved credibility and interfere unduly with the assessment of witness demeanour are assessed in the light of modern psychological research and found to be unpersuasive. Finally, Chapter IV considers the issue of witnesses' rights and the extent to which the duality of the state and individual accused can be said to have been superseded by the adoption of a balancing of interest approach in the context of criminal trial procedure.

Chapters V and VI focus on what is widely considered to be the most traumatic aspect of testifying for many witnesses, namely cross-examination. As stated, cross-examination is lauded within the common law tradition as the definitive forensic device for exposing testimonial infirmity. Victimological study of trial proceedings has however revealed the extent to which cross-examination is used as a tool to humiliate, intimidate, and confuse opposing witnesses. Intrusive and largely unrestrained attacks are made on the character and general credibility of witnesses, causing extreme distress while threatening to seriously distort the fact-finding process and no doubt acting as a deterrent to future witnesses. Furthermore, cross-examination is littered with linguistic devices and interrogative techniques that disadvantage those with language capacity limited by immaturity or disability. The YJCEA does contain a handful of measures aimed at cross-examination (as stated above) but as will be seen, these promise minimal relief for a minority of witnesses.

A central problem, identified in Chapter VI, is that existing explanations for the treatment of witnesses during cross-examination have tended to examine categories of witness in isolation and to focus on those factors that separate them from other witnesses in alternative trial contexts. This has led to a partial and flawed understanding of cross-examination. Specifically overlooked are the deeper structural issues at play which ultimately shape the experience of witnesses generally. This book aims to provide a broader theoretical framework for understanding the documented tactics of adversary advocacy which posits systemic factors as the key determinants of the conduct of cross-examination. Ranked among these are the ethical and attitudinal commitment of defence lawyers to a conception of advocacy that eschews any responsibility towards opposing parties, and the structural barriers to effective regulation of courtroom questioning. The failure to address cross-examination and its abuses is presented as the major limitation of recent initiatives.

Finally, Chapter VII explores the popular contention that inquisitorial-style criminal proceedings hold inherent advantages for vulnerable and intimidated witnesses. This comparative investigation focuses on the experiences of rape complainants within the Dutch trial process, drawing on the author's research of rape proceedings in the Netherlands, which included interviews with Dutch legal practitioners. It will be seen that a general tolerance of hearsay evidence in the Netherlands and reliance on judge-led interrogation greatly facilitate the integration of the witness's perspective, with tangible benefits for those called upon to give evidence. The aim of this analysis is not to advance the wholesale importation of civil law procedures. The advantages of the Dutch process are, as will be explained, rooted in a different institutional framework and their effectiveness crucially depends upon surrounding assumptions, mechanisms, and procedures. Moreover, common law and civil law systems are based on divergent political and epistemological assumptions and are the products of different national and legal cultures. This presents formidable obstacles to successful cross-jurisdictional transplantation. Comparative study of 'inquisitorial' methods and procedures can nevertheless provide a valuable new perspective on the problems of vulnerable witnesses and close study of alternative fact-finding arrangements can, it will be suggested, assist in the crafting of indigenous solutions.

II.

Orality and the Vulnerable Witness

The principle of orality is a foundation of the adversarial trial. It provides that evidence on disputed questions of fact be given by witnesses called before the court to give oral testimony on matters within their own knowledge. The primacy of oral evidence is in part explained by the structure of adversarial proceeding where evidence is presented before an unprepared fact-finder at a single continuous hearing.[1] A deep-seated belief that oral evidence is invariably best is also rooted in basic assumptions of adversarial theory regarding the optimal testing of informational sources.[2] Great faith is specifically placed in the capacity of cross-examination to expose the dishonest, mistaken, or unreliable witness, and to uncover inconsistency and inaccuracy in oral testimony.[3] The absence of an opportunity to cross-examine is thought sufficient reason alone to exclude hearsay evidence. Additional assurances of reliability are assumed to stem from the oath, the observation of a declarant's demeanour, public scrutiny, and (to a lesser degree) the solemnity and officialty of the court-room.[4] In the case of accusatory witnesses great importance has additionally attached to the physical proximity of the accused. These assumptions together dictate that witnesses appear in court to give evidence in all but a number of very limited circumstances.[5] Heavy reliance on live oral testimony places onerous demands on witnesses, as they

---

[1] 'Unlike the continental system of trials, based on the Civil Law, the English system is an adversary system, in which the contest is waged on a day in court': Egglestone, R., *Evidence, Proof and Probability* (1978, London: Wiedenfeld and Nicolson) 35. The majority of defendants of course never experience the full panoply of the English criminal trial.

[2] Ellison, L., 'The Protection of Vulnerable Witnesses in Court: An Anglo-Dutch Comparison' (1999) 3 *International Journal of Evidence and Proof* 29.

[3] Thus Allan writes: 'First hand witnesses must lay open their memory and perception of the events in question to a process in which virtually any query might be made. In front of the trier of fact the witness's powers of observation, deficiencies of memory, reasoning ability and possible dishonesty are all subject to the most critical examination. In a sense he is vouching for their accuracy. As regards hearsay evidence though, the witness in court need only vouch for the accuracy and honesty of what he heard someone else say. The declarant's frailties and susceptibilities can be hinted at but never probed. Thus hearsay evidence, were it always to be admitted, would be allowed to go to the trier of fact for consideration without this safety check': Allan, J., 'The Working and Rationale of the Hearsay Rule and the Implications of Modern Psychological Knowledge' (1991) 44 *Current Legal Problems* 217.

[4] See generally Choo, A., *Hearsay and Confrontation in Criminal Trials* (1996, Oxford: Clarendon).

[5] In modern debates the hearsay rule is increasingly presented as a means of protecting the confrontation rights of criminal defendants. See, for example, Ho, L., 'A Theory of Hearsay' (1999) 19(3) *Oxford Journal of Legal Studies* 403; Massaro, T., 'The Dignity Value of Face to Face Confrontations' (1988) 40 *University of Florida Law Review* 863. These arguments are addressed in Chapter IV below.

must generally testify to events that occurred months, sometimes years, previously in circumstances widely regarded as stressful. The adversarial process assumes that witnesses will not be unduly affected by delays or overly intimidated by the court process. However, it is increasingly accepted that certain witnesses, due to age, incapacity, the nature of the offence, and other situational factors, may be unable to give their best evidence under conventional conditions.

Ethnographic study, surveys, interviews, and experimental research have combined to produce a substantial international literature on the topic of witnesses. However, there has as yet been little attempt to piece this research together and to address the position of vulnerable witnesses as a class. When research findings are combined, as they are in this Chapter, certain commonalities emerge. Key aspects of the adversarial trial process are identified repeatedly as significant sources of witness stress and dissatisfaction. A negative correlation between high levels of stress and the ability of observers to recall and relay information accurately and effectively is indicated in psychological research. Of equal concern is the work of psychologists on the detrimental effects of lengthy retention intervals on the fullness and reliability of recalled events and the susceptibility of stored memories to distortion. Overall, psychological research suggests that trial delay and court-related stress can significantly undermine the quality of witness testimony and this is supported by victimological studies of criminal trials and witnesses' own comments. In criminal proceedings this situation is compounded by evidentiary rules governing the admissibility of previous consistent statements that ensure that everything, by and large, hinges on a witness's court-room recollections. What begins to emerge is a clear and seemingly irreconcilable conflict between the needs and interests of vulnerable and intimidated witnesses and the basic assumptions and resultant evidentiary safeguards of the adversarial trial process.

A. COURT-RELATED STRESS

1. Child Witnesses

Child complainants of physical and sexual abuse have been the focus of much that has been written on the subject of child witnesses.[6] A common theme throughout the voluminous literature is the stress which child witnesses experience when called upon to testify in court and the possible long-term deleterious impact of legal involvement. In a much cited study, Goodman *et al.* examined the emotional effects of criminal court testimony on child sexual assault victims

---

[6] See generally Dent, H. and Flin, R., *Children as Witnesses* (1992, Chichester: Wiley); Goodman, G. and Bottoms, B., *Child Victims, Child Witnesses* (1993, London: Guilford Press); Spencer, J. R. and Flin, R., *Evidence of Children: The Law and the Psychology* (1993, London: Blackstone).

in a sample of 218 children.[7] The researchers specifically examined the behavioural disturbance of a group of 'testifiers' and compared it to that of a matched control group of 'nontestifiers' at three points following testimony: three months, seven months, and approximately one year later. It was found that testifiers evinced greater emotional disturbance at seven months, though these adverse effects did diminish by the time of the final follow-up. In interviews conducted both before and after testifying the main fear expressed by children concerned having to face the defendant. According to Goodman *et al.*, seeing the defendant in court revived traumatic memories, and reawakened feelings of anger, hurt, and helplessness for children, regardless of age.[8] When questioned some children complained that facing the accused in court 'brought the memory all back again' while others clearly found the experience extremely frightening: 'I was scared. I didn't look at him. If I would have looked at him, I would have freaked.'[9] Overall, Goodman *et al.* conclude that testifying in court was distressing for the majority[10] of child sexual assault victims and that children required greater protection within the criminal process if they were to serve as 'effective and less traumatised witnesses'.[11]

In 1989 the Advisory Group on Video Evidence ('Pigot Committee') reported that testifying in court was a 'harmful, oppressive and often traumatic experience' for child witnesses.[12] The report identified 'confrontation with the accused, the stress and embarrassment of speaking in public especially about sexual matters, the urgent demands of cross-examination, the overweening nature of court-room formalities and the sense of insecurity and uncertainty induced by delays' as key stressors of the criminal process.[13] In the committee's view, these difficulties inhibited the giving of a full account and on occasion prevented the court from receiving any coherent evidence at all when children broke down in the witness box and were unable to continue. As a result, the report maintained, 'some child victims are left with feelings of anger, resentment, frustration and even guilt ... Other consequences are that because offenders are not dealt with by the courts they are free to reoffend ...'[14] Describing then existing procedures as 'fundamentally flawed', the committee

---

[7] Goodman, G., Taub, E., Jones, D., England, P., Port, L., Rudy, L. and Prado, L., *Testifying in Criminal Court: Emotional Effects on Child Sexual Assault Victims* (1992, Chicago, Illinois: University of Chicago Press). See also Lipovsky, J., 'The impact of court on children: Research findings and practical recommendations' (1994) 9(2) *Journal of Interpersonal Violence* 238.

[8] Goodman *et al.*, above n. 7, 120.

[9] Goodman *et al.*, above n. 7, 101. Murray likewise describes the Scottish children she interviewed as 'haunted by the fear of confronting the accused in the court-room': Murray, K., *Live television link: An evaluation of its use by child witnesses in Scottish criminal trials* (1995, Edinburgh: The Scottish Office) ii. See also Childline, *Going to court: Child witnesses in their own words* (1996, London: Childline).

[10] A small number of child victims were upset because they did not take the stand.

[11] Goodman *et al.*, n. 7 above, 126.

[12] Home Office, *Pigot Committee: Report of the Advisory Group on Video Evidence* (1989, London: HMSO). The group was established to consider the use of video recordings as a means of taking the evidence of children and other vulnerable witnesses in criminal trials; see Chapter III below.

[13] Ibid. para. 2.10.   [14] Ibid. para. 2.15.

recommended that children in sexual and physical abuse violence cases ought never to appear in public as witnesses in the Crown Court, whether in open court or protected by screens or closed-circuit television, unless they wished to do so. The committee attached particular importance to the expressed opinions of paediatricians, psychiatrists, and social workers on the prolonged and sometimes severe adverse effects of testifying in open court.

Although child witnesses in abuse cases have been the primary focus of research, it is generally accepted that the same stressors affect children who either experience or witness other criminal events. A report by the Australian Law Reform Commission, for example, acknowledges that children are generally intimidated and confused by the appearance of court personnel in unfamiliar costumes, distressed by the presence of members of the public in court, and particularly fearful of confronting the accused.[15] Other studies confirm that the size and physical layout of the court-room are sources of considerable anxiety.[16] Children's lack of exposure to formal situations of any kind, their relative naïvety about the legal system, particularly its adversarial nature, and their less developed social, emotional, intellectual, and linguistic capacities all serve to compound the stress of the event.

Measures have of course been introduced in England and Wales to ameliorate the ordeal of child witnesses in sexual and physical abuse cases.[17] Screens have been used for a number of years to shield child witnesses from the gaze of a defendant.[18] The Criminal Justice Act 1988 made it possible, with the leave of the court, for a child witness to give evidence by means of a live television link from a room adjacent to the court.[19] This innovation was followed a few years later by the possibility of allowing a video-taped investigative interview to replace a child's examination in chief.[20] How effective these measures have since proved in reducing stress and promoting fuller more accurate evidence is discussed in Chapter III below.

---

[15] Australian Law Reform Commission, *Report 84, Seen and heard: Priority for children in the legal process* (1997, Sydney: Australian Law Reform Commission) para. 14.116. See also Queensland Law Reform Commission, *The Receipt of Evidence by Queensland Courts: The Evidence of Children Discussion Paper No. 53* (1998, Brisbane: Queensland Law Reform Commission).

[16] See for example Flin, R. H., Davies, G. and Tarrant, A., *The child witness: Final report to the Scottish Home and Health Department* (1988, Aberdeen: Robert Gordon's Institute); Flin, R., 'Hearing and Testing Children's Evidence' in (eds.) Goodman, G. and Bottoms, B., *Child Victims, Child Witnesses* (1993, New York: Guilford Press) 279.

[17] See Bull, R. and Davies, G., 'The effect of child witness research on legislation in Great Britain' in (eds.) Bottoms, B. and Goodman, G., *International Perspectives on Child Abuse and Children's Testimony: Psychological Research and the Law* (1996, California: Sage) 96; Myers, J., 'A decade of international reform to accommodate child witnesses' in the same volume, 221.

[18] The practice was approved by the Court of Appeal in *R v XYZ* (1990) 91 Cr App R 36.

[19] Criminal Justice Act 1988, s. 32(1)(b). Child users are accompanied by a support person, usually the court usher, whose role it is to ensure the child's privacy and offer social support during periods of waiting.

[20] S. 32A of the Criminal Justice Act 1991. S. 54 amends s. 32, Criminal Justice Act 1988.

2. Witnesses with a Learning Disability

According to Mencap, there are over a million people with learning disabilities in the UK. The term encompasses a wide variety of conditions and manifestations:[21]

> With some individuals, learning disability is the direct result of organic damage, such as malfunction of the nervous system brought about during or shortly after birth. Others have chromosomal abnormality such as Downs Syndrome and a larger group have no organic defects. People with learning disabilities differ not only in the cause of their disability but also differ considerably as a group in terms of the degree of their intellectual impairment whether or not they have significant social impairments, and other problems such as hearing and visual impairments.[22]

Learning disability may or may not affect information processing, recall ability, communication skills, and linguistic capacity. There is a general perception that such adaptive deficits necessarily make people with learning disabilities incompetent or less competent witnesses. However, research suggests that competence is not simply a quality arising from the personal characteristics of a witness but also reflects the way in which evidence is obtained, as well as the way in which the characteristics of certain social groups are perceived.[23] Significantly, studies suggest that situational variables have a major impact on the capacity of people with learning disabilities to provide reliable, complete, and coherent accounts.[24] A recent report by the organization Voice, for example, explains that an individual with a learning disability might behave well in a structured setting but may not be able to use what she or he has previously learnt when placed in stressful or frustrating situations.[25] The court setting and the presence of the defendant have been identified as environmental factors that cause particular difficulties for those with an intellectual impairment. Sanders *et al.*, for example, report that a significant source of stress for learning disabled witnesses is the need to give their evidence in a court-room that is public.[26] 'The presence of friends, relatives or other supporters of the defendant in the public gallery can be intimidating, and where the witness is a victim of a sexual offence, recounting physical details in front of an audience can

---

[21] Some 200 causes of learning disability have been identified: Home Office, *Achieving Best Evidence in Criminal Proceedings: Guidance for Vulnerable or Intimidated Witnesses, including Children* (2000, Home Office: London) para. 2.2.1.

[22] VOICE, *Competent to tell the truth* (1998, Derby: Voice UK) 14.

[23] See Sanders, A., Creaton, J., Bird, S. and Weber, L., *Victims with Learning Disabilities: Negotiating the Criminal Justice System* (1997, Oxford: Centre for Criminological Research, University of Oxford).

[24] Ericson, K., Perlman, N. and Isaacs, B., 'Witness competency, communication issues and people with developmental disabilities' (1994) 22 *Developmental Disabilities Bulletin* 101; Kebbell, M. and Hatton, C., 'People with retardation as witnesses in court: A review' (1999) 37(3) *Mental Retardation* 180.   [25] Voice, n. 22 above, 16.

[26] Sanders *et al.*, n. 23 above. The core of this research consisted of a study of 33 prosecuted cases in which the main witness was learning disabled. See also Mencap, *Barriers to Justice: A Mencap study into how the Criminal Justice System treats people with learning disabilities* (1997, London: Mencap).

be a source of embarrassment.'[27] The presence of judge and counsel in archaic dress can serve to make this process even 'scarier'. Direct confrontation with an accused was also clearly very difficult for witnesses involved in the study. One witness stated: 'It was not nice. He was staring at me the whole time . . . he was looking at me. It was horrid, mean . . . Did not want to see him'. Another complained: 'I was nervous . . . I was just frightened to go in that box. That was the scariest thing . . . especially with him staring at me.'[28] Sanders *et al.* conclude that the general requirement that witnesses appear in open court on the day of the trial adversely affects the ability of learning disabled witnesses to give their best evidence.

A recent report by the Law Commission of New South Wales, based on a five-year study, similarly states that anxiety at the prospect of testifying in a court-room full of people and in close proximity to a defendant can make it difficult and sometimes impossible for intellectually disabled witnesses to testify in criminal proceedings.[29] Fear of a defendant, the Commission was keen to emphasize, was not limited to the victim of the alleged offence. As people with an intellectual disability often live in group homes the defendant, the victim, and the other witnesses may all live together. Moreover, the defendant's relationship with a witness may be the same as his or her relationship with the victim; for example, the defendant may be the carer of both. According to the Commission, the witness may be equally reluctant to give evidence against the alleged offender in court and the quality of his or her evidence may be similarly affected.[30]

Although there is very little empirical research upon which to draw, it seems reasonable to assume that witnesses with other psychological vulnerabilities, including mental disorders, are similarly disadvantaged within the criminal process.[31]

3. Adult Complainants in Sexual Offence Cases

The vulnerability of this category of witness to court-related stress stems from the intimate nature of the offence and the evidence to be given. Criminal trials do not allow for modesty in the disclosure of intensely personal matters and complainants can find it profoundly embarrassing to give evidence of a sexually explicit nature in a public court-room and harrowing to be in the physical presence of their attacker. In a study by Lees, a majority of complainants described their experiences in court as humiliating and distressing.[32] The study was based

---

[27] Sanders *et al.*, n. 23 above, 65.   [28] Ibid. 69.
[29] Law Reform Commission NSW, *Report 80 People with an Intellectual Disability and the Criminal Justice System* (1996, Sydney: Law Reform Commission NSW) para. 7.12.
[30] Ibid. para. 7.13.
[31] See Gudjonsson, G., 'The vulnerabilities of mentally disordered witnesses' (1995) 35(2) *Medicine, Science and Law* 101.
[32] Lees reports that 72% of women whose cases had gone to court complained of being treated unsympathetically in court and 83% of women felt as though they were on trial and not the defendant: Lees, S., *Carnal Knowledge Rape on Trial* (1996, London: Hamish Hamilton). See also Adler,

on the transcripts of thirty-one rape trials and 116 questionnaires completed by victims. Having to speak loudly about intimate matters was identified as one of the worst aspects of taking a case to court. In the words of one complainant: 'It's horrible, because your mouth goes dry and you walk into that court and they've all got wigs on and it's awful really. I thought I was going to drop. I must have a strong heart not to have had a heart attack from all this.'[33] In a study conducted by the organization Victim Support, the experience of seeing the accused in court was described as 'terrifying' and 'traumatic'.[34] One woman interviewed remarked: 'It was horrible. It's like you are up on stage. I am very shy and sitting there and having to talk about that, with everyone staring at you, it's vile. I wanted the ground to open up.'[35] Women were similarly intimidated by the presence of a defendant's relatives and supporters in court: '[I was] paralysed by everybody—all their friends and family—staring and looking at me. It shouldn't have been so bad if they hadn't been in the room when I gave evidence, that should not have been allowed. They were laughing and calling me a liar. No one told them to shut up.'[36]

In a survey of witness services in contact with rape complainants 35 per cent reported that women felt embarrassed having to relate intimate details in court and 47 per cent reported that women had felt fearful of facing the defendant and his supporters.[37] In the United States Konradi conducted interviews with thirty-two rape complainants and reports that many had an intense emotional response when they encountered the defendant in the court-room.[38] For some the defendant's presence was a visual reminder of what they had gone through and of the injuries they had suffered. One woman reported that testifying in the same room as the accused was tantamount to re-experiencing the rape: 'I was crying because of fear from him, seeing him for the first time brought all those memories back, and goin' through the story with him in the same room um, just brought it all to life again.'[39] Such is the distress and powerlessness that many complainants claim to experience in court that it is not uncommon for alleged victims of rape to compare the judicial process to a second assault.[40]

Z., *Rape on Trial* (1987, London: Routledge and Kegan Paul); Dublin Rape Crisis Centre, *The Legal Process and Victims of Rape* (1998, Dublin: Dublin Rape Crisis Centre); Lees, S., 'Judicial Rape' (1993) 16 *Women's Studies International Forum* 26; Temkin, J., *Rape and the Legal Process* (1987, London: Sweet and Maxwell).

[33] Lees (1996) n. 32 above, 142.

[34] Victim Support, *Women, Rape and the Criminal Justice System* (1996, London: Victim Support) 45. In a study of rape trials in Victoria, Australia, complainants felt similarly 'distressed', 'terrified', and 'unsafe' being close to the defendant. As one woman reported: 'I felt sick. I thought I was going to vomit when I looked at him. I just felt terrible. Absolutely. Like you were being raped again it felt': Heenan, M. and McKelvie, H., *Evaluation of the Crimes (Rape) Act 1991* (1997, Melbourne: Department of Justice) 104. See also *Heroines of Fortitude: The Experiences of Women in Court as Victims of Sexual Assault* (1996, Sydney: Department for Women).

[35] Victim Support, n. 34 above, 16.   [36] Ibid.   [37] Ibid. 15.

[38] Konradi, A., '"I Don't Have to be Afraid of You": Rape Survivors' Emotion Management in Court' (1999) 22(1) *Symbolic Interaction* 45.   [39] Ibid. 52.

[40] 'I has put my trust and faith in the legal system; afterwards I felt like I had been again but this time by the legal system itself': Dublin Rape Crisis Centre, n. 32 above, 150.

4. Intimidated Witnesses

Relatively little is known about witness intimidation.[41] It is generally accepted that it can involve verbal abuse, threats of physical or financial harm, or physical assaults and damage to property with the purpose of deterring a witness from reporting a crime or from giving evidence in court.[42] Concerns that the problem may be increasing have fuelled awareness in recent years and prompted calls for the implementation of protective measures. The new offences of intimidating a witness and harming or threatening to harm a witness were recently created to help combat the problem.[43] Fear of intimidation is generally considered as much a problem as actual occurrence, leading to a presumed increased reluctance to come forward on the part of witnesses as well as undermining public confidence in the criminal justice system at a wider level. Research suggests that certain groups may be at greater risk of such intimidation. The 1998 British Crime Survey ('BCS') found that women in particular were likely to experience intimidation following a violent offence, especially in cases of domestic violence. In the vast majority of cases (85 per cent) the harasser was the original offender and subsequent intimidation was significantly more likely if the offence had been reported to the police.[44] The majority of incidents of intimidation involved verbal abuse, followed by threats and physical assault. The BCS also indicates that intimidation is inextricably bound up with the phenomenon of 'multiple' or 'repeat' victimization.[45] Complainants of racially motivated offences[46] and stalking are therefore likely to rank among those susceptible to intimidation; so are the elderly and those with either physical or intellectual disabilities who may be viewed as easy targets. There is also some evidence gleaned from interviews with rape complainants to suggest that retaliatory threats are often made against victims of sexual offences.[47]

In terms of court-room intimidation, Maynard's random house-to-house survey of witness intimidation on high-crime housing estates included face-to-face interviews with some fifty victims of intimidation, some of whom had been

---

[41] See Costigan, R. and Thomas, P., 'Anonymous Witnesses' (2000) 51(2) *Northern Ireland Law Quarterly* 326.

[42] In 'rare and exceptional circumstances' intimidated witnesses may be granted anonymity. See *R v Watford Magistrates' Court, ex p Lenman* [1993] Crim LR 388; *R v Taylor* [1995] Crim LR 253.

[43] Criminal Justice and Public Order Act 1994, s. 51. In 1996 there were almost 320 convictions for these offences in England and Wales: see Elliott, R., 'Vulnerable and intimidated witnesses: A review of the literature' in Home Office, *Speaking Up For Justice* (1998, London: Home Office) 113.

[44] 41% of women who experienced intimidation did so from a partner or ex-partner. In other cases the harasser was the offender's friends or family: Home Office, *Victim and Witness Intimidation: Findings from the British Crime Survey* (2000, Home Office: London).

[45] Intimidation was more likely following incidents that were regarded as part of a series (23%) than with incidents that were single events (8%): ibid.

[46] Multiple victimization is known to be common in cases of racially motivated crimes.

[47] Lees (1996), n. 32 above, 108.

intimidated whilst giving evidence in court.[48] The intimidation at trial ranged from verbal abuse and threats being shouted from the public gallery, to a defendant 'staring' at a witness.[49] More recently in Scotland, Fyfe and MacKay interviewed twenty witnesses considered to be at a high or very high risk of life-threatening intimidation.[50] The intimidation experienced was wide-ranging. In some cases there was a single attempt to frighten a witness, while in others intimidation took the form of sustained campaign: 'I was getting a lot of threats and someone had already tried to knock me down in a car. I had my windows smashed and my name splashed across walls in spray paint and that I was a "grass" . . . After that they tried to blow my house up . . . After that the police heard that I was to get shot.'[51]

A number of witnesses experienced direct intimidation while testifying. One witness complained: 'Every time you happened to look down someone put their fingers across their throat. It was out of order.' Another stated: 'The intimidation at court was horrendous. The witness box is far too close to the dock. That did intimidate me. He was shouting at me when I was giving my evidence.'[52]

Alleged victims of intra-familial violence have been identified as a group especially vulnerable to the latent psychological pressure that defendants can exert on witnesses in court. A recent recommendation of the Council of Europe, for example, states that the effective protection of such witnesses, alongside those in cases of serious organized crime, may require the avoidance of simultaneous attendance at court hearings, either by removing the defendant from the court-room or by allowing the witness to give evidence from a location other than where the defendant is situated.[53]

B. THE EFFECTS OF STRESS

Given that many witnesses are likely to experience high levels of stress when giving evidence in court it is important to examine the possible effects of stress on the quality of testimony. According to psychological research, stress induces a high state of arousal that hinders effective memory function, interfering

[48] Maynard found that 6% of crimes were not reported by victims, and 22% of crimes not reported by witnesses went unreported due to fear of intimidation. Moreover, 13% of crimes reported by victims and 9% reported by witnesses led to subsequent intimidation: Maynard, W., *Witness Intimidation: Strategies for Prevention* (1994, London: Home Office Police Research Group Crime Detection and Prevention). In the 1998 British Crime Survey, fear of reprisals accounted for 3% of all incidents not reported to the police, though this rose to 10% for incidents of violence: Mirlees-Black, C., Budd, T., Partridge, S. and Mayhew, P., *The 1998 British Crime Survey England and Wales* (1998, London: Home Office).   [49] Maynard, n. 48 above, 26.
[50] Fyfe, N. and McKay, H., 'Desperately seeking safety: Witnesses' experiences of intimidation, protection and relocation' (2000) 40 *British Journal of Criminology* 675.
[51] Ibid. 680.   [52] Ibid. 686.
[53] Council of Europe, Recommendation No. R (97) 13 on Intimidation of Witnesses and the Rights of the Defence.

specifically with the ability to retrieve and process information.[54] Psychologists have sought to gauge the impact on stress triggered by the court-room environment on the effectiveness of child witnesses in a series of experimental studies. In one such study, conducted by Hill and Hill, children were questioned about an incident they had observed on video tape.[55] Half of the children were interviewed in a large mock court-room by actors dressed in robes in the physical presence of an 'unpleasant man' from the video portrayal. The other half was questioned in a small room that contained two-way mirrors and a microphone. Hill and Hill report that the children who were interviewed in the relatively informal environment of the small room answered specific questions correctly more frequently and overall they gave fewer 'I don't know' or 'no' responses. Overall, their evidence was more accurate and more complete. The researchers conclude that an intimidating environment diminishes the accuracy and efficiency of recall and thus damages a child witness's ability to testify.

In another study Peters found that stress experienced at the time of retrieval had an adverse effect on children's ability or willingness to identify a suspected 'thief' in a live line-up.[56] Children in the sample who were physically confronted with a man they had previously observed 'stealing' made significantly more false non-identifications (incorrectly saying that the thief was not in the line-up) than children who were shown photographs of possible suspects. These findings were interpreted by Peters as an indication that confrontational stress impairs eyewitness testimony. A similarly negative correlation between stress and the completeness and accuracy of children's evidence was reported in a study by Saywitz and Nathanson.[57] Children questioned in a simulated court-room produced less complete descriptions of past events in free recall than children interviewed at school. The children also made more errors in response to direct questions and acquiesced more often to misleading questions. Confronting the accused and the presence of the public were accordingly identified by Saywitz and Nathanson as characteristics of the court-room context which interfere with children's optimal testimony. Summarizing their findings and those of earlier studies the researchers conclude:

Clinical observation and psychological theory suggest that under conditions of heightened emotional arousal, children's memory performance may be less than complete. For motivational reasons, children may shut down, say as little as possible, or refuse to testify altogether. For reasons of ineffective information processing, child witnesses under

[54] Goodman, G. and Helgeson, V., 'Child Sexual Assault: Children's Memory and the Law' (1985) 40 *Miami Law Review* 181, 203.

[55] Hill, P. and Hill, S., 'Videotaping children's testimony: An empirical view' (1987) 85 *Michigan Law Review* 809.

[56] Peters, D., 'The influence of stress and arousal on the child witness' in (ed.) Doris, J., *The Suggestibility of Children's Recollections: Implications for Eyewitness Testimony* (1991, Washington: American Psychological Association) 60.

[57] Saywitz, K. and Nathanson, R., 'Children's testimony and their perception of stress in and out of the courtroom' (1993) 17 *Child Abuse and Neglect* 613.

high levels of stress may be unable to translate their memories into verbal responses, or unable to generate or employ needed retrieval strategies. If the courtroom environment engenders a significant amount of anxiety, children's memory performance may be impaired when compared to performance in a familiar, informal setting.[58]

Overall, psychological theory suggests that heightened emotional arousal disrupts cognitive and communication skills, leading to less complete descriptions of past events and an increase in errors and inconsistencies.[59] According to Goodman and Helgeson, court-related anxiety may also render witnesses particularly vulnerable to suggestion. High levels of stress, they explain, reduce short-term memory, interfering with the retrieval process; and retrieval failures in turn predict heightened suggestibility.[60]

The reported experiences of actual witnesses support the findings of experimental research. Goodman *et al.* observed children as they testified in court and found that a child's feelings about testifying in front of the defendant were associated with his or her ability to answer prosecution questions. Specifically, the more frightened a child was of the defendant, the fewer questions he or she could answer.[61] Myers *et al.* have further described how the stress of testifying can cause some children to regress to a more immature level of behaviour. A child who is intelligent, articulate and confident at home might, they state, show immature language and memory difficulties in the formal environment of the court-room.[62] According to Sanders *et al.*, the strain of testifying resulted in learning disabled witnesses in their case studies giving less coherent and less detailed evidence in court than was contained in their earlier police statements.[63] In a similar vein, adult rape complainants have described feeling 'paralysed' in a defendant's presence and unnerved by the general atmosphere of the court-room to such an extent that their ability to testify was impaired.[64] The psychologists Goodman and Helgeson have compared this to the anxiety people suffer at the time of a test, causing them to fail to perform despite knowing the material well. A similar anxiety may well, they claim, inhibit sexual assault complainants from telling their stories under certain conditions, such as when facing the defendant in a court-room.[65] In Konradi's study, the proximity of the

---

[58] Ibid.

[59] According to King, giving evidence in a criminal trial is for most people a stressful experience that may adversely affect recall of traumatic events: King, M., 'Use of video in child abuse trials' (1988) 1(5) *The Psychologist* 167.

[60] Goodman *et al.*, n. 54 above, 203.   [61] Goodman *et al.*, n. 7 above, 121.

[62] Myers, J., Saywitz, K. and Goodman, G., 'Psychological research on children as witnesses: Practical implications for forensic interviews and courtroom testimony' (1996) 28 *Pacific Law Journal* 3, 70.

[63] Sanders *et al.*, n. 23 above. A recent report by Mencap states that pressure on learning disabled witnesses in court can lead to unreliable evidence: Mencap, n. 26 above, 8. The Law Commission of New South Wales similarly concluded that the tendency of people with learning difficulties to become tired and lose concentration more quickly than non-disabled persons was greatly exacerbated by court-related anxiety making it difficult and sometimes impossible for a witness with a learning disability to give evidence: see n. 29 above.

[64] Heenan *et al.*, n. 34 above, 105.   [65] Goodman *et al.*, n. 54 above, 190.

defendant had a reportedly negative impact on the ability of complainants to testify, to listen to questions, and to formulate coherent responses.[66] The presence of the defendant was, according to Konradi, a distraction that caused some complainants to be less attentive to both the questions posed in court and to their replies.[67] Practising barristers have also acknowledged the 'incredible psychological influence' some defendants exert over rape complainants in court that in their experience caused the minds of some complainants to 'go blank'.[68]

If the prospect of testifying in court proves too daunting, of course, witnesses will be lost to the system altogether. Witnesses may elect to withdraw from a case or fail to report an offence at all. The Home Office recently published a report addressing the issue of attrition in rape cases.[69] The proportion of recorded rapes resulting in a conviction has declined from 24 per cent in 1985 to just 9 per cent. The study examined 483 incidents initially recorded as rape by the police in 1996 and followed their progress through the criminal justice system. The study found that only 6 per cent of cases originally recorded as rape by the police resulted in convictions for rape. A striking finding of the study was the high level of complainant withdrawal at the pre-trial stage of the criminal process. In the 31 per cent of cases in which no further action was taken and the 25 per cent of cases which were 'no-crimed' by the police the most common reason was complainant withdrawal. While recognizing that victims decide not to pursue allegations for many reasons, the report significantly attributes the disturbingly high levels, in part, to fears that giving evidence in court would be a 'harrowing ordeal'.[70] At the same time, it is acknowledged in other contexts that Crown Prosecution Service lawyers are often reluctant to put young or learning disabled complainants through the 'trauma of testifying' if they are ultimately unlikely to come up to proof because of overwhelming court-room anxiety.[71]

Finally, studies suggest that court-related stress may have a prejudicial effect on the perceived credibility of affected witnesses. The risk to credibility stems, in part, from the noted tendency of observers to intuitively associate witness confidence with testimonial accuracy.[72] Psychological research suggests that any correlation between the two is illusionary but this does not, studies suggest,

---

[66] Konradi, n. 38 above, 53.

[67] In rape trials observed by Adler some complainants cried almost continuously, 'had difficulty getting words out', and 'spoke almost inaudibly': n. 32 above, 51.

[68] Temkin, J., 'Prosecuting and defending rape: Perspectives from the Bar' (2000) 27(2) *Journal of Law and Society* 219, 237.

[69] Harris J. and Grace, S., *A question of evidence? Investigating and prosecuting rape in the 1990s* HORS 196 (1999, London: HMSO).   [70] Ibid. 14.

[71] Davies *et al.*, for example, report that police and Crown prosecutors believe that the experience of testifying at trial is traumatic for children and this is an important factor in the decision whether to proceed. See Davis, G., Hoyano, L., Keenan, C., Maitland, L. and Morgan, R., *An Assessment of the Admissibility and Sufficiency of Evidence in Child Abuse Prosecutions* (1999, London: Home Office) x.

[72] Confidence has been shown in consecutive studies to be a poor guide to reliability and truthfulness. See O'Sullivan, M., Ekman, P. and Freisen, W.V., 'The effect of behavioral comparison in detecting deception' (1988) 12 *Journal of Non-verbal Behavior* 203.

prevent observers being swayed by an eyewitness who exudes confidence, nor from being correspondingly distrustful of those who appear nervous and hesitant. The position of alleged victims is probably more complex. In the context of a rape case, for example, it has been remarked that a complainant who appears lucid, controlled, and calm may be in danger of not coming across as a victim. Conversely, if a complainant appears too upset she runs the risk of being seen as hysterical and therefore not believable.[73] To compound matters, non-verbal behavioural manifestations popularly identified with deception, such as fidgeting, blushing, and avoidance of eye contact, are also recognized signifiers of anxiety and embarrassment. The diffident demeanour of vulnerable witness occasioned by the court-room environment or other situational variables may therefore be misinterpreted as betraying a lack of veracity.[74]

C. The Effects of Delay

Research suggests that the perennial problem of delay within the criminal justice system constitutes a further threat to the quality of oral testimony in criminal proceedings and to the welfare of vulnerable witnesses. Despite official efforts to speed up the completion of cases, witnesses must often testify at trial to events that occurred many months earlier. Delays of a year are not uncommon in the prosecution of serious offences. For example, a recent study found that child abuse cases took on average fifty-seven and a half weeks from referral to the police to the first day of trial.[75] In rape cases it is reported that a 'delay of around eight months is average, but some women have to wait for as long as a year and a half before they are called upon to appear in court'.[76] Psychological research suggests that such lapses of time undermine the reliability of witness testimony in numerous ways. For example, it is generally accepted that people are less accurate and complete in their eyewitness accounts after a long retention interval.[77] Scientists appear to agree that people experience a sharp decline in memory immediately after an event that becomes more gradual as time

---

[73] Lees, n. 32 above, xiii.

[74] See generally DePaulo, B. M., Stone, J. I. and Lassiter, G. D., 'Deceiving and Detecting Deceit' in (ed.) Schlenker, B. R., *The Self and Social Life* (1985, New York: McGraw-Hill); Edelman, R., 'Non Verbal Behaviour and Deception' in (eds.) Canter, D. and Alison, L., *Interviewing and Deception* (1999 Aldershot: Ashgate) 162; Ekman, P., *Telling Lies: Clues to Deception in the Marketplace, Marriage and Politics* (1986, New York: W. W. Norton); Kohnken, G., 'The evaluation of statement credibility: Social judgment and expert diagnostic approaches' in (eds.) Spencer, J. R., Nicolson, G., Flin, R. and Bull, R., *Children's Evidence in Legal Proceedings: An International Perspective* (1990, Cambridge: Selwyn College); Miller, G. R. and Stiff, J. B., 'Applied issues in studying deceptive communication' in (ed.) Feldman, R. S., *Applications of Non-verbal Behavioral Theories and Research* (1992, Hillsdale, New Jersey: Erlbaum).   [75] See Davis *et al.*, n. 71 above.

[76] Adler, n. 32 above.

[77] See generally Loftus, E., *Eyewitness Testimony* (1979, Cambridge, Mass.: Harvard University Press).

passes: the so-called 'forgetting curve'.[78] 'After a year, memory will be less accurate than after a month; after a month it will be less accurate than after a week'.[79] Witnesses for whom memory retention is a problem will naturally be disproportionately disadvantaged by delay.

Among the most important variables affecting memory performance is age. While account must always be taken of personal and situational factors, elderly witnesses can generally be expected to do less well when it comes to recalling information than young or middle-aged adults. At the other end of the spectrum, the long-term memory of children is widely, though not universally, thought to deteriorate more rapidly than that of adults.[80] Studies certainly indicate that child witnesses struggle greatly at trial to recall the details of events that allegedly took place months previously. Accordingly, there is general agreement on the wisdom of interviewing children promptly. Another group potentially susceptible to 'memory fade' are witnesses with learning disabilities who are generally considered to be poorer in aspects of encoding, storing, and retrieving information compared to the general population. However, it is important to stress that not all learning disabilities lead to memory problems. Autism, for example, is associated with good memory performance.[81] Less attention has typically focused on the difficulties encountered by those individuals who have experienced or witnessed traumatic incidents. There is however evidence to suggest that psychological factors or personal circumstances can induce such witnesses to forget important details over time as a conscious effort is made to avoid thinking about the incident each time it comes to mind. So-called 'motivated forgetting' or trauma-induced amnesia remains a controversial issue, especially in cases of recovered memories of childhood abuse.[82] While more research is clearly required, theories of active forgetting may account for the real difficulties which witnesses can experience when narrating traumatic events after a significant time lapse. Barristers have, for example, given accounts of trying, often unsuccessfully, to elicit detailed evidence in chief from rape complainants a year after the events complained of:

Rape victims often needed to forget what had happened to them in order to cope with their lives and expended much effort in seeking to do so. Where, after a year or so, they had managed to put the experience behind them, it was traumatic then to be forced to recall the event in court and they frequently had a reluctance to talk about it. Their minds sometimes went blank. Very often they had not spoken in any detail

[78] Ebbinghaus, H., *Memory: A Contribution to Experimental Psychology* (1913, New York: Teachers College, Columbia University).   [79] Loftus, n. 77 above, 54.

[80] Myers, J., Saywitz, K. and Goodman, G., 'Psychological research on children as witnesses: Practical implications for forensic interviews and court-room testimony' (1996) 28 *Pacific Law Journal* 3, 14.

[81] See Kebbell, M. and Hatton, C., 'People with retardation as witnesses in court: A review' (1999) 37(3) *Mental Retardation*, 179.

[82] Yuille, J. and Daylen, J., 'The Impact of Traumatic Events on Eyewitness Memory' in (eds.) Thompson, C., Herrmann, D., Read, J., Bruce, D., Payne, D. and Toglia, M., *Eyewitness Memory* (1998, Mahwah, New Jersey: Lawrence Erlbaum Associates) 155.

about the rape for months and it was difficult for them to recall the sequence of events.[83]

The effectiveness of those trying to come to terms with severe personal difficulties and trauma is no doubt further undermined by the accumulated stress of waiting for trial. As a result, examination at the earliest possible stage is likely to provide the best and most reliable information.[84]

The risk of a witness's original memories being contaminated or transformed by information received from others also increases with the delay between reporting and giving evidence. Memory does not, of course, operate like video tape, recording and then storing information for subsequent retrieval. Instead, memory is malleable and subject to a large number of external and internal influences. Memories of an event can be overlaid or over-written by information acquired after the fact. There is therefore always a danger that erroneous 'post-event information' will be inadvertently integrated or implanted into memory for the event. Loftus has shown, for example, how non-existent objects can be introduced into memory through the use of deliberately misleading questioning, and how substantively incorrect details can be insinuated by exposure to false 'external' information.[85] This risk appears to increase with the length of the retention interval. As Loftus notes, 'giving the event information a chance to fade in the memory makes it easier to introduce misleading information'.[86] While all witnesses are potentially affected, the risk of distorted testimony may be greater in the case of learning disabled witnesses and young children. Both groups are widely regarded as being more susceptible to suggestion, although recent research does indicate that generalizations may be misleading.

An insistence on direct oral evidence also carries with it huge emotional costs for many vulnerable witnesses, particularly when therapy or counselling is postponed pending trial. Victims of terrible crimes are unable to face up to what has happened by talking it through with a trained counsellor and as a result cannot be induced to put events behind them.[87] Parents of children testifying in abuse cases have ranked long delays between the report of an offence and the trial as one of their worst experiences. In Murray's study 65 per cent of parents said their children's anxiety was manifested in 'nightmares, sickness or school refusal'.[88] According to the Queensland Children's Commission, as a result of lengthy delays children's lives are effectively put on hold at a crucial stage of their cognitive, emotional, and social development. The anticipated ordeal of giving evidence frequently overshadows everything they do and often limits their capacity to come to terms with what has occurred as well as preventing them from developing new interests, taking on new challenges, or just

---

[83] Temkin, n. 68 above, 222.   [84] See Home Office, n. 12 above, para. 112.
[85] Loftus, n. 77 above, 58.   [86] Ibid. 66.
[87] New guidelines on pre-trial therapy have recently been published: Home Office, *Provision of Therapy for Child Witnesses Prior to a Criminal Trial: Practical Guidance* (2001 London: Home Office).
[88] Murray, n. 9 above, 61.

continuing with their everyday lives.[89] Adult rape complainants have also similarly described the wait for trial as traumatic and as prolonging their ordeal. One complainant interviewed by Victim Support explained how a trial delay had affected her: 'It is now fourteen months since I was raped and I feel that I cannot get on with my life until the trial is over . . . I have been very close to packing it in, I can tell you. I continue to relive the trauma—an you imagine how that feels?'[90] Naturally, opportunities for witness intimidation also increase the longer the delay.

D. Exclusion of Out of Court Statements

In adversarial proceedings the significant problems associated with stress and delay are compounded by the rules governing the admissibility of prior consistent statements, which allow direct oral evidence to be supplemented or supported only in very limited circumstances. Previous statements retain their hearsay character even where a witness testifies at trial and are thus inadmissible as evidence of the facts contained within them. The related but separate rule against narrative excludes previous consistent statements as evidence of consistency and credibility on the part of a testifying witness. To a large extent vulnerable witnesses therefore stand or fall by what they manage to recall and recount 'on the day' as their earlier statements are deprived of evidential status irrespective of their apparent reliability. Such disclosures may include specific allegations against an accused to family members, friends, or carers and statements to the police. This 'one-shot' philosophy undoubtedly means that better quality evidence gathered at the investigative stage of the criminal process is often rejected in favour of less complete and less compelling evidence given at trial. As the Law Reform Commission of Western Australia recently commented this carries with it the risk of the trial itself being a 'flawed forensic process with the potential for missing the "truth"'.[91]

The rationale for maintaining the hearsay status of previous consistent statements is far from clear. The perceived weaknesses of hearsay evidence said to stem from the absence of the oath, demeanour evidence, and most importantly cross-examination are far less apparent when a witness testifies at trial. These testing conditions may not have prevailed at the time when the statement was made but this seems little justification for their limited admissibility. The limited utility of the oath as a truth-promoting device and the deficiencies of demeanour evidence as an indicator of veracity are both now

---

[89] Queensland Children's Commission, *Response to Queensland Law Reform Commission Discussion Paper* WP No. 53 (1998); *The Receipt of Evidence By Queensland's Courts: The Evidence of Children* (1999, Brisbane: Queensland Children's Commission).

[90] Victim Support, n. 34 above, 31.

[91] Law Reform Commission of Western Australia, *Review of the Criminal and Civil Justice System Final Report* (1999, Perth: Law Reform Commission of Western Australia) para. 7.13.

widely acknowledged.[92] The notion that contemporaneous counter-interrogation would uncover testimonial infirmities which subsequent cross-examination could not is also unconvincing. 'While it is true that a witness may, given time, prepare some explanation or justification for a previous statement, which might have been forestalled by immediate cross-examination, he may equally do so in regard to the facts in issue themselves and his evidence at trial concerning the facts in issue'.[93] The treatment of previous consistent statements as hearsay is all the more questionable when the rules governing refreshing memory are considered. As a concession to the fragility of human memory, witnesses are allowed to read their earlier statements outside the court-room and may refer to a previous statement in the witness box at the court's discretion.[94] When this occurs the witness's memory is uniformly said to be 'refreshed' and his or her testimony is accepted unhesitatingly as first hand evidence. This is, of course, a long-standing fiction as full revival of present recollection on sight of a previous statement is likely to be rare.[95] In many cases, there will be no independent recollection and a witness will simply recite a prior note, giving what is, in effect, hearsay evidence. Furthermore, it is doubtful that jurors use admitted prior consistent statements as they are directed for the limited purpose of assessing credibility. The subtle distinction between evidence that shows consistency and evidence of the truth of facts stated will often be meaningless and the complex jury directions which the distinction inspires have been rightly described as 'wholly unrealistic and difficult for a jury to appreciate'.[96]

1. The Rule against Narrative

The rule against narrative shores up the orality principle by excluding previous statements as evidence of consistency except in very limited circumstances.[97] One of the principal justifications advanced for the rule is that evidence of previous consistent statements will generally be superfluous, adding little to direct testimony.[98] This argument assumes that evidence delivered orally in

---

[92] See for example Law Commission, *Evidence in Criminal Proceedings: Hearsay and Related Topics*, Consultation Paper No. 138 (1995, London: HMSO) 78.

[93] Murphy, P., 'Previous Consistent and Inconsistent Statements: A Proposal to Make Life Easier for Juries' [1985] *Criminal Law Review* 270, 280.

[94] The rules governing refreshing of memory have been considerably relaxed. See *R v South Ribble Magistrates, ex p Cochrane* [1996] 2 Cr App R 544. This case confirms that a trial judge has a wide discretion to permit a witness to refresh his or her memory from a non-contemporaneous document in the course of testifying.

[95] See Ashworth, A. and Pattenden, R., 'Reliability, Hearsay Evidence and the English Criminal Trial' (1986) 102 *Law Quarterly Review* 292, 298.

[96] Criminal Law Revision Committee, *Eleventh Report Evidence* Cmnd. 4991 (1972, London: HMSO) para. 232.

[97] See generally Gooderson, R., 'Previous Consistent Statements' (1968) 26 *Cambridge Law Journal* 64.

[98] 'The necessity of saving time by avoiding superfluous testimony and sparing the court a protracted inquiry into a multitude of collateral issues which might be raised about such matters as the

court will be at least equal in terms of quality and quantity to out of court statements. This ignores the fact that stress and delays often militate against such parity, especially in cases involving vulnerable witnesses. As previously stated, the debilitative effects of both time and system-induced anxiety mean that statements made nearer to the events in question are in most cases likely to provide a fuller, more reliable account than any emerging subsequently from the witness box.[99] In any event, the inherent power of the court to exclude insufficiently relevant evidence seriously weakens arguments based on a potential influx of material of too little weight. A second justification for the rule against narrative is the alleged ease with which previous consistent statements may be manufactured. This argument is as tenuous as the first, given that the admission of such a statement presupposes the availability of the witness for cross-examination where motivation and opportunity for fabrication can be fully explored. The risk of manufacture is anyway a matter of weight and to treat it as a condition of admissibility usurps the fact-finder's role.

Exceptions[100]

The rule against narrative is subject to a number of exceptions, but a combination of limited scope and dubious psychological foundation mean that these are of very limited value to vulnerable witnesses. The best known and most criticized of these exceptions is, arguably, the doctrine of recent complaint which provides that evidence of a complaint made by an alleged victim of a sexual offence is admissible as evidence of consistency and, in cases where consent is in issue, as evidence inconsistent with consent.[101] As conditions of admissibility, the statement must amount to a complaint, be spontaneous or voluntary,[102] and made at the first reasonable opportunity.[103]

The continued restriction of the recent complaint rule to sexual offence complainants is its most glaring limitation. By way of justification, little more is offered than vague and unpersuasive assertions that more often hinges on the credibility of such complainants given a customary absence of bystander witnesses.[104] In truth, the singling out of sexual offence complainants is a dated monument to the common law requirement of 'hue and cry' from which the

---

precise terms of the previous statement is undoubtedly a sound basis for the general rule': Tapper, C., *Cross and Tapper on Evidence* 9th edn. (1999, London: Butterworths) 272.

[99] The Criminal Law Revision Committee stated that if a witness was honest then 'what he said soon after the events in question is likely to be at least as reliable as his evidence at trial and will probably be more so': n. 96 above, para. 239.

[100] The admission of video-taped interviews in lieu of examination in chief in child abuse cases is discussed in Chapter III below.   [101] *R v Lillyman* [1896] 2 QB 167.

[102] 'If the circumstances indicate that but for the questioning there probably would have been no voluntary complaint, the answer is inadmissible. If the question merely anticipates a statement the complainant was about to make, it is not rendered inadmissible by the fact that the questioner happens to speak first': *R v Osborne* [1905] 1 KB 551.

[103] *R v Cummings* [1948] 1 All ER 551; *R v Valentine* [1996] 2 Cr App R 213.

[104] Tapper, n. 98 above, 274.

doctrine originally evolved. According to this medieval rule, victims of violent crimes, later reduced to victims of sexual offences, were expected to cry out immediately and alert their neighbours of an assault if their appeals were to succeed. By the 1800s the absence of a complaint was no longer an absolute bar to a successful rape prosecution but a strong presumption against a complainant could be drawn from a failure to complain contemporaneously. The recent complaint rule emerged to allow the prosecution to rebut this adverse inference by leading evidence of a fresh complaint in chief, in effect permitting the anticipatory rehabilitation of a witness who faced unusual suspicion. Today there appears to be no sound reason for excluding complaints made by all categories of complainant. As Spencer notes, 'it is surely most important for the court to be able to hear the terms in which any victim originally complained, irrespective of the nature of the offence'.[105]

The conditions of admissibility further diminish the value of this exception because they reflect misconceived notions about how 'reliable' people react to and communicate traumatic events.[106] The recent complaint doctrine is based on the implicit assumption that it is natural for a person who has been sexually assaulted to complain immediately,[107] admitting only those statements made 'as speedily as could be reasonably expected'.[108] The exception also expects alleged victims to provide spontaneous accounts of abuse and excludes statements made in response to suggestive or leading questioning. Research has, however, shown that victims of sexual offences are often unwilling or unable to disclose details of an assault without the kind of prompting and encouragement that render a complaint inadmissible. It is also clear that victims of sexual offences very often delay reporting for lengthy periods due to fear of reprisals, embarrassment, fear of not being believed, and shame.[109] Belated reporting is also consistent with behavioural manifestations associated with Rape Trauma Syndrome and more generally with Post Traumatic Stress Disorder.[110] In the case of *Valentine* the temporal requirement was relaxed in recognition that 'victims of sexual offences, be they male or female, often need time before they can bring

---

[105] See Spencer, J., 'Hearsay Reform: A Bridge Not Far Enough' [1996] *Criminal Law Review* 29, 33. See also Spencer, J., 'Orality and the Evidence of Absent Witnesses' [1994] *Criminal Law Review* 628.

[106] Wigmore describes the rationale for the rule as follows: 'Now, when a woman charges a man with a rape . . . and the accused denies the act itself, . . . the circumstance that at the time of the alleged rape the woman said nothing about it to anybody constitutes in effect a self contradiction . . . It was entirely natural, after becoming the victim of an assault against her will, that she should have spoken out. That she did not, that she went about as if nothing had happened, was in effect an assertion that nothing violent had been done': Wigmore, J. H., *Evidence* vol. 4 (1976, Boston, Mass.: Chadbourn revision) 298.

[107] See Stanchi, K., 'The Paradox of the Fresh Complaint Rule' (1996) 37 *Boston College Law Review* 441. [108] *R v Valentine* [1996] 2 Cr App R 213.

[109] See Bronitt, S., 'The rules of recent complaint: Rape myths and the legal construction of the "reasonable" rape victim' in (ed.) Easteal, P., *Balancing the Scales: Rape, Law Reform and Australian Culture* (1998, Sydney: Federation Press) 41.

[110] See Burgess, A. W. and Holmstrom, L., 'Rape trauma syndrome' (1974) 131 *American Journal of Psychiatry* 981.

themselves to tell what has been done to them; that some victims will find it impossible to complain to anyone other than a parent or member of their family whereas others may feel it quite impossible to tell their parents or members of their family.'[111] However, this is unlikely to help those who postpone the act of reporting for months and even years.

Other exceptions to the rule against narrative are equally narrow in scope.[112] Statements admissible to rebut a suggestion made in cross-examination that a witness's testimony is a recent invention, for example, serve a very limited rehabilitative function. The exception is triggered only by a specific accusation of having fabricated testimony for the purposes of the trial.[113] If a witness is discredited in cross-examination by damaging allegations of contradiction and inconsistency, evidence of confirmatory statements cannot be introduced to redress the balance and restore credibility. The *res gestae* exception which allows for the introduction of 'spontaneous statements'[114] is also of very limited application. Like a number of hearsay exceptions, the *res gestae* rule is explained by the presumed trustworthiness of the evidence it admits. Here, approximate contemporaneity is assumed to preclude the reflection necessary for concoction, rendering such statements sufficiently reliable to warrant admission.[115] Moreover, it is assumed that stress or the excitement of involvement 'stills the reflective faculties', diminishing the dangers of insincerity, mistake, and distortion. Modern psychological theory, of course, disputes both notions.[116]

E. CONCLUSION

The principle of orality and its concomitant, the principle of immediacy, are premised in part on an assumption that live testimony delivered in open court is subject to key testing conditions that enhance the rationality of fact-finding. It was Wigmore's view, for example, that public scrutiny produces: 'In the witness' mind a disinclination to falsify; first, by stimulating the instinctive responsibility to public opinion, symbolised in the audience, and ready to scorn a demonstrated liar; and next, by inducing the fear of exposure of subsequent falsities through disclosure by informed persons who may chance to be present or to hear of the testimony from others present'.[117]

---

[111] *R v Valentine* [1996] 2 Cr App R 213, 293.

[112] Exceptions not discussed include: statements made upon accusation, *R v Pearce* (1979) 69 Cr App R 365; *R v Tooke* (1989) 90 Cr App R 417; statements made on discovery of incriminating articles, *R v Abraham* (1848) 3 Cox CC 430; and statements of prior identification of the accused, *R v Christie* [1914] AC 545.   [113] *R v Oyesiku* (1971) 56 Cr App R 240.

[114] As evidence of the truth of what it contains under the *res gestae* exception to the hearsay rule or, where a witness testifies at trial, as evidence of consistency. *R v Fowkes* (1856) *The Times*, 8 March.

[115] Exact contemporaneity was of course once required, as illustrated in the celebrated case of *R v Bedingfield* (1879) 14 Cox CC 341.

[116] For a critical analysis of the *res gestae* doctrine in the guise of excited utterances see Orenstein, A., '"My God!": A Feminist Critique of the Excited Utterance Exception to the Hearsay Rule' (1997) 85 *California Law Review* 159.   [117] Wigmore, n. 106 above, vol. 6, 435.

Direct confrontation has also assumed great significance in adversarial theory due to an assumption that it is 'more difficult to tell a lie about a person to his face than behind his back'.[118] Compelling a witness to testify in the physical presence of an accused is said to afford the latter some protection against unfounded allegations and contrived testimony. Furthermore, the general atmosphere and formal nature of trial itself are intended and expected to impress upon participants the solemnity of the occasion and the importance of 'truth-telling'. Research reviewed in this Chapter challenges the validity of these basic assumptions, at least in their application to witnesses who are vulnerable by virtue of age, disability, intimidation, or the nature of the offence. Rather than promote the reliability of evidence, these so-called safeguards have been shown to be counter-productive, seriously impairing the ability of young, traumatized, intellectually disabled, and intimidated witnesses to provide full, coherent, and accurate accounts in criminal proceedings. The proposition that conventional evidentiary safeguards may hamper rather than enhance the fact-finding process has been accepted for some time in relation to child victims of sexual and physical abuse. It is however clear that rules and procedures sustaining the orality principle operate to deny the courts access to the best evidence potentially available in many more cases. When attendant trial delays are taken into account the perceived advantages of direct oral evidence are, in the case of vulnerable witnesses, significantly outweighed by far-reaching and detrimental effects. The extent to which these effects are mitigated by the statutory regime introduced in the Youth Justice and Criminal Evidence Act 1999 is the subject of the following Chapter.

---

[118] *Coy v Iowa* 487 US 1012, 1019 (1988). A witness, the Court opined, 'may feel quite differently when he has to repeat his story looking at the man whom he will harm greatly by distorting or mistaking the facts. He can now understand what sort of human being that man is . . .'

III.

Accommodating Vulnerable and Intimidated Witnesses

In 1997 Home Secretary Jack Straw established an interdepartmental working group to examine ways of improving the treatment of vulnerable and intimidated witnesses within the criminal justice system. The report, *Speaking up for Justice*, was published in June 1998 and contained a total of seventy-eight recommendations, a number of which were aimed at trial procedure. In terms of court measures, the working group was apparently motivated by the twin concerns of reducing the stress typically associated with conventional live testimony and enabling witnesses to give the best evidence they were capable of giving. To this end the working group recommended the use of various 'Special Measures', including screens, live television links, intermediaries, and videotaped testimony. The recommendations form the basis of chapter I of Part II of the Youth Justice and Criminal Evidence Act 1999 ('YJCEA').

This Chapter examines the special measures provisions and assesses just how effective they are likely to prove in securing the best evidence from vulnerable and intimidated witnesses. The measures have been directly imported (with the exception of pre-trial cross-examination) from the domain of child witnesses. In this context, recent evaluative study and psychological research provide some support for court-room modifying measures and for television links but also raise important concerns about their use in shoring up an attachment to direct oral evidence. Significant questions have also been raised regarding the utility of video-taped investigatory interviews as replacements for examination in chief, challenging the apparent assumption that the video-taping provisions of the Criminal Justice Act 1991 were operating sufficiently well to warrant their wholesale extension. Overall, research appears to indicate that the measures which deviate most from the paradigmatic adversarial model provide witnesses with greatest assistance and the courts with access to the best evidence.

A. Special Measures

As stated above, many of the special measures available under the new Act simply extend or place on a statutory footing, practices which were developed and followed under previous law. Section 23 of the Act, for example, provides for the use of screens to shield a witness from seeing the defendant. Screens have been used increasingly since the 1980s to shield child witnesses from the physical presence of an accused in court.[1] Where a screen is authorized, section 23(2) provides that the judge, legal representatives, and the jury must be able to observe and be observed by the witness at all material times. Section 24 of the Act extends the availability of the live link from child witnesses in cases of physical and sexual abuse to other children and eligible adults.[2] The procedure takes the witness outside the court-room but he or she will still be seen and heard by the judge, jury, and legal representatives and will be able to see the same. A neat description of the form of the live link procedure as it has applied to child witnesses is provided by Davies:

> The judge, defence, and prosecution counsel have access to electronic workstations that can both send pictures to and receive pictures from the interview view. They question the child via a live interactive link. The child is seated in front of a monitor that contains a concealed camera. The child always sees whomever is talking to her or him, while the court always sees the child. In addition to the workstations, large screen television monitors are set up in the court for the benefit of the accused, the jury and the public . . . the cameras are always arranged so that the defendant is not visible to the child.[3]

Section 25 provides for the exclusion of certain persons from the court-room while the witness gives evidence. The courts have an inherent power to hold a trial wholly or partly in camera but have been traditionally been reluctant to derogate from the principle of open justice.[4] The measure is only available in sexual offence cases or in cases where the court is persuaded that someone other than the accused has sought or will seek to intimidate the witness.[5] A court may not exclude by virtue of this section the accused, legal representatives, or any interpreter or other person appointed to assist the witness. Special provision is made in relation to members of the press.[6] The accepted discretion of trial judges to order the removal of wigs and gowns is placed on a statutory footing by section 26. It may be assumed that this measure will be invoked in cases involving children and those with learning disabilities although it is also available to witnesses outside these categories.[7]

Section 27 of the Act extends the use of video-taped interviews to vulnerable and intimidated adult witnesses and children who were previously exempt. In line with existing practice, video interviews are to be conducted

---

[1] The practice was approved by the Court of Appeal in *XYZ* (1990) 91 Cr App R 36.

[2] Criminal Justice Act 1988, s. 32(1)(b).

[3] Davies, G., 'The impact of television on the presentation and reception of children's testimony' (1999) 22 (3-4) *International Journal of Law and Psychiatry* 241, 242.

[4] *Attorney General v Leveller Magazine* [1979] AC 440. Certain statutory powers enable a court to sit in camera without the public or the press being present: s. 8, Official Secrets Act 1920 and s. 37, Children and Young Persons Act 1933.

[5] S. 25(4). In Scotland it is common practice to clear courts of non-essential personnel when a rape complainant is giving evidence: s. 92(3), Criminal Procedure (Scotland) Act 1995.

[6] The court will have to allow at least one member of the press to remain if one has been nominated by the press: s. 25(3).

[7] The benefits of removing wigs are said to be mixed as some people with learning difficulties, having seen court-room dramas, expect wigs and are thrown by their absence.

in accordance with a suitably updated Memorandum of Good Practice.[8] Subsections (2) and (3) allow video recordings to be excluded and edited if the interests of justice so require. In deciding whether to allow only an edited recording to be used in evidence, courts will have to consider whether any potential prejudice to the accused is outweighed by the desirability of receiving the whole recording.[9] A video-taped interview will not be admitted if it appears to the court that the witness will not be available for cross-examination (whether in court or on video-tape) or that the disclosure rules relating to the interview have not been complied with to the satisfaction of the court.[10] Where a recording is admitted, section 27(5) provides that the witness may not give evidence in chief as to any matter which, in the opinion of court, has been dealt with adequately in the pre-trial interview.[11] Where further questioning of a witness is permitted the witness may testify by means of a live television link.[12]

The only entirely new measure introduced by the Act is pre-trial video-taped cross-examination. Section 28 provides for cross-examination and re-examination to be video-recorded for use at trial where a court has provided for a video-taped interview to be admitted as a witness's evidence in chief. Such a recording must be made in circumstances in which the judge and legal representatives are able to see and hear the examination of the witness and to communicate with the witness.[13] The recording may be made in the absence of the accused but the accused must be able to see and hear any such examination and communicate with his or her legal representative throughout.[14] If any of these requirements are not met, or if the court is not satisfied that the terms of a direction have been complied with, the recording may be excluded. To meet concerns that vulnerable witnesses may be subjected to repeated cross-examination, there are restrictions on the extent to which further cross-examination or re-examination is allowed. Section 28(5) provides that witnesses who have been cross-examined on video are not to be cross-examined again unless the court makes a direction permitting another videorecorded cross-examination. A court may only give such a further direction if a party wishes to raise a matter which it could not, with reasonable diligence, have raised at the first recording[15] or if the judge determines that it is otherwise in the interests of justice to allow further questions.[16] Pre-recorded cross-examination is in principle available to all witnesses, regardless of age or offence charged.

---

[8] See Home Office Consultation Paper, *Achieving Best Evidence in Criminal Proceedings: Guidance for Vulnerable or Intimidated Witnesses, including Children* (2000, London: Home Office).
[9] S. 27(3).   [10] S. 27(4).
[11] In order to question a witness about matters not dealt with adequately in the interview a party must first obtain the permission of the court: s. 27(7).
[12] S. 27(9). In the case of witnesses who are not subject to the special presumptions that apply to children, the court may alternatively decide that the witness should give evidence in court, protected if necessary by a screen.   [13] S. 28(2).
[14] S. 28(2)(b).   [15] S. 28(6)(a).   [16] S. 28(6)(b).

Sections 29 and 30 provide for the use of intermediaries and communication aids by child witnesses and those with mental or physical disorders or with significant impairment of intelligence and social functioning. These measures are discussed in Chapter VI below. It should however be noted that the role of the intermediary is to communicate questions put to the witness and the witness's replies, and to explain both of these so far as is necessary to enable both to be understood.[17] Intermediaries will thus have an important role to play not only at trial but during each examination of an eligible witness, including video-recorded pre-trial interviews and cross-examination.

B. Eligibility

In *Speaking Up for Justice* the working group considered several different definitions of vulnerable witness.[18] Models based on limited categories and listed individual characteristics were rejected in favour of a combined approach[19] which took account of both personal qualities and what the group described as circumstantial or situational factors which made it likely that a witness would suffer such emotional trauma or intimidation as to be unable to give best evidence without protection. The option of an offence gateway was rejected by the group, who reasoned correctly that a witness was either vulnerable or he or she was not. Sections 16 and 17 of the YJCEA adopt the working group's combined approach essentially laying down three basic categories of eligibility: age, incapacity, and fear or distress about testifying.[20] The first category of eligible witnesses includes all witnesses under the age of seventeen, who qualify automatically for special measures in line with the working group's recommendations.[21] The second category of witness comprises those with a mental[22] or physical disorder or impairment of intelligence and social functioning which the court considers significant enough to affect the quality of their evidence. The term 'quality' refers to the completeness, coherence, and accuracy of evidence.[23] 'Coherence' refers to a witness's ability to give answers in evidence which both address the questions put to him or her and can be understood both individually and collectively.[24] It appears that any diminution in quality would

---

[17] The use of an intermediary is not an entirely new measure. Evidence of a video-taped interview between a social worker and a disabled witness with severe speech difficulties was, for example, received in *R v Duffy* [1999] 1 Cr App R 307.

[18] Home Office, *Speaking Up For Justice: Report of the Interdepartmental Working Group on the Treatment of Vulnerable or Intimidated Witnesses in the Criminal Justice System* (1998, London: Home Office) 19.

[19] This is the model adopted in Western Australia: Western Australia Acts Amendment (Evidence of Children and Others) Act 1992.

[20] Any witness may qualify for assistance except for the accused, who is specifically excepted in s. 19(1).

[21] The relevant date for determining age is when the court decides whether to offer assistance: s. 16(3).   [22] Within the meaning of the Mental Health Act 1983.

[23] S. 16(5).   [24] S. 16(5).

suffice to qualify a witness for assistance. The final category of eligible witness comprises those who the court considers likely to suffer fear or distress in giving evidence to an extent that is expected to affect its quality. To satisfy this test something more than the ordinary apprehension or 'stage fright' which afflicts most witnesses will be required. It is not for the court to explore whether the fear or apprehension is justified; it is enough that fear exists.[25]

Section 17(2) is intended to give trial judges some guidance as to factors that should properly be taken into account in assessing someone's degree of apprehension or fear about giving evidence.[26] These include the nature of the offence, the age of the witness, and if deemed relevant, the witness's social and cultural background and ethnic origin, domestic and employment circumstances, and any religious beliefs or political opinions.[27] The behaviour of the accused and that of his or her relatives and associates is also to be considered.[28] Somewhat puzzlingly, the court is not directed in section 17(2) to consider the relationship of a witness to the defendant, although this will clearly be a highly significant factor in many cases adding to a witness's fear and apprehension.[29] The views of the witness must also be considered but are not to be binding.[30] It should be emphasized that some witnesses who qualify for assistance will want to have their 'day in court' and will value the opportunity to confront an accused publicly at trial. In such cases research suggests that it would be counterproductive, as well as inappropriate, to press special measures on a witness.[31]

To a laudable extent the eligibility provisions of the YJCEA dispense with artificial restrictions, recognizing that vulnerability is neither a prerogative of youth nor confined to specified offences. Rightly, no distinction is made between witnesses who are alleged victims and those who are eyewitnesses to offences against others. The court has a discretion to allow the special measures for any eligible witness, whatever the offence charged. The Act does however apply special rules to child witnesses and sexual offence complainants. Recognizing that 'giving evidence of an intimate nature in a public courtroom was likely to be an intimidating experience for the majority of rape and serious sexual assault complainants', the working group recommended that there should be a rebuttable assumption that such a witness should have special measures available to him or her.[32] Section 17(4) of the Act goes one step further and provides that a complainant in a sexual offence case is to be considered eligible for special measures

---

[25] Fear or distress must be felt by the witness and not, for example, by a close family member.
[26] The list is not meant to be exclusive.   [27] S. 17(2).   [28] S. 17(2)(d).
[29] Home Office Circular 19/2000 *Domestic Violence: Revised Circular to the Police* states that victims of domestic violence are likely to fall into the category of 'vulnerable witness'.
[30] S. 17(3).
[31] For example, research conducted by Cashmore and Haas suggests that the most important factor in ensuring the success of a prosecution is allowing a witness to decide how his or her evidence will be presented, because witnesses given a choice perform better: Cashmore, J. and De Haas, N., *The Use of Closed Circuit Television for Child Witnesses in the ACT: A Report for the Australian Law Reform Committee and the Australian Capital Territorial Magistrates Court* (1992, Sydney: Australian Law Reform Commission).   [32] Home Office, n. 18 above, para. 9.1.

unless she informs the court that she does not wish to be so. The automatic qualification of rape complainants has the welcome effect of precluding challenges to eligibility in cases of acquaintance or 'date rape' on the unwarranted ground that the complainant knows the defendant and is therefore less likely to be intimidated by him than a victim of rape by a stranger.[33]

Section 21 imposes special obligations on courts when they deal with witnesses under the age of seventeen.[34] Essentially, it creates three groups of child witnesses: those giving evidence in a sexual offence case; those giving evidence in a case involving an offence of violence, abduction, or neglect; and children giving evidence in all other cases. The first two groups are described as being in need of 'special protection' and such children benefit from strong presumptions about how they will give evidence. Specifically, the 'primary rule' in section 21 provides that a video interview of a child deemed to be in need of special protection must be admitted if available unless the video recording falls within the section 27(2) requirement to exclude it in the interests of justice. Strikingly, the court is not required to consider whether the special measures will improve the quality of the witness's evidence. In a sexual offence case the court is then bound to provide that cross-examination and re-examination should also be pre-recorded unless the witness informs the court that she does not want the measure to apply to her. In the case of a child witness giving evidence in a violent offence case, section 21 provides that the witness is entitled to give further evidence by live link at trial and will do so unless an optional order for pre-recorded cross-examination is granted. Child witnesses not deemed to be in need of special protection will, as a general rule, give evidence in chief in the form of video testimony if available and be cross-examined by live link. In these cases, however, the court is required to consider whether the special measure is likely to maximize the quality of a witness's evidence as far as practicable. Having applied these measures as available, the court must in all cases return to section 19 (see below) and consider whether any further measures are necessary.

The presumptions which apply to child witnesses do inject a welcome measure of certainty into the process which was missing under the old regime. Research indicates that it was previously quite common for children to arrive at court without knowing whether video-taped interviews would be admitted or whether a video link or screen would be made available. Decisions were not made at plea and direction hearings and the position taken by counsel could differ on the day of the trial.[35] Less satisfactory is the complexity of the provisions and the differential treatment of children in sex and violence cases, which

---

[33] There are anecdotal reports of rape complainants being refused screens on the grounds that they had known their alleged attacker for years and could not be intimidated by him.

[34] See generally, Bates, P., 'The Youth Justice and Criminal Evidence Act: The evidence of children and vulnerable adults' (1999) 11(3) *Child and Family Law Quarterly* 289.

[35] See Plotnikoff, J. and Woolfson, R., *Prosecuting Child Abuse: An Evaluation of the Government's Speedy Progress Policy* (1995, London: Blackstone) 77.

appear to be based upon the unproven assumption that children falling within the latter category will be less traumatized by a court appearance.

C. PROCEDURE

Applications for special measures will be made at plea and direction hearings, either by the parties or the court may raise the issue of its own motion.[36] Where the court determines that a witness is eligible for assistance by virtue of section 16 or 17 it must then consider whether any of the special measures, or any combination of them, would be likely to improve the quality of the evidence given by the witness.[37] The court is obliged to consider all the circumstances of the case including, in particular, any views expressed by the witness and the extent to which measures might inhibit the evidence being effectively tested by a party to the proceedings.[38] If this test is satisfied, the court must determine which measure or combination of measures would be likely to maximize, so far as practicable, the witness's evidence.[39] Section 20 provides that a special measures direction will normally be binding until the end of a trial, although the court may vary or discharge a direction if it seems to be in the interests of justice to do so. To create some certainty for witnesses the party seeking the alteration or discharge of a direction must show that there has been a material change in circumstances since the direction or an application for it to be altered was last made.[40] Where a court refuses such an application, or alters or discharges an application for special measures it must state its reasons in open court.[41]

At this juncture much will depend on the accuracy and fullness of information provided to the court. This will, in turn, depend heavily on the ability of investigators to establish at an early stage whether a witness is in need of special protection and, if so, the measures which might be appropriate.[42] The fact that children are defined as vulnerable by reason of their age would seem to augur ready identification of this group. However, the minefield of statutory presumptions created by section 21 provides ample scope for error. There is evidence that police officers, social workers, and Crown Prosecution Service lawyers have experienced difficulty in identifying eligible witnesses under the old regime which is less complex in comparison to the new statutory framework.[43] This has resulted in written statements being taken from alleged victims of sexual assault aged between fifteen and seventeen who were entitled to be interviewed by video. Investigators will also require clear and effective guidance

---

[36] S. 19(1).   [37] S. 19(2)(a).

[38] The working group considered that a court would be unlikely to force measures upon a witness against his or her wishes: n. 18 above, para. 3.26.   [39] S. 19(2)(b).

[40] S. 20(2).   [41] S. 20(5).

[42] The working group commended the appointment of specialist officers responsible for identifying vulnerable witnesses: n. 18 above, para. 5.14.

[43] See Hoyano, L. C. H, 'Variations on a theme by Pigot: Special measures directions for child witnesses' [2000] *Criminal Law Review* 250, 253.

if they are to identify witnesses who are vulnerable by reason of learning disability, mental disorder, or illness.[44] Past research suggests that police performance in identifying suspects and witnesses within this category has been poor.[45] The training implications are clear and substantial. The government is currently in the process of devising detailed guidance for the various criminal justice agencies involved.

D. Maximizing Quality?

As stated, the declared aim of the YJCEA is to assist vulnerable and intimidated witnesses to give the best evidence they are capable of giving through the provision of special measures. The court is required to determine not only whether special measures would improve the quality of a witness's evidence but also the measure or combination of measures that would *maximize* the quality of that evidence. Recent research based on experimental study, interviews with witnesses, and trial observation indicate a clear gradation in terms of the protection and assistance which individual measures can be expected to afford.

1. Clearing the Gallery

In the previous Chapter it was seen that the public nature of criminal trials can expose witnesses to acts of intimidation in the court-room and add to the embarrassment and anxiety of witnesses who are required to give evidence of a necessarily intimate nature. Also detailed were the debilitating effects stress can have on the ability of individuals to recall and relate information accurately. A special measure allowing for the exclusion of spectators or specified persons from the public gallery is therefore highly welcome and likely to have a positive effect on the quality of oral testimony. The benefits of this provision are however limited in both scope and effect. Psychological research suggests that the environment most conducive to the disclosure of painful, traumatic events

---

[44] The Home Office consultation paper *Achieving Best Evidence in Criminal Proceedings* provides a series of prompts to be used as an aid in making an overall assessment of an individual witness's needs. Investigating officers are, for example, advised to establish whether a witness lives in sheltered accommodation, attended a special school, receives benefits relating to disability, or has a social worker. Behavioural prompts include slow or confused responses, difficulty in answering simple questions, speech difficulties, inability to read and write, and an unclear concept of time and place. When in doubt, officers are advised to request an early assessment by an expert, such as a clinical psychologist, speech therapist, or psychiatrist: Home Office, *Consultation Paper Achieving Best Evidence in Criminal Proceedings: Guidance for Vulnerable or Intimidated Witnesses, including Children* (2000, London: Home Office).

[45] ACPO has already developed a list of prompts to identify intimidated witnesses. The document *Achieving Best Evidence in Criminal Proceedings* provides further guidance, advising officers to consider, *inter alia*, the offence, the relationship of the witness to the accused, the motivation for the offence, whether it is racism or homophobia; and whether the witness lives in close proximity to the alleged offender, their family or associates: ibid.

would contain a minimum number of unfamiliar persons. Sexual offence complainants, towards whom the measure is primarily aimed, will still have to testify before an audience of court officials, lawyers, and jurors. For many, this is likely to prove a stressful and potentially inhibiting process. In non-sexual offence cases the measure is narrowly confined to situations where the court is persuaded that someone has sought or will seek to intimidate the witness. This fails to cater for witnesses with an intellectual impairment or a mental disorder who may be intimidated by the mere presence of strangers in court.

2. Screens

The inclusion of screens among the special measures provisions of the 1999 Act appears to be a somewhat retrograde step given that screens were at one point officially regarded as a mere stop-gap measure pending full implementation of the television link.[46] In terms of protection, screens rate poorly, an obvious limitation being that the witness is not insulated from the impact of the courtroom.[47] Child witnesses interviewed after giving evidence using screens have, for example, spoken of the disturbing effects of looking directly at the defendant's supporters sitting in the public gallery and of the embarrassment of having to speak about the intimate details of an alleged sexual assault before a room full of strangers.[48] Notwithstanding the power of the court to exclude the public in limited cases, the protection which screens afford is slight. Being in the *same room* as the defendant is the source of stress for many witnesses. When screens are employed a witness is still aware that the accused is only feet away and any sound coming from the dock may be as unsettling to a witness as being able to see him or her. For these reasons screens are only likely to be of benefit where a witness has expressed a desire to remain in the court-room but to be shielded from the eye contact with the accused.

3. Live Television Links

Research into the effectiveness of a live television link in reducing witness anxiety has yielded more positive results.[49] In the first evaluative study of the live link procedure in England and Wales, Davis and Noon observed 154 children

---

[46] See Morgan, J. and Plotnikoff, J., 'Children as victims of crime: Procedure in court' in (eds.) Spencer, J., Nicolson, G., Flin, R. and Bull, R., *Children's Evidence in Legal Proceedings: An International Perspective* (1990, Cambridge: Selwyn College) 191.

[47] There is some evidence to suggest that lawyers are more favourably disposed towards screens than towards other protective measures. See, for example, Plotnikoff *et al.*, n. 35 above, 77.

[48] See, for example, O'Grady C., *Child Witnesses and Jury Trials: An Evaluation of the Use of Closed Circuit Television and Removable Screens in Western Australia* (1996, Perth: Western Australia Ministry of Justice) v.

[49] See generally Davies, G., 'The impact of television on the presentation and reception of children's testimony' (1999) 22 (3–4) *International Journal of Law and Psychiatry* 241; Westcott, H., Davies, G. and Spencer, J., 'Protecting the child witness: Hearsay techniques and other innovations' (1999) 5 *Psychology, Public Policy and Law* 282.

who testified via this medium and assessed their behaviour and performance as witnesses.[50] The study itself contained no control group, but tentative comparisons were made with the reported observation of some eighty-nine children who testified in open court in Scotland. Compared to this sample, children who gave evidence via the television link were, the researchers report, appreciably less distressed and more self-confident. Specifically, a significant majority of the children who used the live link were, in contrast to their Scottish counterparts, able to give evidence without being reduced to tears at any point. Importantly, the study found no support for concerns expressed previously by the Pigot Committee that the use of television links could make a child feel more isolated and insecure and ultimately place a greater burden upon child witnesses.[51] Furthermore, Davis and Noon report that the live link had a positive and facilitating effect on the evidence of the child witnesses they observed. Children who used the live link were more consistent and fluent in their testimony and more resistant to leading questions about peripheral details, correcting barristers when they were wrong. Lawyers interviewed by Davis and Noon largely confirmed that children who used the live link were less frightened, more relaxed, and (some believed) more forthcoming in their evidence as a result. Significantly, it was accepted that the live link enabled some children to give evidence who would otherwise have been unable to speak.

A second study evaluated the introduction of the live link in Scotland.[52] Murray observed forty-eight children giving evidence via the live link and a further seventeen who testified in court. The study was also able to draw on interviews with children and their parents conducted both before and after testifying.[53] Murray reports that, with very few exceptions, the children who had testified over a live link were very glad that they had done so, many expressing the view that the television link had made the process of testifying much less distressing than it might have been had they had to confront the accused in the court-room. Compared to children who testified in court, children who testified by means of a live television link were significantly less likely to report feeling fear while testifying and were significantly more likely to report that the mode of presenting their evidence was fair. It was the opinion of the majority of parents that without the use of the television link the evidence of their children would not have reached the trial at all.[54] Moreover, when questioned, the

---

[50] Davies, G. M. and Noon, E., *An Evaluation of the Live Link for Child Witnesses* (1991, London: Home Office). The study examined the implementation and use of the live link scheme over its first 21 months of operation.

[51] 'It may place a greater burden upon the child witness who must cope with intrusive technology and a sense of remoteness from contemporaneous proceedings': Home Office, *Pigot Committee: Report of the Advisory Group on Video Evidence* (1989, London: HMSO) para. 2.13.

[52] Murray, K., *Live television link: An evaluation of its use by child witnesses in Scottish criminal trials* (1995, Edinburgh: The Scottish Office). Legislation permitting the use of the live link was introduced in Scotland in 1990: Law Reform (Miscellaneous Provisions) (Scotland) Act 1990.

[53] Interviews were conducted with 71 parents pre-trial and 38 parents and 56 children post-trial.

[54] Murray n. 52 above, 107.

participating children who had testified in open court were unanimous in their view that they would have felt more comfortable using the live link facility.[55] Lawyers interviewed by Murray also described the children who testified by live television link as less anxious and more able to recount complete and consistent information than they might have done in the court-room. Nevertheless, children's televised testimony was rated after analysis as slightly less consistent and detailed than that delivered in open court. This may be explained by the fact that the live link users were generally younger and were giving evidence in more serious cases. It is important to note that a significant number of children (58 per cent) 'felt scared' even when using the television link. According to Murray, those using the link were unnerved by anything that triggered images of an accused: 'a shadow on the television screen, a footstep in the corridor, the sound of a cough, peals of laughter coming from the jury, the occasional abrupt interruption to the continuity of their testimony'.[56]

A third evaluative study followed the introduction of the live link in courts in Western Australia.[57] O'Grady reports that witnesses who used television links were very appreciative of the facility and none regretted using it. Users also appeared to adapt well and quickly to the experience of speaking to a television image. Significantly, the majority of children who testified in the conventional manner in open court stated in interviews that they would have preferred some sort of barrier between themselves and the accused and other people in the court-room.[58]

Experimental research findings lend some support to the claim that live link technology reduces stress and in so doing improves the quality of children's testimony. Saywitz and Nathanson, for example, conducted a study in which thirty-four children aged between eight and ten years of age participated in an activity and were questioned about it two weeks later.[59] Half of the children were questioned in a simulated court-room environment and the remainder in their school, both by the same interviewer. The study found that children who answered questions in the mock court-room perceived their experiences as more stressful than the children who were interviewed at school. The former group of children also demonstrated poorer memory performance producing less complete and less detailed descriptions. In a more recent study Goodman *et al.* directly examined the effect of closed-circuit testimony on children giving

---

[55] Ibid. 72.   [56] Ibid. 71.

[57] O'Grady, n. 48 above. In the course of the evaluation observers watched 75 jury trials where children gave evidence. Interviews with 32 witnesses, 26 lawyers, and 8 judges, and opinions of 138 jurors who served on trials where children gave evidence were obtained through a mail survey.

[58] An evaluation by Cashmore and de Haas following the introduction of television links in Canberra also reported that children who testified via television links appeared significantly less anxious than those giving evidence in the conventional manner: see n. 31 above. See also Whitney, L. and Cook, A., *The Use of Closed Circuit Television in New Zealand Courts: The First Six Trials* (1990, Wellington: Department of Justice).

[59] Saywitz, K. and Nathanson, R., 'Children's testimony and their perception of stress in and out of the courtroom' (1993) 17 *Child Abuse and Neglect* 613.

evidence in elaborately staged mock jury trials. One hundred and eighty-six children individually participated in a play session with an unfamiliar male confederate and two weeks later were taken to a local court-room and questioned about what had taken place at the session.[60] Mock juries observed the trials, with the children's evidence presented either live in open-court or over closed-circuit television. Prior to each trial the children answered questions about their anxiety level. Testifying in open court, Goodman *et al.* report, was associated with higher levels of pre-trial stress. Pre-trial anxiety was, in turn, associated with children refusing to testify or becoming too upset to testify. Goodman *et al.* report a small but significant positive impact on children's answers to direct questions compared to live testimony in open court. In particular, use of closed-circuit technology was associated with decreased suggestibility for younger children. Children who testified in the court-room were found to make more errors in answering misleading questions than other children of the same age who used television links. Expressing the usual caveats about generalizing their findings to forensic settings, Goodman *et al.* conclude that television links generally promoted more accurate testimony in the children in their sample. The protective nature of the closed-circuit arrangement specifically helped children feel less anxious about testifying, helped them agree to testify, and reduced suggestibility in younger children.[61]

Caution is always advisable when applying the results of experimental research to actual criminal trials and researchers themselves are quick to point out variables which may compromise the ecological validity of their experiments. However, when considered in conjunction with children's perspectives and observational trial data, these studies support the view that the live link removes a significant source of stress without evident ill effect. No strong conclusions may be drawn about the impact of the live link on the quality of children's evidence, but the effects do appear to be positive rather than negative. Moreover, it seems reasonable to assume that vulnerable adult witnesses would derive similar benefits from the live link facility. In New Zealand television links have been available, at the court's discretion, to adult learning disabled complainants in sexual cases since 1989. The Law Commission reported in 1996 that no major problems had arisen in its use. A small-scale study on the use of television links concluded that, in the case of learning disabled complainants, the equipment allowed for concentration and focus that would probably not occur in the court-room setting.[62] Nevertheless, the live link is not a panacea. Removing a witness from the court-room may eliminate key environmental stressors but in many cases this will be insufficient to give the courts access to the best evidence potentially available. As the previous Chapter described, a lengthy retention interval between a given incident and the recording of a

---

[60] Goodman, G., Tobet, A., Batterman-Faunce, J., Orcutt, H., Thomas, S., Shapiro, C. and Sachsenmaier, T., 'Face to face confrontation: Effects of closed circuit technology on children's eye-witness testimony and jurors' decisions' (1998) 22 *Law and Human Behaviour* 165.

[61] Ibid. 199.   [62] Whitney *et al.*, n. 58 above, 26.

witness's testimony represents as much, if not more, of a threat to the quality of evidence and the welfare of vulnerable witnesses. Television links do not resolve the sizeable problem of trial delay, which results in memory deterioration, 'motivated forgetting', and memory contamination and distortion. Nor do they provide a remedy to the accumulated stress caused by delays and postponements in the run-up to a trial which can so debilitate a witness. These issues are likely to have an adverse effect on a large proportion of witnesses eligible for assistance under the Act. Thus, to the extent that the live television link reinforces and perpetuates detrimental reliance on live oral testimony, it may be viewed as a doubled-edged sword.

Freer to Lie?

It is necessary at this point to address claims that the quality of evidence elicited from a witness shielded by protective measures will necessarily suffer from the absence of key testing conditions: namely, direct confrontation and public scrutiny.[63] It is often said that a witness who gives evidence via a live link is freer to lie and to do so undetected than a witness exposed to the physical presence of the accused and the formality of a public forum. Scottish lawyers interviewed by Murray, for example, expressed a belief that children who testified by means of the live link were more likely to tell lies. Defence lawyers surveyed by Davis and Noon in England and Wales and by O'Grady in Western Australia voiced similar fears. It may be common 'wisdom' at the Bar, but there is no persuasive empirical support for the assumption that a physical confrontation between an accusatory witness and the defendant encourages the former to tell the truth. Nor do there appear to be sound grounds for assuming that examination in public deters a witness from providing false testimony. What evidence there is suggests that these so-called evidentiary safeguards are counter-productive in certain cases, making it more difficult, if not impossible, for some vulnerable and intimidated witnesses to testify.[64] This was the conclusion reached by the New Zealand Law Commission in a recent report addressing the problems encountered by vulnerable witnesses within the criminal trial process:

The fact that the complainant may not be present in the same room as the defendant, or is behind a screen, does raise the concern that the lack of face to face confrontation may take away what some may view as an important deterrent to lying. There is, however, simply no empirical evidence that people are less likely to lie when faced with the person

[63] As an exponent of this view Graham asserts that 'People are more careful and sincere when they accuse someone face to face rather than when they are spreading rumor': Graham, M., 'Indicia of Reliability and Face to Face Confrontation: Emerging Issues in Child Sexual Abuse Prosecutions' (1985) 40 *University of Miami Law Review* 19, 74. See also Beckett, J., 'The true value of the confrontation clause: A study of child sexual abuse trials' (1994) 82 *Georgetown Law Journal* 1605, 1607.

[64] As Spencer and Flin note, 'It should be obvious that it makes it harder rather than easier to tell the truth about another to have that person there, particularly if the truth is unpleasant': Spencer, J. R. and Flin, R., *Evidence of Children: The Law and the Psychology* (1993, London: Blackstone) 278.

they are accusing and, from the point of view of promoting reliability, there is no basis to conclude that alternative ways of giving evidence detract from either the rational ascertainment of facts or procedural fairness.[65]

4. Video-taped Interviews

Video-taping a witness's evidence in advance of trial appears to offer a solution to both court-related stress and, if conducted promptly, to the substantial problems associated with trial delay. Specifically, a witness's account can be accurately recorded while still relatively fresh, in an environment more conducive to full and frank disclosure. Moreover, witnesses are questioned by skilled interviewers trained to accommodate their special needs in accordance with guidelines grounded in psychological research. As Birch and Leng note, the 'net result of accumulation of expertise is likely to be an interview that is of better "quality", in all the senses in which that term is used in the 1999 Act, than an exchange conducted in the form of an examination in chief in court'.[66] While the merits of video-taped testimony are widely recognized, recent research has raised significant questions regarding the evidential use of video-taped investigatory interviews in criminal trials. This research suggests that such interviews may compare unfavourably to testimony extracted by experienced counsel in important respects. While some of the problems identified relate to the advice given to interviewers, others are of a structural nature, stemming from the bipartisan nature of evidence presentation within the adversarial trial process.

Background

In 1989 the Pigot Committee recommended a scheme under which in certain cases the entire evidence of children would routinely be taken in advance of trial and recorded on video-tape.[67] Under its proposals the admissibility of a video-recorded interview with a child would be decided at a preliminary hearing attended by the accused and by counsel for each side. The committee envisaged that such interviews would be conducted by specially trained interviewers, usually social workers or police officers, in line with an official code of practice. The examination and cross-examination of a child witness would take place at a subsequent preliminary hearing held in relatively informal surroundings, with only the judge, counsel for each side, the child, and a supporter present. The defendant would view the proceedings through a two-way mirror or television link, and be able to instruct defence counsel through an audio link. The video-recorded evidence would later be shown at trial, substantially replacing oral examination in chief and cross-examination. According to the Committee,

---

[65] New Zealand Law Commission, *The Evidence of Children and other Vulnerable Witnesses* (1996, Wellington: New Zealand Law Commission) 28.

[66] Birch, D. and Leng, R., *Blackstone's Guide to the Youth Justice and Criminal Evidence Act 1999* (2000, London: Blackstone Press) 29.   [67] Home Office, n. 51 above.

allowing children to give video-taped evidence made as early as possible in informal surroundings would give the courts access to an important and often crucial source of evidence and would spare child witnesses the acknowledged trauma of testifying in court.[68]

To the disappointment of many the government chose to implement the Pigot recommendations only in part.[69] The 'watered down' scheme introduced, known colloquially as 'half-Pigot', allowed for the admission of pre-recorded investigatory interviews with the leave of the court in sex and violence cases. However, leave was only to be granted if, *inter alia*, the child witness was available for cross-examination at trial.[70] Subject to the power of the court to exclude otherwise admissible evidence, section 32A of the Criminal Justice Act 1988 provided that leave should be granted unless, in the opinion of the court, the recording ought not to be admitted in the interests of justice or if the rules requiring disclosure had not been complied with.[71] Where recordings were admitted, the court could direct that parts of the video recording be edited or excluded.[72] Police officers and social workers have typically been assigned the task of conducting interviews in accordance with guidance contained in the *Memorandum of Good Practice* published by the Home Office and Department of Health in 1992.[73] An important feature of the half-Pigot scheme is that video-taped interviews were expected to replace conventional examination in chief completely, with supplementary questions by prosecution counsel permitted only where the trial judge is satisfied that a matter was not 'dealt with

---

[68] Ibid. para. 2.18. In 1996 the New Zealand Law Commission recommended the introduction of pre-trial cross-examination in the case of child complainants who have given evidence in chief on video-tape and any witness whose evidence in chief the court has directed be given on video-tape and who are shown to have an inability to retain and recall information over time. New Zealand Law Commission, *The Evidence of Children and other Vulnerable Witnesses* (1996, Wellington: New Zealand Law Commission). However, in 1999 the Law Commission decided not to recommend pre-trial cross-examination, apparently as a result of 'unanimous opposition from the defence bar' following the publication of its initial proposals: New Zealand Law Commission, *Evidence Report 55 Volume 1: Reform of the Law* (1999, Wellington: New Zealand Law Commission) 460.

[69] See Birch, P., 'Children's Evidence' [1992] *Criminal Law Review* 262; Spencer, J. R., 'Children's Evidence and the Criminal Justice Act: A Lost Opportunity' (1991) November, *Magistrate*, 182; Spencer, J. R., 'Reforming the law on children's evidence in England: The Pigot Committee and after' in (eds.) Dent, H. and Flin, R., *Children as Witnesses* (1992, Chichester: Wiley) 113.

[70] The same age limits applied as for live links.

[71] S. 32A(3)(b) and (c). The admissibility of the video-taped interview in criminal proceedings is also subject to the Police and Criminal Evidence Act 1984, s. 78.

[72] S. 32A(3). The court is required to consider whether any prejudice to the accused which might result from the admission of some part of the recorded interview is outweighed by the desirability of showing the whole, or substantially the whole: s. 32A(4).

[73] The *Memorandum* provides interviewers with guidance on the conduct of investigative interviews and appropriate questioning techniques. It advocates a four-stage approach to the investigative interviewing of children, comprising rapport building, free narrative, questioning, and closure. The provisions of the *Memorandum* are not mandatory but those conducting investigatory pre-trial interviews are under considerable pressure to adhere to its guidance: Home Office, *Memorandum of good practice on video recorded interviews with child witnesses for criminal proceedings* (1992, London: Home Office).

adequately' in the recorded evidence.[74] A recent CPS Inspectorate Report indicates that the submission of an application to show a video-taped interview is now the norm in cases of alleged child sexual abuse.[75]

Weaknesses of the 'Half-Pigot' Scheme

In recent years few have seriously questioned the use of video-taped interviews as replacements for children's examination in chief in criminal trials. In an early evaluative study child protection professionals did express strong reservations about the continuing need for cross-examination at court while lawyers voiced concerns about the likely impact of video-taped evidence relative to live testimony.[76] The conformity of video-taped interviews with the rules of evidence was also a matter of concern for defence lawyers who cited the overuse of leading questions, the inclusion of inadmissible hearsay evidence, and improper comforting by interviewers. Overall however the professionals surveyed generally favoured the introduction of video-taped evidence, the main perceived advantage being the reduction of stress and trauma for the children involved.[77] The same study interviewed children about their experience of making a video and the majority made positive comments, preferring the use of a video recording to giving evidence via a live link.[78] Court-room ratings also suggested that children who testified live were considerably more anxious than those seen on tape.[79]

However, more recent studies have raised concerns regarding the quality of evidence recorded in video-taped interviews. An evaluative study commissioned by the Home Office and carried out by a team of researchers from the University of Bristol[80] significantly found that initial memorandum interviews with

---

[74] Criminal Justice Act 1988, s. 32A(5) as amended by the Criminal Justice and Public Order Act 1994, s. 50 and further amended by the Criminal Procedure and Investigations Act 1996, s. 62(2).

[75] According to the report 93% of cases were accompanied by an application to show a video; 77% of the applications were granted; 23% of applications granted were not taken up; 56% of children had their video-tapes played in court: Crown Prosecution Service, *The Inspectorate's Report on Cases Involving Child Abuse* (1998, London: Crown Prosecution Service Inspectorate).

[76] Davies, G., Wilson, C., Mitchell, R. and Milsom, J., *Videotaping Children's Evidence: An Evaluation* (1994, London: Home Office). There were 640 video applications made between 1 October 1992 and 30 June 1994 and 470 of these were granted. Of the remainder, 25 were refused whilst the others were rendered unnecessary by a late guilty plea from the defendant.

[77] Most judges favoured the admission of video-taped interviews, although under half of barristers did so.

[78] A review of 40 video-taped interviews found the visual and sound quality of interviews to be generally satisfactory, though technical difficulties had rendered a significant minority of video-tapes unusable.

[79] Trained observers attended 93 separate trials and assessed the demeanour and competence of the children testifying. Of the 150 children observed, some 73% had their video-tape played as evidence in chief while the remainder were examined via the live link. Questionnaires were also completed by 17 children who had made a video-tape and had appeared in court.

[80] Davis, G., Hoyano, L., Keenan, C., Maitland, L. and Morgan, R., *An Assessment of the Admissibility and Sufficiency of Evidence in Child Abuse Prosecutions* (1999, London: Home Office). The study included an examination of 94 cases involving 124 complainants in 2 police force areas and examination of 79 video-taped interviews. The cases involved allegations of physical

children often produced incomplete, inadmissible, and sometimes incoherent accounts from children that jurors found difficult to understand.[81] The study endorsed the findings of earlier research by Wade *et al.* which found that children's evidence in investigative interviews often lacked specificity, structure, and clarity compared to evidence as it emerged in a carefully staged examination in chief.[82]

Criticism of the *Memorandum of Good Practice*

The deficiencies of children's pre-trial disclosures have been attributed in part to weaknesses in the *Memorandum of Good Practice*. A particular concern has been the guidance that no video-taped interview should last for longer than one hour and that children should ideally be interviewed only once.[83] Underlying this guidance is an assumption that lengthy and repeated questioning causes undue stress to a child by reviving the trauma he or she experienced at the time of the event and a concern that multiple interviews may increase the risk of evidence contamination. According to the Bristol team, this advice adds unnecessarily to the pressure on interviewers as it is based on unrealistic expectations regarding the capacity and willingness of children to recall all relevant information relating to an offence at one sitting. Full disclosure may, for example, be inhibited at a first interview by a child's natural reluctance to discuss intimate sexual matters with a stranger and possible fear of naming a perpetrator who has threatened them into silence. Moreover, the fullness of an initial disclosure may depend on the interviewer's developmental sensitivity, or the child's ability to retrieve relevant information at a given moment in time.[84] Although initial disclosures were often incomplete, the Bristol study found that second interviews were rarely instigated. Officers tended to believe that a second interview might be both harmful to the child and damaging to the prosecution case, inviting the suggestion that the child had been coached between the two interviews. CPS lawyers admitted rarely sanctioning a second interview. The view that supplementary interviews are inevitably harmful and thus to be avoided has recently been challenged. For example, Martin and Thomson maintain that second or even third interviews need not necessarily be traumatic for a child witness. As they note, '[m]any therapeutic approaches involve recall of a traumatic event—whether in part or the entire episode—and repeated recall is a particular feature of grief counselling which often accompanies interventions after

---

assault, neglect, or sexual assault. See also Keenan, C., Davis, G., Hoyano, L. and Maitland, L., 'Interviewing Alleged Abused Children with a View to Criminal Prosecution' [1999] *Criminal Law Review*, 863.   [81] Davis *et al.*, n. 80 above, 68.

[82] Wade, A., Lawson, A. and Aldridge, J., 'Stories in Court' (1998) 10(2) *Child and Family Law Quarterly* 179. According to the researchers, as a result video testimony placed greater demands on jurors in terms of concentration.

[83] Although this advice is not mandatory it has, in practice, been treated as such.

[84] Myers, J., Saywitz, K. and Goodman, G., 'Psychological research on children as witnesses: Practical implications for forensic interviews and courtroom testimony' (1996) 28 *Pacific Law Journal* 3, 20.

traumatic experiences'.[85] The researchers also suggest that the risk of contamination need not increase if interviews are properly conducted.

The *Memorandum* guidance has also been criticized for taking insufficient account of the special needs of children who are disabled,[86] black,[87] young, or highly traumatized as a result of long-term and organized abuse.[88] The *Memorandum*'s phased approach to interviewing has, for example, been characterized as inapt for certain children with special needs.[89] A lack of adequate pre-interview preparation has also been blamed for children's less than satisfactory performance in video interviews. For example, Wade *et al*. found that it was rare for children to have been consulted about the arrangements for the interview, and very often they did not understand the implications of making a statement.[90] This, Wade *et al*. report, had a negative impact on the completeness and quality of children's evidence. In interviews children described their own experiences:

The first [video] they made, I didn't really tell them anything . . . I didn't know what was happening and what it was about . . . I didn't even know she was a police lady until I got there. If they would have told me before I even got there then it wouldn't have been upsetting, but it was when I got there that I found out. That was what got to me. [Nine-year-old girl.]

I was just sort of shoved in the room and interviewed, really. I was introduced but I wasn't, I didn't really feel very comfortable at first . . . I didn't want to speak to them because I didn't know anything about them and you know—complete strangers. I didn't know whether I could trust them or not.[91]

The *Memorandum* is currently being updated and revised to take into account the wider range of eligible witnesses and special measures available under the 1999 Act. It is encouraging that the consultation draft document *Achieving Best Evidence in Criminal Proceeding* has taken many of the above criticisms on board.[92] The revised and updated document, which will apply not only to children but to all vulnerable and intimidated witnesses, draws upon practical experience and research completed since the publication of the original

---

[85] Martin, S. and Thomson, D., 'Videotapes and Multiple Interviews: The Effects on the Child Witness' (1994) 1(2) *Psychiatry, Psychology and Law* 119, 120.

[86] See Marchant, R. and Page M., 'The Memorandum and disabled children' in (eds.) Westcott, H. and Jones, J., *Perspectives on the Memorandum, Policy, Practice and Research in Investigative Interviewing* (1997, Aldershot, Hants: Arena) 67.

[87] Gupta, A., 'Black Children and the Memorandum' in Westcott *et al*., n. 86 above, 81.

[88] Davies, L., 'The investigation of organised abuse: Considering alternatives' in Westcott, n. 86 above, 109.

[89] See Davies, G. and Westcott, H., *Interviewing Child Witness under the Memorandum of Good Practice: A Research Review* Police Research Series Paper 115 (1999, London: Home Office).

[90] Wade *et al*., n. 82 above.

[91] Wade, A. and Westcott, H., 'No easy answers: Children's perspectives on investigative interviews' in Westcott *et al*., n. 86 above, 55. Children interviewed by Wade also attributed incomplete *Memorandum* disclosures to: the difficulty of talking about their abuse; anxiety about what the investigation might lead to; concern that what they would say would cause distress to people they cared for; the stress of the interview itself; or their dislike of the interviewer.

[92] Home Office Consultation Paper, *Achieving Best Evidence in Criminal Proceedings: Guidance for Vulnerable or Intimidated Witnesses, including Children* (2000, London: Home Office).

Memorandum in 1992. Significantly, the new guidance is broader in scope and covers not only interviewing but also witness support and preparation at the interview, pre-trial, and court stages. The greatly criticized one-hour rule on interviews has disappeared. In relation to children, the new document states that shorter times will usually be necessary for developmentally younger children with limited attention spans, while older children may be comfortable with an interview which lasts longer than an hour.[93] It also recognized that a supplementary interview with a child may be necessary in some circumstances. More than one such interview, the guidance states, is unlikely to be appropriate except when interviewing very young or psychologically disturbed children or where a case is exceptionally complex or involves multiple allegations. In relation to witnesses with a learning disability the document states that several short interviews are more likely to lead to a satisfactory response than one long interview. As well as giving advice on identifying witnesses in need of assistance and the measures that may be open to them, the document provides special detailed guidance on interviewing different categories of witness while emphasizing the need to tailor responses to the witness's particular needs and circumstances. Only time will tell whether the new guidance has struck an appropriate balance between the special needs of vulnerable and intimidated witnesses and evidential concerns.

Structural Problems

More intractable are the deeper structural problems affecting the quality of children's testimony in video-taped interviews which have been identified in recent studies. The Bristol team specifically notes the multiple functions that video-taped interviews are required to serve which are extremely difficult to reconcile. The interview is the initial exploratory step in a criminal investigation and is intended to ascertain whether an offence has been committed; at the same time, it is expected to constitute a child's examination in chief at trial.[94] The interviewer is thus required to perform simultaneously the roles of investigator and counsel adducing evidence. Little thought appears to have been given to the nature of examination in chief and whether interviewers can realistically be expected to do the job of barristers given that the latter's role within an adversarial process extends well beyond the simple eliciting of a narrative account.

Persuasion is commonly presented as the ultimate goal of a trial advocate within an adversarial process. In examination in chief a barrister does not simply seek to elicit relevant factual information from a witness, but to promote a version of reality in antithesis to the account advanced by the other side. This reflects the basic assumption of adversarial theory that 'truth' best emerges from an orchestrated clash of opposing views.[95] Each party is expected to

---

[93] Ibid. para. 7.3.2.

[94] The interview is also an inquiry into whether the child needs protection in civil proceedings.

[95] The central precept of the adversary process is that out of a sharp clash of proofs presented by adversaries in a highly structured forensic setting is most likely to come the information upon which

present the facts in the light most favourable to its own side in the belief that party self-interest will bring a greater number of facts to light. Advocacy manuals are replete with advice on the methods and organizational principles that advocates should adopt in order to maximize the persuasiveness of their respective cases.[96] In relation to examination in chief, these manuals uniformly identify careful pre-trial preparation as the key to trial success. Counsel are specifically advised to identify clear goals for direct examination and to formulate questions and a structure that will enhance these defined objectives.[97] Before embarking upon examination in chief counsel are instructed to develop a theory of the case and to identify the themes that will provide a fact-finder with a framework for interpreting evidence presented at trial. During pre-trial preparation counsel are further advised to anticipate difficult areas in cross-examination and to use examination in chief to draw out possible weaknesses in a witness's testimony, thus stealing a cross-examiner's 'thunder' and neutralizing the effect of detrimental evidence.

At trial barristers seek to elicit testimony from witnesses in a manner that enhances its persuasive impact. Counsel often decide simply to present events in the form of an easy-to-follow chronological narrative. Alternatively, counsel may for strategic reasons elect to extract testimony in a sequence different from that in which events are claimed to have occurred. Advocacy texts refer to the doctrines of primacy and recency which provide that the first and last moments of any given exchange will be the most memorable.[98] Hence, sequencing is used deliberately in criminal trials to highlight and reinforce favourable facts and to minimize the impact of contrary evidence.[99] Advocates are, for example, advised to bury potentially embarrassing or counter-productive material deeply in the middle of examination in chief.[100]

In recent years advocacy texts have been particularly influenced by the work of social scientists on the importance of story-telling in criminal proceedings.[101] Many trial commentators now urge lawyers to engage in the explicit construction of stories in court and offer guidance on the properties of credible narratives. For

---

a neutral and passive decision maker can base the resolution of a litigated dispute acceptable to both parties and society': Landsman, S., *The Adversary System: A Description and Defense* (1984, Washington, DC: American Enterprise Institute for Public Policy Research) 2.

[96] See Evans, K., *The Golden Rules of Advocacy* (1993, London: Blackstone); Munkman, J., *The Techniques of Advocacy* (1991, London: Butterworths); Napley, D., *The Technique of Persuasion* (1970, London: Sweet & Maxwell); Turbak, N., 'Effective Direct Examination' (1998) 34 *Trial* 68.

[97] See, for example, Kerper, J., 'The Art and Ethics of Direct Examination' (1998) 22 *American Journal of Trial Advocacy* 377, 383.

[98] Ibid. In scientific studies of memory this is known as the 'serial position effect': see Ainsworth, P., *Psychology, Law and Eyewitness Testimony* (1998, Chichester: Wiley) 25.

[99] In a similar vein, Marcus Stone states that it may be tactically advantageous to call a good witness last, so as to leave the court with a good final impression: Stone, M., *The Proof of Facts in Criminal Trials* (1984, Edinburgh: Green) 270.

[100] Lubet, S., 'Persuasion at Trial' (1997) 21 *American Journal of Trial Advocacy* 325, 328.

[101] Miller, M. and Mauet, T., 'The Psychology of Jury Persuasion' (1999) 22 *American Journal of Trial Advocacy* 549.

example, some refer to the work of Bennett and Feldman on the relationship between story structure and narrative plausibility and acceptance.[102] According to Bennett and Feldman's narrative theory, stories which exhibit greater structural coherence are more likely to be believed than those containing structural ambiguities.[103] Advocates are accordingly advised to strive for 'internal coherence' during examination in chief and to ensure that a basic story line is not submerged in a welter of sequential detail. According to Doan:

A well-designed story should comport reality, touch appropriate emotions and human values and be told from a well chosen point of view. It must use colourful language coupled with attention extending, memory enhancing and knowledge increasing visual aids. It needs to repeat the case theory and persuasive facts without appearing to do so. It has to be delivered in enough detail to be convincing, but in a timely fashion.[104]

Through the use of controlled questioning[105] and various preventative techniques an advocate guides a witness through his or her testimony in court avoiding troublesome elaboration and equally damaging omission.[106] Other discursive devices or advocacy tools used in the task of persuasion include deliberate juxtaposition, repetition, and duration to emphasize or disguise the significance of certain information. Variations in pace and tone are also used both to maintain juror interest and to reflect the story counsel wants to tell. For example, Lubet notes that counsel may speak rapidly to make events seem faster, closer together, and more intense, and slowly to make events seem unhurried, further apart, and more relaxed.[107]

The highly stylized, nigh theatrical nature of examination in chief contrasts sharply with questioning conducted in *Memorandum* interviews. The investigative nature of such interviews first and foremost precludes adequate opportunity for preparation and planning. Interviewers necessarily embark upon questioning without an overview of the whole case or even a clear idea of the nature of a child's allegations. As a consequence interviewers are unable to

---

[102] 'Stories have implicit structures that enable people to make systematic comparisons between stories. Moreover, the structural form of a completely specified story alerts interpreters to descriptive information in a story that might be missing, and which, if filled in, could alter the significance of the action. The inadequate development of setting, character, means, or motive can, as any literature student knows, render a story's action ambiguous. In a novel or film, such ambiguity may be an aesthetic flaw. In a trial, it is grounds for reasonable doubt': Bennett, W. L. and Feldman, M., *Reconstructing Reality in the Courtroom* (1981, New Brunswick: Rutgers University Press) 10.

[103] 'A prosecution case that fails to define all the elements of a story in a consistent way will generally succumb to a defense strategy that simply attacks the structural adequacy of the prosecution case': ibid. 97. For a critique of Bennett and Feldman's theory see Jackson, J. D., *Law, Fact and Narrative Coherence* (1988, Liverpool: Deborah Charles) ch. 3.

[104] Doan, L., 'The Art of Trial Advocacy for Prosecutors' (1999) 33 *Prosecutor* 34, 38.

[105] 'If the witness must not be led, he must be guided. The evidence is given responsively, in answer to questions, not spontaneously, and the advocate must keep the witness under control': Du Cann, R., *The Art of the Advocate* (1993, London: Penguin) 97.

[106] See Jackson, J. D., 'Law's Truth, Lay Truth and Lawyers' Truth: The Representation of Evidence in Adversary Trials' (1992) 3 *Law and Critique* 31, McBarnet, D., 'Victim in the Witness Box: Confronting Victimology's Stereotype' (1983) 7 *Contemporary Crises* 293.

[107] Lubet, n. 100 above, 334.

impose the same order on children's pre-trial disclosures. Chronological sequencing is almost impossible, resulting in accounts which are frequently 'rambling and incoherent'.[108] The difficulty of assessing the relevance of specific disclosures as they emerge can also lead to detrimental gaps in a child's evidence:

With no clear idea of the specific nature of the allegations, it is difficult for interviewers to maintain an overview of the child's allegations during an interview so as to ensure that all the questions that could be asked are asked. It is very easy for interviewers to fail to pursue a point when they have a series of questions they wish to ask and are trying to listen to the child at the same time.[109]

At the same time, interviewers may not rely on predictability of response and cannot guard against breaches of the rules of evidence, for example the introduction of hearsay information. Those conducting *Memorandum* interviews will also inevitably find it more difficult to identify the boundaries of propriety in leading a witness. In court experienced counsel may, with the permission of the court, make judicious use of focused and even leading questions in chief in order to extract testimony from a reticent witness.[110] Research suggests that some police officers and social workers are extremely reluctant to employ such questioning techniques for fear of being accused of unduly influencing a child's account, using leading questioning only as 'a last resort'.[111] According to Davis *et al.* officers were given little guidance on the legal principles which underlie the various protocols they are asked to follow. As a result officers tended to lack confidence in their knowledge of the law, and were apprehensive about the courts' reactions to their interviewing techniques. They were particularly concerned lest they be found to have asked leading questions and so jeopardized the whole prosecution case.[112] This is significant because clinical experience and psychological research indicate that victims of sexual or physical abuse find it extremely difficult to disclose without the prompting that these forms of questioning allow.[113]

Of course, not all interviewers exercise the same degree of caution. Video-taped interviews are regularly rejected by the courts or Crown Prosecution Service due to the use of unacceptable questioning techniques. In the Bristol study most of the objections raised by defence counsel to the use of video tapes were based upon the interviewer's style of questioning and specifically the use of

---

[108] Davis *et al.*, n. 80 above, 27. The recent Crown Prosecution Service Inspectorate report states 'It could be better for the quality of the prosecution evidence if it were extracted by experienced counsel using the television link, rather than in a more discursive account on video': n. 75 above, para. 8.51.   [109] Davis *et al.*, n. 80 above, 21.

[110] In court, of course, defence counsel may make an objection before a witness replies to an improper leading question posed by prosecution counsel.

[111] Leading questions are generally discouraged (though not prohibited) during video-taped interviews on the ground that they may elicit unreliable information from a suggestible child witness.   [112] Davis *et al.*, n. 80 above, ix.

[113] See, for example, Dent, H. and Newton, S., 'The conflict between clinical and evidential interviewing in child sexual abuse' (1994) 1 *Psychology, Crime and Law* 181.

leading questions.[114] The Crown Prosecution Service Inspectorate also recently reported that 54 per cent of video interviews required editing with the result that some child witnesses did not benefit from the measures available to them.[115] This is perhaps to be expected in a trial system characterized by a complex body of exclusionary rules which tax even experienced lawyers and are 'quite alien to the interviewer's professional culture'.[116]

Overall, the prompt recording of a witness's evidence elicited by a trained interviewer in a relatively informal environment promises to provide access to fuller, more reliable testimony in ways that alternative trial arrangements do not. The contentious nature of evidence presentation with its accent on persuasion and body of exclusionary rules nevertheless serve to undermine the potential utility of video-taped investigatory interviews within the context of adversarial trial proceedings. To date, this position has been compounded by the 'inflexible approach of the 1991 legislation to the use of the interview as the child's evidence in chief'.[117] Under the 1991 regime an interview was expected to replace direct examination completely and limitations were imposed on supplementary questioning in court.[118] According to the Bristol study, this meant in practice that the prosecution could often not improve its case beyond a child's initial incomplete or otherwise deficient video-taped disclosure. Accordingly, when confronted with a poor quality video-taped investigatory interview prosecutors had little choice other than to 'jettison the interview and proceed with live examination in chief at trial, or abandon the prosecution altogether'.[119]

Lamentably, the Youth Justice and Criminal Justice Act 1999 does nothing to remedy this situation. Indeed, the Act may be said to place the prosecution in an even tighter strait-jacket by placing further restrictions on additional direct examination.[120] Section 27(5)(b) provides that supplementary questioning can only be conducted with the permission of the court and this can only be given in relation to matters which have not been dealt with adequately in the witness's recorded testimony. The court must be further satisfied that it would be in the interests of justice to do so.[121] Subsection (7) allows a court to give such permission on an application by a party to the proceedings only if there has been a material change of circumstances since the direction to admit the video

---

[114] Davis *et al.*, n. 80 above, 57.

[115] This occurred in just over 54% of cases on file samples which were listed for trial and were invariably instigated by the defence or the court: n. 75 above.   [116] Hoyano, n. 43 above, 254.

[117] Ibid. 255.

[118] Criminal Justice Act 1988, s. 32A(5) amended by the Criminal Justice and Public Order Act 1994, s. 50 and further amended by the Criminal Procedure and Investigations Act 1996, s. 62(2). The CPIA 1996, s. 62(2) has somewhat relaxed the prohibition on asking supplementary questions. It allows the court to give permission for the child to give further live testimony in chief respecting matters dealt with in the video recording where there has been 'a material change of circumstances' since the court first gave leave to admit the video recording in evidence and it appears to the court 'to be in the interests of justice to give such permission'.

[119] Hoyano, n. 43 above, 254. Judges told the Bristol team that it was rare in their experience for supplementary questions to be asked: Davis *et al.*, n. 80 above, 60.

[120] Hoyano, n. 43 above, 264.   [121] S. 27(7).

recording was made.[122] As Birch points out, the new rules also appear to remove from prosecutors the option of abandoning an admissible but deficient video-taped interview in favour of live examination in the case of child witnesses deemed in need of 'special protection'. When a child gives evidence in a sexual or violent offence case section 21 provides that the court will not have to consider whether special measures will improve the quality of her or his evidence. The argument that use of a possibly disjointed and rambling video-taped interview would not maximize the quality of a vulnerable child's evidence does not therefore appear to be open to prosecutors.[123] This runs contrary to the spirit of the legislation which is avowedly committed to securing access to a witness's best evidence.

Possible Remedies?

According to the Bristol team, many of the problems identified in their report could be resolved, or at least alleviated, if prosecution lawyers were granted greater latitude in the use of video-taped interviews. Prosecutors should, they argue, be able to decide whether to use a video-taped interview as a complete substitute for oral examination in chief or as only one segment of that evidence. This would give interviewers greater freedom to act as investigators and would enable prosecutors to fill in any serious omissions in a witness's evidence at trial.[124] Moreover, it would allow prosecutors to ease a child into the process of giving evidence rather than confronting him or her immediately with a hostile cross-examiner. The researchers point out that prosecutors in other jurisdictions are currently subject to far fewer constraints than their counterparts in England and Wales. In Canada and New Zealand, for example, Crown prosecutors have an unfettered choice as to how to use a video-taped interview as part of a child's examination in chief. In Canada prosecutors often opt to use a video-taped interview as an introduction to oral examination in chief, either to supplement the child's narrative or simply as a historical record of how the disclosure occurred.[125] Such a move would, however, require child witnesses to testify at trial. Any advantage gained by flexible supplementary questioning would arguably be outweighed by the detrimental effects of pre-trial delay and additional stress on the integrity of children's testimony and their welfare. Davis *et al.* themselves report that even children afforded the protection of a video link or screen at trial in their study showed signs of stress which affected the quality of their evidence.[126]

A more radical alternative would be to adopt a procedure similar to that already operating in a number of common law jurisdictions, including a

---

[122] The consultation paper *Achieving Best Evidence in Criminal Proceedings* states that witnesses will be asked to give further evidence 'exceptionally': Home Office, n. 8 above, para. 3.6.7.

[123] According to Birch the 'new regime generates intolerable pressures on the interviewers of children to get it right first time': Birch, D., 'A Better Deal for Vulnerable Witnesses?' [2000] *Criminal Law Review* 223, 246.

[124] Barristers and several judges interviewed in the Bristol study supported this reform.

[125] Davis *et al.*, n. 80 above, 72.   [126] Ibid. 68.

number of US states and Western Australia.[127] In these jurisdictions eligible witnesses are examined by prosecution counsel in advance of trial at a court-ordered pre-trial hearing. These hearings are video-taped and are admitted at trial in lieu of a witness's examination in chief.[128] Pre-trial hearings of this kind were a key feature of the proposals made by the Pigot Committee in 1989. The Committee recommended that child witnesses in certain cases should give evidence in a pre-trial informal hearing at which no one would be present except the witness, the judge,[129] and a lawyer for each side. The possible advantage of this model is that the prosecution would, under a suitably flexible procedure, have the choice of asking a witness supplementary questions to fill lacunae in an account preserved in a *Memorandum* interview or, if necessary, the option of taking a witness step by step through his or her evidence. The prosecution would thus be able to compensate for any evidential deficiencies in a *Memorandum* interview and organize a witness's evidence into a more cohesive and persuasive narrative. Although the procedure would necessarily have an air of formality about it, since the judge would be involved and questions would be put by a lawyer, such a process would no doubt be less stressful than traditional examination at trial. In some cases it may be thought appropriate to allow a witness to answer questions from a video-linked room accompanied only by an approved support person and, where necessary, an intermediary or interpreter. From the perspective of the defence, advantages may lie in the presence of defence counsel during the examination and the ability of the defendant to view the examination via a live television link and instruct counsel through an audio link.

In summary, recent research calls into question the readiness with which the Criminal Justice Acts 1988 and 1991 were seized upon as templates for reform. Much would have been gained from examining alternative models for taking and recording the evidence of vulnerable and intimidated witnesses in advance of trial.

5. Pre-trial Cross-examination

Insistence upon live cross-examination at trial, albeit via a television link, is a more widely recognized and criticized weakness of the half-Pigot scheme. The procedure spares child witnesses neither the acknowledged stress of going to court nor the trauma associated with invariably lengthy delays. Moreover, witnesses are plunged directly into hostile cross-examination at trial without the 'warm up' that examination in chief arguably provides. The only conceivable

---

[127] See Evidence Act 1906 (WA), s. 1061(1).

[128] In Scotland, s. 271 of the Criminal Procedure (Scotland) Act 1995, as amended, makes provision for vulnerable witnesses to give evidence on commission at a pre-trial hearing. However, these new procedures have as yet rarely been implemented: Scottish Office, *Towards a Just Conclusion: Vulnerable and Intimidated Witnesses in Scottish Criminal and Civil Cases* (1998, Scottish Office) para. 5.3.2.   [129] Ideally the same judge should preside over the trial, to ensure continuity.

benefit for child witnesses is the reduction of time spent in the witness box or video link room.[130] The separation between examination in chief and cross-examination has also been shown to have an adverse impact on both the quality of evidence received by the courts and the perceived credibility of children. As Hoyano explains:

> The accumulating stress while awaiting the trial can make the child a less effective witness in cross-examination. Inconsistencies may develop between the videotaped interview and the child's testimony in court, which may cast doubt on the credibility of earlier disclosures. Deterioration of memory may adversely affect the defence case as well as the prosecution: the child may have genuinely forgotten points favourable to the defence case, or may shelter behind avowals of forgetfulness to avoid making admissions helpful to the defence. Juries may discount the credibility of what the child does remember, because of the effluxion of time.[131]

These problems were publicly played out in the case against two Shieldfield Day Nursery workers accused of abusing three- and four-year-old children in their care.[132] Concerns regarding the capacity of these children to recall reliably events which occurred two years previously accounted, in part, for the trial judge's controversial decision not to admit video-taped interviews in the case.[133] The subsequent collapse of the case fuelled calls for full implementation of the Pigot Committee proposals.

The potential advantages of video-taped pre-trial cross-examination as introduced in the YJCEA are listed by Hoyano. Apart from the obvious benefit of capturing a witness's entire evidence at a relatively early stage, conducting cross-examination in advance of trial may, she notes, facilitate pre-trial decision-making by both prosecution and defence.[134] The prosecution can specifically decide on the basis of a witness's actual performance rather than speculating about whether to proceed, withdraw, or downgrade charges. Defence lawyers can advise their client at an earlier stage to be realistic about their prospects of conviction. Where a witness retracts or stands up poorly to defence questioning early withdrawal will shorten the length of time a defendant spends in custody and result in savings to the judicial system. For witnesses there are clear substantial benefits in being able to testify at an earlier stage. Witnesses can avoid the stress of trial postponements, adjournments, and additional delay and begin to put events behind them and get on with their lives.

It is true that sizeable question marks still hang over this so far untested special measure. There are fears that in practice cross-examination will be conducted only shortly before the trial thus losing its principal advantage of preserving an accurate record of a witness's evidence while still relatively fresh.

---

[130] See Davies, G. and Westcott, H., 'Videotechnology and the child witness' in (eds.) Dent, H. and Flin, R., *Children as Witnesses* (1992, Chichester: Wiley) 211.

[131] Hoyano, n. 43 above, 255.   [132] 'Seen and not heard' *The Guardian* 11 May 1999.

[133] *Lillie and Reed* unreported 13 July 1994.

[134] As Hoyona points out, having a witness's testimony video-taped before trial may also facilitate the scheduling and conduct of the trial: n. 43 above, 266.

This rests on concerns regarding the feasibility of ensuring timely disclosure under current procedural arrangements thus allowing the defence adequate time for preparation. A second concern is that vulnerable witnesses will be put through the ordeal of cross-examination on two or more occasions if further questioning becomes necessary after a recording has been made.[135] Additional cross-examination may be permitted, it will be recalled, if a party wishes to raise a matter which it could not, with reasonable diligence, have raised at the first recording[136] or if the judge determines that it is otherwise in the interests of justice to allow further questions.[137] Applications to reopen cross-examination may be anticipated in the majority of cases. Much then will depend on the efficacy of disclosure procedures and the preparedness of the courts to sift out unmeritorious applications to conduct additional questioning. As Home Office Minister Paul Boateng stated, this will require a radical change in the culture of the courts. However, some grounds for optimism are arguably provided by the experience of Western Australia where a version of the full Pigot scheme was introduced as long ago as 1992.[138] Initially, hearings to record pre-trial cross-examination were conducted not long before the trial.[139] However, as the system has bedded down the interval has lengthened and children's evidence is now said to be complete up to six months earlier than if it were given at trial, and on average within seven months of the start of criminal proceedings.[140] Furthermore, according to reports, the further questioning of children at trial has rarely been required.[141]

E. Summary

Under Part II of the Youth Justice and Criminal Evidence Act 1999 ('YJCEA') the courts will have a range of measures available to them which they can award to any witness who needs help to give his or her best evidence, whether because of age, disability, the risk of intimidation, or other personal circumstances. Research analysed in this Chapter suggests a clear ranking among the special

---

[135] Another apparently unanswerable concern is that witnesses will be put through cross-examination which is rendered unnecessary when a defendant subsequently changes a plea to guilty.
[136] S. 28(6)(a).   [137] S. 28(6)(b).
[138] Evidence Act 1906, s. 106I as amended by the Acts Amendment (Evidence of Children and Others) Act 1992. The provisions apply to child complainants under 16 at the time when proceedings are initiated in cases of alleged sexual abuse, intra-familial assault, or kidnapping. The legislation is based on the recommendations of the Law Reform Commission of Western Australia in its report *Evidence of Children and Other Vulnerable Witnesses* (1991, Perth: Law Reform Commission of Western Australia).
[139] The physical arrangements for pre-trial hearings are prescribed in detailed guidelines agreed by judges of the Supreme Court of Western Australia.
[140] See Davis *et al.*, n. 80 above, 271.
[141] This is according to information received by the Australian Law Reform Commission, *Seen and heard: Priority for children in the legal process* (1997, Sydney: Australian Law Reform Commission) para. 14.46.

measures in terms of the protection and assistance they can be expected to afford. Overall, screens and other court-room modifying measures emerge as poor substitutes for the live television link; that in turn emerges as an inferior alternative to video-taped testimony. Notwithstanding the sizeable problems inherent within the adopted scheme for video-taping testimony, the questioning of witnesses entirely in advance of trial in a non-intimidating environment while events are still relatively fresh stands out clearly as the method most likely to furnish the court with the best evidence a witness is capable of giving. Yet it appears that conservative use is to be made of the video-taping provisions. Speaking of video-taped pre-trial cross-examination, the Home Secretary in the seconding Reading of the Youth Justice and Criminal Evidence Bill emphasized that the measure would not become routine, stating that it would be used sparingly and in special situations.[142] Initial government estimates were that some 900 witnesses a year would benefit from pre-recorded cross-examination.[143] The courts will have no choice but to grapple with the measure in the case of child sexual offence complainants, but with respect to other vulnerable and intimidated witnesses pre-trial cross-examination looks set to be very much the exception rather than the rule. This is no doubt linked to the costs and time involved in video-taping evidence, but it also betrays a reluctance to undermine the oral nature of criminal trials and to depart too resolutely from the adversarial model. This unwillingness to set aside conventional adversarial methods has given rise to a complex assortment of compromise measures that will afford vulnerable and intimidated witnesses a greatly reduced standard of protection and assistance.

1. Attitudinal Barriers

The remainder of this Chapter considers how perceived strategic disincentives may yet militate against the widespread use of alternative trial arrangements introduced in the YJCEA. The government has acknowledged that many lawyers will 'react instinctively against the taking of special measures'.[144] Resistance can be expected not only from opposing parties but also (perhaps less predictably) from the parties calling witnesses who may require assistance. Empirical research suggests, for example, that prosecutors will be strongly predisposed to keeping complainants in the court-room whenever possible. This relates to concerns that the emotional impact of testimony relayed by a live link is reduced or flattened relative to evidence delivered in the court-room, translating into a loss of empathy and sympathy on the part of jurors.[145] Televised testimony is specifically regarded by many lawyers as artificial, remote, and less compelling. As one lawyer interviewed by Heenan and McKelvie explained: 'I

---

[142] *Hansard*, 15 April 1999, col. 390.
[143] Minister of State, Paul Boateng, Standing Committee E 22 June 1999.
[144] Minister of State, Paul Boateng, Standing Committee E, 17 June 1999.
[145] Birch, P., 'Children's Evidence' [1992] *Criminal Law Review* 273.

just think that when juries see . . . the whole person they relate to them as a human being. People watch so much television these days, they see a complainant on the television and it has a displacement effect, whereas the accused is sitting in front of them as a real live person. I just feel that it doesn't help.'[146]

In the case of child witnesses, prosecution counsel have complained that the live link minimizes cues as to height and size, leading jurors to overestimate a child's maturity and build.[147] Prosecutors have also bemoaned the loss of direct eye contact, rapport, and customary control when live television links are used.[148]

A recent Crown Prosecution Service Inspectorate report suggests that prosecutors may finally be accepting the benefits of the television link for child witnesses in sexual abuse prosecutions.[149] The report found a substantial increase in prosecution applications to use television links in these cases. However, lawyers and judges interviewed by Harris and Grace in a recent Home Office study were strongly opposed to the use of live link technology in most rape cases, stating that evidence delivered in person had a more positive impact.[150] Barristers interviewed recently by Temkin also expressed unanimous and strong opposition to the suggestion that a live television link should be routinely available to adult rape complainants.[151] Prosecutors in particular considered that their task would be rendered more difficult if television links were introduced for adults. It was believed to be very difficult to establish rapport with a witness through a television screen, and they thought that the medium 'neutralised', 'anaesthetised', and diminished the effect of evidence. One barrister with experience of prosecuting explained: 'It's so difficult to bring home a rape case. You need evidence, you need spontaneity. It's awful for women but once they get going they're normally all right. OK they do burst into tears and it's terrible for them but if you're going to make an impact, then they do make it.'[152] The anguish of complainants was thus seen to translate into an increased probability of successful prosecution.[153] In a similar vein, the value of a visibly distressed child in convincing a sceptical jury was mentioned by prosecutors interviewed by Davis and Noon.[154] Video-taped testimony has evoked a similarly ambivalent response from prosecution lawyers who have described it as 'remote, anonymous and anodyne'.[155] Davies *et al.* report that barristers viewed the loss of

---

[146] Heenan, M. and McKelvie, H., *Evaluation of the Crimes (Rape) Act 1991* (1997, Melbourne: Department of Justice) 76.   [147] O'Grady, n. 48 above, 45.
[148] See Murray, n. 52 above, 113.   [149] N. 75 above, para. 12.2.
[150] Harris, J. and Grace, S., *A question of evidence? Investigating and prosecuting rape in the 1990s*, HORS 196 (1999, London: HMSO) 48.
[151] Temkin, J., 'Prosecuting and defending rape: Perspectives from the Bar' (2000) 27(2) *Journal of Law and Society* 219.   [152] Ibid. 237.
[153] Sanders *et al.*'s study provides an example of a prosecution barrister asking a 23-year-old woman with a mild learning disability to give evidence without a screen because he felt it would not be a 'real' situation: Sanders, A., Creaton, J., Bird, S. and Weber, L., *Victims with Learning Disabilities Negotiating the Criminal Justice System* (1997, Oxford: Centre for Criminological Research, University of Oxford) 68.   [154] Davies *et al.* n. 50 above, 135.
[155] For a survey of prosecutors' perceptions of alternative methods in the United States see Goodman, G., Quas, J., Bulkley, J. and Shapiro, C., 'Innovations for child witnesses: A national survey' (1999) 5 *Psychology, Public Policy and Law* 255.

immediacy and diminished impact of video-taped evidence compared to live testimony to be the medium's principal drawback. Video-taped evidence was generally regarded as second-hand and so less likely to sway a jury.[156]

2. An Australian Perspective

Experience in other jurisdictions shows that the attitudes of lawyers and judges can impact significantly on the implementation of innovative trial procedures aimed at improving the position of witnesses. In Queensland, for example, the courts have had discretion to authorize special arrangement including television links in cases involving vulnerable witnesses since 1989.[157] A report published recently by the Queensland Law Reform Commission acknowledged that judges have been generally reluctant to exercise their discretion in favour of the use of television links and attributed the low rate of use, in part, to a belief that the right of defendants to a fair trial would be compromised.[158] In Victoria the Crimes (Rape) Act 1991 extended the use of protective measures, previously available only to children and complainants with an intellectual disability, to adult complainants of sexual offences.[159] The Act provided for the use of television links, screens, and the exclusion of specified persons from the court-room while a complainant gave evidence.[160] In 1997 the Victorian Department of Justice published an evaluative study of the reforms which examined the extent to which the alternative arrangements for giving evidence were used during rape proceedings, and explored the attitudes of both legal practitioners and judges towards the reforms.[161] Heenan and McKelvie report that the broad intentions of the new legislation were often confounded by the assumptions made by legal practitioners and members of the bench about who ought to use the arrangements and the effect their use might have on juror decision-making.[162] In particular, the research highlighted the extent to which the outcome of applications often hinged on the personalities of the legal professionals involved, rather than on any standard practice or consistent approach being adopted. Television links

---

[156] See Davies et al., n. 76 above.

[157] S. 21A Evidence Act 1977 (Qld). Such arrangements include: excluding the accused from the court; obscuring the accused from the view of the witness; excluding other persons from the court; permitting the witness to give evidence in another room; permitting the presence of another person to provide emotional support for the witness; and video-taping the evidence of the witness and presenting it in court in lieu of direct testimony from the witness.

[158] Queensland Law Reform Commission, The Receipt of Evidence by Queensland Courts: The Evidence of Children Discussion Paper No. 53 (1998, Brisbane: Queensland Law Reform Commission).

[159] In such cases the court must be satisfied that without alternative arrangements being made the witness is likely in giving evidence to suffer severe emotional trauma, or to be so intimidated or stressed as to be severely disadvantaged as a witness.

[160] S. 37C. In cases where alternative arrangements are used at the trial proceedings, the judge must warn the jury not to draw any inference adverse to the defendant, or to give the evidence any greater or lesser weight because of the making of those arrangements.

[161] Heenan et al., n. 146 above.

[162] Just over 25% of complainants who gave evidence at trial used an alternative arrangement.

and screens were used in a relatively small proportion of sexual assault cases. Prosecutors were often reluctant to make applications on behalf of adult complainants, and judges rarely exercised their own discretion to order that these arrangements be used.[163] There was a strong assumption held by many practitioners and members of the bench that television links, in particular, lessened the emotional impact of evidence and made complainants seem less real and believable. A number of prosecutors specifically spoke of attempting to persuade complainants to give their evidence in the court-room if they possibly could.[164] It is also worth noting that a significant number were unconvinced of the need for protective measures:[165] 'I mean where is the threat? That person is not going to jump out of the dock and attack you, that person is removed by 30, 40, 50 feet of the room.'[166] In one case a rape complainant was told that she did not need to use a television link as 'she ha[d]n't been brutalised'.[167]

A study in New South Wales, conducted over a decade after the introduction of procedural changes to protect adult sexual assault complainants, similarly found that little had changed in the day-to-day practice of the courts.[168] Television links were rarely used, and orders to close the court while the complainant gave evidence were only made in a minority of cases.[169] According to the study's authors, judges and barristers widely considered the public interest in having open trials to be more important than the interests of vulnerable complainants. As one judge commented: 'I acknowledge there is likely stress, likely embarrassment for a complainant but unless extreme difficulty can be shown, [it is important that] courts be open for scrutiny by ordinary citizens'.[170] Overall, the study found courts to be inflexible and insensitive to the need to provide facilities to make the process of testifying less traumatic for adult sexual assault complainants.

3. Findings on Televised Testimony

Evaluative studies of both the live link and video-taping provisions have found no empirical support for the notion that video technology reduces the perceived credibility of children's evidence. In Davies *et al.*'s study, for example, analysis

---

[163] Heenan *et al.*, n. 146 above, 109.   [164] Ibid. 83.

[165] Obviously not all complainants will want to use television links. A small number of victims spoke of it being 'empowering' for them to describe what had happened in the accused's presence: ibid. 114.   [166] Ibid. 73.

[167] Ibid. 112.

[168] Department for Women (NSW), *Heroines of Fortitude: The Experiences of Women in Court as Victims of Sexual Assault* (1996, Sydney: Department for Women). The study was based on a sample of 111 sexual assault trials.

[169] S. 77A of the Crimes (Personal and Family Violence) Amendment Act 1987 NSW allows for part of proceedings to be held in camera where the court so directs. In 9 of the 11 trials involving complainants with disabilities, the court was open to the public throughout the trial.

[170] N. 168 above, 123. The study showed that in refusing applications to close the court judges considered many factors, such as the age of the complainant, which are not specified by the legislation as relevant factors in deciding to close the court.

of trial data showed that prosecutions were successful in 44 per cent of cases where children testified live, compared to 49 per cent in cases using video-taped evidence.[171] Experimental research has similarly failed to disclose a causal link between perceived credibility and modes of presentation. In a study conducted by Swim et al. mock jurors viewed video-tapes of a sexual abuse trial in which the eight-year-old complainant gave evidence in open court and a second trial in which video-taped testimony was shown.[172] The jurors' reactions to the defendant's testimony were monitored during the trial, after which the jurors were required to reach a verdict. The researchers report that the medium of presentation had few effects on mock juror responses. In a similar study conducted by Ross et al. 3 mock juries watched a video-taped simulation of a sexual abuse trial which included the testimony of the ten-year-old complainant delivered either in open court, or in court from behind a protective screen, or through a video monitor.[173] The mock jurors judged the guilt of the defendant after watching the entire trial. Ross et al. report that the modality of the child's testimony had no impact on conviction rates and there was no statistically significant impact on the perceived credibility of the child complainant. A more recent study by Goodman et al. did find that children who testified via television links were viewed as less believable by mock jurors than children who testified in open court despite the fact that, if anything, the children who testified via television links were more accurate.[174] Significantly, however, this positive attributional effect proved to be short-lived, not surviving the deliberation process.[175] Although no firm conclusions can be drawn, the weight of research to date suggests that the impact of the use of video technology is broadly neutral.[176] It may be, as media theorists suggest,[177] that the mode of presentation inevitably alters the message communicated, but the greater composure of vulnerable witnesses appears to wipe out any advantage associated with a live court appearance.

[171] Davies et al., n. 76 above.

[172] Swim, J., Borgida, E. and McCoy, K., 'Videotaped versus in court witness testimony: Does protecting the child witness jeopardize due process?' (1993) 23 Journal of Applied Social Psychology 603.

[173] Ross, D., Hopkins, S., Hanson, E., Lindsay, R., Hazen, K. and Eslinger, T., 'The impact of protective shields and videotape testimony on conviction rates in a simulated trial of child sexual abuse' (1994) 18(5) Law and Human Behavior 553.

[174] Goodman, G., Tobet, A., Batterman-Faunce, J., Orcutt, H., Thomas, S., Shapiro, C. and Sachsenmaier, T., 'Face to face confrontation: Effects of closed circuit technology on children's eyewitness testimony and jurors' decisions' (1998) 22 Law and Human Behaviour 165.

[175] According to Westcott et al., any loss of immediacy needs to be traded off against the reduced stress for the child as this is likely to have benefits for the child's long-term mental health and may improve the quantity and quality of their evidence: Westcott, H., Davies, G. and Spencer, J., 'Protecting the child witness: Hearsay techniques and other innovations' (1999) 5 Psychology, Public Policy and Law 282, 291.

[176] See Westcott, H., Davies, G. and Clifford, B., 'The credibility of child witnesses seen on closed circuit television' (1991) 15(1) Adoption and Fostering 14.

[177] See generally Roth, M. D., 'Laissez faire videoconferencing: Remote witness testimony and adversarial truth' (2000) 48 UCLA Law Review 185.

IV.
Orality and the Right to a Fair Trial

The preceding Chapters have analysed the orality principle in terms of an evidentiary dimension, centring on the reliability of testimony tendered in evidence. However, the general insistence upon direct oral testimony in adversarial criminal proceedings is increasingly presented in modern debates as an effective means of safeguarding the fair trial rights of criminal defendants.[1] A number of objections have been raised by opponents of special protective procedures based upon due process concerns. First, the claim is made that measures which shield a witness from direct contact with an accused infringe the latter's right to challenge contrary evidence. Exponents of this view maintain that the right to challenge is a corollary right to face-to-face confrontation which is violated when physical or technological barriers are interposed between accuser and accused. It is further contended that the use of screens and the video medium generally in criminal trials is *per se* prejudicial to the position of the defendant. This argument assumes that the testimony of witnesses allowed to use either screens or video links is somehow imbued with unwarranted credibility while that of a defendant is necessarily tainted. Finally, it is asserted that alternative modes of presentation interfere unduly with jurors' assessment of non-verbal cues to witness credibility and that this disadvantages defendants. This claim centres on orthodox legal assumptions regarding the utility of demeanour evidence in evaluating the reliability of oral testimony. Drawing upon recent jurisprudence of the European Court of Human Rights and relevant contemporary psychological research, the first part of this Chapter examines the strength or otherwise of each of these claims.

The second part of this Chapter examines more generally the issue of witnesses' rights. Traditionally, the interests of witnesses have not been balanced against the rights of defendants to a fair trial but have been marginalized, the relationship between the state and the offender dominating all aspects of the criminal process. The proposition that the scope of fair trial rights can be assessed without reference to the rights and legitimate expectations of those who testify as witnesseses in criminal proceedings is, however, no longer tenable. The precise extent of witnesses' rights is still ambiguous, but is widely regarded as including a right to appropriate protection for both privacy and physical safety and an expectation of being treated with dignity and respect at each stage of the criminal process.

---

[1] Choo, A., *Hearsay and Confrontation in Criminal Trials* (1996, Oxford: Clarendon); Ho, L., 'A Theory of Hearsay' (1999) 19(3) *Oxford Journal of Legal Studies* 403.

A. A RIGHT TO PHYSICAL CONFRONTATION?

A charge commonly made against the use of shielding procedures, as yet mostly by child witnesses, is that such measures constitute an unwarranted infringement of an accused's right physically to confront his accusers in court. The abuses in the 1603 trial of Sir Walter Raleigh and even biblical accounts of the trial of St Paul are cited as evidence of the deep historical roots of this 'right'.[2] Friedman, a leading exponent, maintains that the testimony of a witness who refuses to give evidence according to the principles of face-to-face confrontation and public disclosure should be rejected unless attributable to the wrongdoing of the accused.[3] However, English common law does not recognize the right of a defendant physically to face accusatory witnesses. In the 1919 case of *Smellie* the trial judge ordered the accused to sit on steps out of sight of his eleven-year-old daughter as she gave evidence against him. On appeal it was argued that an accused has a common law right to be within sight and hearing of all witnesses throughout the trial. Dismissing the appeal, the Court of Appeal stated that where a judge considers that the presence of an accused will intimidate a witness, there is nothing to prevent him or her from securing the ends of justice by removing the former from the presence of the latter.[4] In the more recent case of *XYZ*, the Court of Appeal approved the practice of shielding child witnesses from an accused through the use of screens.[5] It was held that the trial judge had a duty to see that the system operated fairly not only to the defendant but also to the prosecution and to witnesses. On occasion, the necessity of trying to ensure that child witnesses were able to give evidence would, it was held, outweigh any possible prejudice to a defendant that attached to the employment of a screen. Similarly in the case of *Brown*, the Lord Chief Justice, Lord Bingham, stated that trial judges had a clear duty to do everything they could, consistently with giving the defendant a fair trial, to minimize the trauma suffered by other participants. Lord Bingham stated that if a defendant sought by his dress, bearing, or manner to dominate, intimidate, or humiliate the complainant, trial judges should not hesitate to order the erection of a screen.[6] Furthermore, in *X v UK* the European Commission found that a decision to screen witnesses did

---

[2] The Roman Governor Festus is reported to have refused to render judgment against Paul until he was physically confronted with his accusers: 'It is not the manner of the Romans to deliver any man to die, before that he which is accused have the accusers face to face, and have licence to answer for himself concerning the crime laid against him:' Blumenthal, J., 'A wipe of the hands, a lick of the lips: The validity of demeanour evidence in assessing witness credibility' (1993) 72 *Nebraska Law Review* 1157, 1175. See also Hamilton Thielmeyer, L., 'Beyond Maryland v Craig: Can and should adult rape victims be permitted to testify by closed circuit television?' (1992) 67 *Indiana Law Journal* 797.

[3] Slightly more moderate rules might, he concedes, be appropriately adopted for child witnesses and those suffering a substantial mental disability: Friedman, R., 'Thoughts from across the water on hearsay and confrontation' [1998] *Criminal Law Review* 697, 703.

[4] (1919) 14 Cr App R 128.   [5] (1989) 91 Cr App R 36.

[6] The case involved an unrepresented defendant but the principle may be assumed to apply more widely: *R v Brown (Milton)* (1998) 2 Cr App R 364.

not interfere with an accused's rights under Article 6 of the European Convention on Human Rights, as the defendant's legal representative was able to see the witness and question him on the defendant's behalf.[7]

1. Jurisprudence of the European Court of Human Rights

The relevant paragraphs of Article 6 of the European Court of Human Rights are 1 and 3(d), which provide:

1. In the determination of his civil rights and obligations or of any criminal charge against him, everyone is entitled to a fair and public hearing within a reasonable time by an independent and impartial tribunal established by law. Judgment shall be pronounced publicly but the press and the public may be excluded from all or part of the trial in the interests of morals, public order or national security in a democratic society, where the interests of juveniles or the protection of the private life of the parties so require, or to the extent strictly necessary in the opinion of the court in special circumstances where publicity would prejudice the interests of justice.
3. Everyone charged with a criminal offence has the following minimum rights: . . .
(d) to examine or have examined witnesses against him and so obtain the attendance and examination of witnesses on his behalf under the same conditions as witnesses against him.

The nature of the right to challenge prosecution witnesses enshrined in Article 6(3)(d) has been examined chiefly in relation to the issue of witness anonymity.[8] Jurisprudence of the European Court of Human Rights clearly establishes that it is not automatically a breach of an accused's right to a fair trial to refuse the defence the opportunity to cross-examine accusatory witnesses at trial.[9] In *Kostovski v The Netherlands*[10] the applicant's conviction for armed robbery was to 'a decisive extent' based on the statements of two anonymous witnesses. The first was interviewed only by police while the second was additionally examined at a preliminary judicial hearing by an examining magistrate or *rechter commissaris*, although in the absence of the applicant and his counsel. The defence were invited to submit written questions to be put at a second hearing but the majority of these ultimately went unanswered in order to preserve the witness's anonymity. At trial, reports of the statements of the two anonymous witnesses, who did not testify, were admitted. The defence questioned the examining magistrate and police officers who had examined the witnesses but were again prohibited from asking certain questions which would have revealed the witnesses' identity. Slobodan Kostovski alleged a breach of Article 6(1) and 6(3)(d) of the Convention, claiming that he was unable to challenge the witnesses' allegations either directly or through his legal representative.

---

[7] (1992) 15 EHRR CD 113.
[8] See Osborne, C., 'Hearsay and the Court of Human Rights' [1993] *Criminal Law Review* 255.
[9] See generally Cheney, D., Dickson, L., Fitzpatrick, J. and Uglow, S., *Criminal Justice and the Human Rights Act 1998* (1999, Bristol: Jordans); Van Dijk, P. and Van Hoof, G. J. H., *Theory and Practice of the European Convention on Human Rights* 3rd edn. (1998, The Hague: Kluwer) 473.
[10] (1992) 14 EHRR 396.

In its ruling the Court stressed that its task was not to express a view as to whether the statements in question were correctly admitted, stating that the admissibility of evidence is primarily a matter for regulation by national law. Rather, the Court's task was to ascertain whether the proceedings as a whole, including the way in which evidence was taken, were fair. In principle, the Court stated, all evidence must be produced in the presence of the accused at a public hearing with a view to adversarial argument. However, the Court went on to state that the use of pre-trial statements was not in itself inconsistent with paragraphs (3)(d) and (1) of Article 6, provided that the rights of the defence had been respected. As a rule, these rights required that an accused should be given an adequate and proper opportunity to challenge and question a witness against him, *either* at the time when the witness was making the statement *or* at some later stage of the proceedings. Moreover, it was sufficient that witnesses were questioned on behalf of the defendant in the absence of the defendant. In this regard, the importance of defence counsel being able to observe the demeanour of a witness during questioning was emphasized by the Court. In this case the defence had not been present when witnesses were examined and at no stage were they directly questioned on Kostovski's behalf. Moreover, the examining magistrate was not informed of the identity of the witness prior to examination, and the questioning at trial was restricted in scope. In these circumstances the Court held that it could not be said that 'the handicaps under which the defence laboured were counterbalanced by the procedures followed by the judicial authorities' and accordingly Kostovski had not received a fair trial.[11]

The right embodied within Article 6(3)(d) can therefore be more accurately described as a right of challenge rather than a right of confrontation, as confirmed in later cases. In *Windisch v Austria*,[12] for example, the applicant's conviction for burglary was similarly based mainly on statements to the police by two anonymous witnesses. In spite of repeated requests, neither the applicant nor his counsel were given the opportunity to examine the witnesses, who did not give evidence at trial. In ruling that the applicant had not received a fair trial, the Court stated that the ability of the defence to question the investigating officers and to submit written questions could not replace the right to examine prosecution witnesses directly. In *Delta v France* the conviction of the applicant for robbery was again based decisively on the written police statements of two witnesses. Neither witness was examined by an investigating judge and neither, despite the applicants' requests, was summoned to give

---

[11] Following the *Kostovski* judgment new provisions were introduced into the Dutch Code of Criminal Procedure regarding the protection of witnesses: Witness Protection Act 1994. Under the new provisions an anonymous statement can only be used in evidence if it has been taken down by an investigating judge who knows the identity of the witness, who has expressed his opinion as regards the reasons for the witness's desire to remain anonymous and the witness's reliability, and has provided the defence with ample opportunity to question the witness. These provisions were tested in the case of *Doorson* (see n. 16 below) and were found to be compatible with the ECHR, provided that no conviction is based 'solely or to a decisive extent' on evidence provided by anonymous witnesses. See further Chapter VII below.   [12] (1993) 13 EHRR 281.

evidence at trial. At no point, therefore, had the applicant or his counsel had the opportunity to examine the witnesses and test their reliability.[13] The Court held that the rights of the defence were subject to such restrictions that the applicant did not receive a fair trial. In *Unterpertinger v Austria* the applicant was convicted of causing actual bodily harm to his stepdaughter and of causing grievous bodily harm to his wife.[14] The conviction was based mainly on the police statements of his wife and stepdaughter. Both complainants had refused to give evidence at trial, as they were entitled to do by virtue of Article 152 of the Austrian Code of Criminal Procedure. The applicant claimed that, as a result, he had not had an opportunity to examine them or have them examined at any stage of the proceedings. The Court held that the applicant had been convicted substantially on the basis of 'testimony' in respect of which his defence rights were appreciably restricted and, that being so, the applicant had not received a fair trial.

In a number of cases the existence of supporting evidence has been held to compensate for the absence of a direct challenge by the defence. In *Asch v Austria*, for example, the applicant was convicted of inflicting actual bodily harm on the woman with whom he lived.[15] The complainant's statement was read out in court notwithstanding the fact that she had withdrawn her complaint and had refused to give evidence in court. The applicant claimed that his inability to question the complainant at any stage of the proceedings violated his right to a fair trial. The Court held that there had been no violation of Article 6. Above all, the Court noted that the applicant's conviction was not based on the complainant's statement alone but on other corroborative evidence. In this respect, the Court held, the case was distinguishable from that of *Unterpertinger*.

More recently the European Court of Human Rights seems to have moderated its approach towards witness anonymity. In *Doorson v The Netherlands* the applicant was convicted of drug trafficking and sentenced to fifteen months' imprisonment.[16] The evidence against Doorson consisted largely of the statements made to the police by two drug addicts who remained anonymous. Before the Regional Court the defence requested that the witnesses be heard at trial but the request was refused. The defendant appealed and the Appeal Court referred the case to an investigating magistrate to determine whether the anonymity of the witnesses should be preserved. The examining magistrate heard two of the anonymous witnesses at a pre-trial hearing where they were questioned by Doorson's lawyer. The examining magistrate considered their reasons for remaining anonymous and determined them to be valid.[17] Relying on the examining magistrate's conclusions, the Court of Appeal decided not to call any of the anonymous witnesses. The European

---

[13] (1993) 16 EHRR 574. [14] (1991) 13 EHRR 175. [15] (1993) 15 EHRR 597.
[16] (1996) 22 EHRR 330.
[17] While no overt threats were made against either witness, the examining magistrate was satisfied that the general resort to violence by drug dealers was sufficient reason to maintain anonymity.

Court of Human Rights held that there had been no violation of Article 6(3)(d). The handicaps under which the defence had laboured were, the Court opined, sufficiently counterbalanced by the procedures followed by the judicial authorities. Specifically, counsel for the applicant was not only present at the preliminary hearing but was able to ask witnesses whatever questions he considered to be in the interests of the defence, except in so far as they might lead to the disclosure of their identity. The defence was therefore able to challenge the evidence of the anonymous witnesses and to cast doubt on the reliability of their statements. Furthermore, the national court did not base its finding of guilt 'solely or to a decisive extent on the evidence of the anonymous witnesses'[18] and had treated the statements of the witnesses 'with the necessary caution and circumspection'.

However, a more restrictive approach has been adopted towards state agent witnesses. In *Van Mechelen v The Netherlands* evidence identifying the applicants as the perpetrators of an attempted murder and robbery consisted largely of statements made by anonymous police officers.[19] The officers, who did not testify at trial, were questioned at a preliminary hearing by an examining magistrate in the absence of the applicants and their lawyers. All communication was by sound link. The applicants' argument that they had not received a fair trial was upheld by the Court. The Court expressed the view that the position of police officers was to some extent different from that of a disinterested witness or a victim since they usually had links with the prosecution. It accepted that it may, in certain circumstances, be legitimate for police authorities to preserve the anonymity of their agents but stated that any measures restricting the rights of the defence should be strictly necessary. In this case the Court was not satisfied that such far-reaching measures had been necessary because insufficient effort was made to assess the threat of reprisals against the police officers and their families.

From examination of recent European Court of Human Rights rulings the right of challenge can be seen to have two central aims: the facilitation of cross-examination and the opportunity for the defence to observe the demeanour of a witness. Jurisprudence of the European Court of Human Rights provides that cross-examination may legitimately take place at a private preliminary hearing in the absence of an accused provided that his or her legal representative is present. In other words, out of court testimony may be regarded as functionally equivalent to that delivered in court if the defence was afforded sufficient opportunity to challenge the credibility of a witness at the pre-trial stage. Where there is adequate supporting evidence it appears that reliance on the evidence of a witness not subject to direct defence challenge will not necessarily lead the Court to rule the proceedings in violation of Article 6. The Court will examine whether the proceedings *taken as a whole* were fair. Clearly there is no

---

[18] The Court made it clear that a conviction based solely on anonymous statements would violate the Convention even if 'counterbalancing' procedures had been adopted.

[19] (1997) 25 EHRR 547.

requirement for a physical showdown between witness and accused.[20] The use of screens, television links, and video-recorded testimony may preclude direct confrontation but they do not interfere unduly with the defence right of challenge. The significance attached within adversarial theory to unmediated face-to-face confrontation finds no reflection in the contemporary judgments of the European Court of Human Rights.

2. A 'Fair Play' Theory of Confrontation

In the United States, where face-to-face confrontation at trial remains a hotly contested issue, defenders have developed what may be termed a 'fair play' theory of confrontation. This contends that people's sense of 'fairness' is disturbed by the use of protective procedures such as screens and television links within criminal proceedings. People generally, it is maintained, accord innate value to face-to-face encounters, as expressed in commonly held notions about fair play and decent treatment of others in social and business relationships.[21] The communication of bad news in person rather than mediated through some impersonal device is cited as an illustration. According to some commentators, the acceptability of legal decisions to the participants and to the wider community may hinge on whether this emotion is acknowledged in the context of criminal trials. For example, Massaro has advocated an approach to confrontation that rests on what he describes as principles of human dignity.[22] Massaro asserts that this approach provides a theoretical basis for confrontation which accounts for both its instrumental and its intrinsic, non-functional values.[23] Face-to-face confrontation between accused and accuser, he argues, preserves the dignity of the former and maximizes participation in the trial process. The use of shielding mechanisms is alleged to undermine the 'humanness' and equality of courtroom exchanges:

[20] *Recommendation No. R (97) 13 on Intimidation of Witnesses and the Rights of the Defence 1997* states explicitly that Article 6 of the European Convention on Human Rights and the case-law of its organs do not guarantee the right to a face-to-face confrontation between a witness and an alleged offender.

[21] In *Coy v Iowa* 487 US 1012 (1988) the Supreme Court similarly reasoned 'there is something deep in human nature that regards face to face confrontation between accused and accuser as essential to a fair trial in a criminal prosecution'.

[22] Massaro, T., 'The Dignity Value of Face to Face Confrontations' (1988) 40 *University of Florida Law Review* 863. Massaro maintains that protective measures such as video-taped or closed-circuit testimony should be made available only after a witness has been confronted with the defendant in open court and rendered speechless as a result. The attempt to offer live testimony, Massaro argues, offers visible and concrete proof that the government has made every reasonable effort to preserve the defendant's opportunity for a face-to-face confrontation.

[23] According to Massaro, one intrinsic benefit is the chance to respond: 'If the witness lies, the accused may respond with a snort of indignation, a glare, laughter, a cry of dismay, a curse, tears, or stony silence. This opportunity to look the witness in the eye and to respond may not change the witness's testimony. The opportunity to be seen and heard by one's accusers nevertheless is of value—intrinsic value—to the accused. This might be called the "shame on you" value of confrontation. "Tell me to my face" therefore implies not only that you must accuse me in person, but you must remain witness to my reaction', ibid. 906.

The confrontation guarantee reflects a belief that criminal trials of human beings should look human to do 'justice' and should treat the defendant—even an alleged child molester—as an equal, dignified participant in the proceedings against him. These qualities are compromised when government prosecutors use affidavits, depositions, videotaped testimony, one way mirrors, or closed circuit television testimony to prove their central accusations against the criminal defendant no matter how 'accurate' those accusations may be. Procedure which is based on these forms of evidence no longer is an even contest in which the defendant plays an active, equal and dignified role.[24]

Scallen similarly argues that granting defendants an affirmative right to face their accusers corresponds with cultural perceptions of fairness and by so doing strengthens the integrity and legitimacy of the adversarial fact-finding process.[25] Confrontation is also, Scallen contends, a special kind of communication event with identifiable interpersonal effects which have significant value for the individuals involved. Face-to-face encounters provide specifically, she maintains, an outlet for dissatisfaction and frustration, thus serving as a means for catharsis, as well as providing an opportunity for enhanced understanding of the other party.[26] According to Friedman, affording a defendant the opportunity to confront adversarially those lined up against him lends an important sense of completeness to the accused and more widely to society.[27] Direct confrontation is, he asserts, required as much for the appearance of fairness as for fairness itself.

Empirical research has failed to uncover any hard evidence that laypersons, in the guise of jurors, regard the use of non-conventional trial methods as unfair or inequitable. In Western Australia O'Grady surveyed 138 jurors from seventeen criminal trials in which live links and screens had been used.[28] According to O'Grady, most jurors understood that protective procedures were used to protect child witnesses from the stress of testifying in court and to facilitate 'better, more accurate, more truthful evidence'.[29] Experimental studies involving mock jurors have similarly failed to disclose concern among laypersons toward the use of protective measures. In a study by Goodman *et al.*, for example, mock jurors viewed eight-year-old children testifying in a series of mock trials.[30] Half the

---

[24] Massaro, n. 22 above, 903.

[25] Scallen, E., 'Constitutional Dimensions of Hearsay Reform: Toward a Three Dimensional Confrontation Clause' (1992) 76 *Minnesota Law Review* 623.   [26] Ibid. 646.

[27] Friedman, R., 'Confrontation Rights of Criminal Defendants' in (eds.) Nijboer, J. F. and Reijntjes, J. M., 'Proceedings of the First World Conference on New Trends in Criminal Investigation and Evidence', The Hague, The Netherlands, 1–5 December 1995 (1997, Netherlands: Koninklijke Vermande) 534. Choo similarly refers to the 'moral value' and 'emotional appeal' of ensuring, wherever possible, face-to-face confrontation between a defendant and those whose statements are being used against him or her: see n. 1 above, 185.

[28] The survey of television link trials included responses from juries who decided for the accused, as well as from juries who decided against the accused: O'Grady, C., *Child Witnesses and Jury Trials: An Evaluation of the Use of Closed Circuit Television and Removable Screens in Western Australia* (1996, Perth: Western Australia Ministry of Justice).   [29] Ibid. 124.

[30] See Batterman-Faunce, J. M. and Goodman, G., 'Effects of context on the accuracy and suggestibility of child witnesses' in (eds.) Goodman, G. and Bottoms, B., *Child Victims, Child Witnesses* (1993, New York: Guilford Press) 322.

children testified in open court in a 'regular trial' condition, and the other half gave evidence by means of closed-circuit television. At the end of the trial the mock jurors were asked how strongly they would advocate the following court-room techniques: a child testifying live in court, a child testifying on video tape, and a child testifying via closed-circuit television. Of the various techniques suggested, mock jurors were more negative about traditional court-room appearances for children than any other option.

More generally, attention must be paid to the role of public pressure in securing the greater protection of complainants and witnesses within the criminal process. The traditional neglect of both groups is widely regarded as a significant source of public dissatisfaction with the criminal justice system. The use and proposed extension of shielding procedures in criminal trials can thus be seen as part of ongoing attempts to promote greater public confidence in the criminal justice process.[31] Against this backdrop, the claims by advocates of confrontation that deviation from conventional adversarial practice arouses public unease are unpersuasive.

B. The Risk of Prejudice

A second argument advanced against special protective measures maintains that the risk of prejudice which attaches to their use necessarily detracts from the fairness of a criminal trial. In the case of screens, for example, it is commonly said that the presence of a physical barrier in the court-room segregating a witness from the defendant may lead a jury to infer that the latter is dangerous, thus undermining the presumption of innocence. As Massaro writes, 'a person who must be cordoned off . . . is not someone a juror will be likely to believe, empathise with, or want to protect. If the defendant appears to be too alien, too contagious, or too dangerous to be confronted face to face, then the jury may be less inclined to acquit that defendant.'[32] In *XYZ* the Court of Appeal dismissed such arguments, stating that no sensible jury could be prejudiced by the existence of a barrier between a child witness and the dock even in the absence of a suitable judicial direction.[33] The trial judge had in fact warned the jury not to hold the use of such equipment against the defendant because it was common practice and designed to protect young complainants of sexual offences from the inevitable embarrassment of having to give evidence about highly intimate matters in a public court-room. However, in *Cooper and Shaub*, a case involving an adult rape complainant, the Court of Appeal took a different view, stating that the very employment of a screen suggested to a jury that there was a need for the witness to be protected from any contact with the defendant. The

---

[31] See Home Office, *Promoting Public Confidence in the Criminal Justice System* (2000, London: Home Office).   [32] Massaro, n. 22 above, 903.
[33] (1990) 91 Cr App R 36, 40.

inevitably prejudicial effect of screens required, the Court held, that judges should permit screens for adult witnesses only in the most exceptional cases, not as a general course in trials for sexual offences.[34] One year later a differently constituted Court of Appeal held in *Foster* that the appropriate test was that set out in *XYZ*. In this case the Court was satisfied that the 'slim risk of prejudice' which attached to screens had been countered by a warning to the jury couched in suitably neutral terms.[35]

The Youth Justice and Criminal Evidence Act 1999 provides that where evidence in received in accordance with a special measures direction, the judge must give the jury such warning as he or she considers necessary to ensure that the accused is not prejudiced by the fact that the direction was given.[36] This should be sufficient to overcome the possibly stigmatizing presence of a physical barrier in the court-room. However, in light of the very limited protection which screens afford to vulnerable witnesses, the use of alternative measures such as television links and video-recorded testimony, which offer more readily identifiable benefits besides avoidance of the accused, may better serve the interests of justice.

In relation to live television links and video-recorded evidence there is, as stated, a concern that the video medium may imbue a witness's testimony with undeserved credibility.[37] The power or persuasiveness of a 'telegenic' witness may, it is feared, be artificially enhanced or bolstered by the use of video technology, placing an accused at an invisible and unmonitored disadvantage.[38] Televised testimony is also said by some to capture a jury's attention more effectively than a court-room performance, conferring an unfair advantage on the prosecution. Evaluative studies suggest that such concerns are largely overstated. In Davies *et al.*'s study, for example, data analysis revealed no statistically significant difference between the proportion of guilty verdicts delivered for video-taped evidence and evidence given via the live link, or given in open court.[39] This was interpreted by the researchers as an indication that video-taped evidence had the same impact on a jury as a live examination.

Experimental studies similarly suggest that shielding procedures have a limited impact.[40] Mock trials staged by Goodman *et al.*, for example, in which evidence was delivered either live or via a video link failed to uncover direct

[34] 'There can be little doubt in our judgment that the use of screens is prejudicial to an accused person, even where the jury are properly warned not to make any assumptions adverse to the accused person because of the presence or use of screens': R v XYZ [1994] Crim LR.

[35] The case involved a 20-year-old rape complainant: R v Foster [1995] Crim LR 333.

[36] S. 32.

[37] See Montoya, J., 'On truth and shielding in child abuse trials' (1992) 43 *Hastings Law Review* 1259, 1305.   [38] A phenomenon known as 'status conferral'.

[39] Data supplied by the Lord Chancellor's Department showed that prosecutions were successful in 44% of cases where children testified live, compared to 49% in cases using video-taped evidence: Davies, G., Wilson, C., Mitchell, R. and Milsom, J., *Videotaping Children's Evidence: An Evaluation* (1994, London: Home Office).

[40] See generally Davies, G., 'The impact of television on the presentation and reception of children's testimony' (1999) 22 (3–4) *International Journal of Law and Psychiatry* 241.

negative biases towards defendants due to the utilization of the video medium. Specifically, there were no more guilty verdicts rendered when children testified via the television link.[41] In a study conducted by Ross *et al.* mock juries watched a video-taped simulation of a sexual abuse trial in which the testimony of the ten-year-old complainant was delivered either in open court, or in court from behind a protective screen, or through a video monitor.[42] In the first experiment the mock jurors judged the guilt of the defendant after watching the entire trial. Ross *et al.* report that the modality of the child's testimony had no impact on conviction rates. In particular, the perceived credibility of the defendant did not differ over the three experimental conditions. In a second experiment subjects watched the same video but the trial was stopped immediately after the child had testified. This time the medium of presentation had a significant impact on conviction rates. Mock jurors observing witnesses in the open court condition were more likely to convict the defendant than jurors watching the screen and video-tape conditions. These findings were taken by Ross *et al.* to suggest that the use of protective measures did not put defendants at an increased risk of conviction.[43] Any possible impact produced by protective procedures was also seen to be of a transient nature. Specifically, '[n]o support was obtained for the hypotheses that jurors are more likely to convict a defendant or perceive the defendant negatively if a child testifies using a protective device versus testifying while directly confronting the defendant'.[44]

Caution must, of course, be exercised when applying the results of experimental research to forensic settings. However, the failure of consecutive studies to disclose a discernible prejudicial effect when a witness is removed from the 'court-room' does suggest that any adverse impact is slight and is amenable to suitable jury direction. The requirement that trial judges issue such a warning as is determined necessary to prevent adverse inferences being drawn against the accused as a result of the making of a special measures direction under the YJCEA therefore appears sufficient to satisfy concerns about due process. In any event, from a defence perspective the use of shielding mechanisms may be preferable to the admission of written witness statements under section 23 of the Criminal Justice Act 1988.[45] Where such documentary hearsay statements are admitted the defence is denied the opportunity of cross-examining the maker on their contents.

[41] Goodman, G., Tobet, A., Batterman-Faunce, J., Orcutt, H., Thomas, S., Shapiro, C. and Sachsenmaier, T., 'Face to face confrontation: Effects of closed circuit technology on children's eye-witness testimony and jurors' decisions' (1998) 22 *Law and Human Behaviour* 165, 199.

[42] Ross, D., Hopkins, S., Hanson, E., Lindsay, R., Hazen, K. and Eslinger, T., 'The impact of protective shields and videotape testimony on conviction rates in a simulated trial of child sexual abuse' (1994) 18(5) *Law and Human Behavior* 553.

[43] The authors of the study acknowledge that the generalizability of their findings may be limited by the fact that all three conditions were presented on videotape, inevitably compromising any contrast.

[44] Ross *et al.*, n. 42 above, 560. See also Westcott, H., Davies, G. and Clifford, B., 'The credibility of child witnesses seen on closed circuit television' (1991) 15(1) *Adoption and Fostering* 14.

[45] See *R v Radak* (1999) 1 Cr App R 187.

C. Diminution of Demeanour Evidence

A further concern raised by the advocates of confrontation rests upon the importance traditionally attached to the observation of witness demeanour by the fact-
finder in adversarial systems of trial.[46] This in turn is rooted in the assumption
that the dishonest witness will betray himself through facial expression and other
non-verbal behaviour. According to Frank: 'All of us know, in everyday life, the
way a man behaves when he tells a story—his intonation, his fidgeting or composure, his yawns, the use of his eyes, his air of candour or evasiveness—may furnish valuable clues to his reliability. Such clues are by no means impeccable
guides, but are often immeasurably helpful. So the courts have concluded.'[47]

The ability of a defendant to challenge the prosecution case is accordingly
said to be compromised when protective measures 'interfere' with the assessment of non-verbal witness behaviour.[48] It is claimed that live link jurors in
particular are denied the opportunity to consider the full range of
demeanour evidence normally available with live in court testimony.[49] Murray,
for example, reports lawyers' concerns that the nuances of children's testimony are lost through the use of the live link and that their reactions and
responses are consequently less readily monitored and evaluated.[50] However,
such arguments assume that demeanour evidence supplies valuable clues as to
the sincerity and reliability of witnesses, and that jurors are capable of identifying and accurately interpreting these signs.[51] Evidence supporting either
contention is thin on the ground.[52] In fact, an extensive body of psychological and behavioural research contradicts orthodox legal assumptions as to
utility of demeanour in assessing veracity.[53] Specifically disputed are claims
that there are recognizable indicia of deception. Non-verbal behaviours popularly perceived as indicators of mendacity include avoidance of eye contact,
fidgeting, blushing, postural shifts, manipulative hand movements, and
scratching. However, studies indicate that eye contact, for example, may in
fact increase during deception and that some people appear tense and fidgety
when lying while others remain still and appear calm.[54] There is some

---

[46] According to Marcus Stone's definition, 'demeanour' excludes the content of the evidence, and
includes 'every visible and audible form of self-expression manifested by a witness, whether fixed or
variable, voluntary or involuntary, simple or complex': Stone, M., 'Instant Lie Detection?
Demeanour and Credibility in Criminal Trials' [1991] *Criminal Law Review* 821, 822.

[47] Frank, J., *Courts on Trial: Myth and Reality in American Justice* (1963, Antheneum:
Massachusetts) 21.

[48] See Costigan, R. and Thomas, P., 'Anonymous Witnesses' (2000) 51(2) *Northern Ireland Law
Quarterly* 326, 332.   [49] Montoya, n. 37 above, 1306.

[50] Murray, K., *Live television link: An evaluation of its use by child witnesses in Scottish criminal trials* (1995, Edinburgh: The Scottish Office), 168.   [51] Stone, M., n. 46 above, 827.

[52] See Wellborn, O. G., 'Demeanour' (1991) 76 *Cornell Law Review* 1075.

[53] See Blumenthal, n. 2 above; Re, L., 'Oral v. written evidence: The myth of the "impressive
witness"' (1983) 57 *Australian Law Journal* 679.

[54] See DePaulo, B. M., Stone, J. I. and Lassiter, G. D., 'Deceiving and Detecting Deceit' in (ed.)
Schlenker, B. R., *The Self and Social Life* (1985, New York: McGraw-Hill); Miller, G. R. and Stiff,

evidence to suggest that vocal or paralinguistic cues may be more valuable as indicators of deception than visual ones. A number of studies, for example, suggest that vocal pitch increases when lying and so too do the number of speech errors made. However, even these studies acknowledge that these cues are not foolproof and that a truthful speaker may exhibit the same auditory characteristics.[55] Importantly, research suggests that behaviour commonly interpreted as signifying untruthfulness may equally signify stress.[56] This is highly significant given the high levels of stress commonly experienced by witnesses testifying in accordance with conventional adversarial methods. Furthermore, observers have been generally shown to be inefficient in spotting prevarication. As Wellborn has observed, if ordinary people possess the capacity to detect falsehood or error on the part of others by observing their non-verbal behaviour, then it should be possible, indeed easy, to demonstrate such a capacity under controlled conditions. Over the years a large number of experiments involving thousands of subjects have searched for this capacity and have shown with remarkable consistency that it simply does not exist.[57] When the Law Commission for England and Wales examined available evidence it similarly concluded that the chances of an observer correctly concluding that someone is lying from his or her demeanour were little better than the chance of doing so by tossing a coin.[58] To compound matters further, there is evidence to suggest that observers who rely on demeanour evidence are often unduly influenced by peripheral factors unrelated to reliability and truthfulness, such as personal attractiveness, wardrobe, mannerisms, and apparent confidence.[59]

Overall, the primary objections to special trial arrangements which deviate from normal practice appear on examination to be overstated. Each attaches an importance to direct confrontation that is difficult to justify in the light of the available supporting evidence. What is more, the arguments raised rarely take account of the needs, legitimate expectations, and rights of those other than the defendant. The second part of this Chapter endeavours to demonstrate that fairness in criminal trials can no longer be meaningfully discussed in such narrow terms.

J. B., 'Applied issues in studying deceptive communication' in (ed.) Feldman, R. S., *Applications of Non-verbal Behavioral Theories and Research* (1992, Hillsdale, New Jersey: Erlbaum).

[55] See Ekman, P. and Friesen, W. V., 'Non-verbal Leakage and Clues to Deception' (1969) 32 *Psychiatry* 88.

[56] Ekman, P., *Telling Lies: Clues to Deception in the Marketplace, Marriage and Politics* (1986, New York: W. W. Norton); Kohnken, G., 'The evaluation of statement credibility: Social judgment and expert diagnostic approaches' in (eds.) Spencer, J. R., Nicolson, G., Flin, R. and Bull, R., *Children's Evidence in Legal Proceedings: An International Perspective* (1990, Cambridge: Selwyn College).   [57] Wellborn, n. 52 above, 1104.

[58] Law Commission for England and Wales, *Criminal law: Evidence in criminal proceedings: Hearsay and related topics, a consultation paper* (1991, London: HMSO) 80.

[59] See Fife-Shaw, C., 'The influence of witness appearance and demeanour on witness credibility: A theoretical framework' (1995) 35(2) *Medicine, Science and Law* 107.

D. RECOGNIZING WITNESSES' RIGHTS[60]

In determining whether to make a special measures direction a court is bound to consider, *inter alia*, any views expressed by the witness, and whether the measure or measures might tend to inhibit the evidence being tested by a party to the proceedings. The court is in effect required to balance competing interests and values. Traditionally, witnesses' interests and rights have received limited recognition within the criminal process. However, recent decisions of the European Court of Rights have broken new ground in allowing a defendant's 'normal' rights to be curtailed in the interests of witnesses.[61] The landmark ruling was *Doorson v The Netherlands*.[62] In its judgment the Strasbourg Court stated for the first time that a witness's rights must, in line with principles of fairness, be considered alongside those of the defendant in criminal proceedings:

It is true that Article 6 does not explicitly require the interests of witnesses in general, and those of victims called upon to testify in particular, to be taken into consideration. However, the life, liberty, or security of a person may be at stake as may interests coming generally within the ambit of Article 8 of the Convention. Such interests of witnesses and victims are in principle protected by other, substantive provisions of the Convention, which imply that Contracting States should organise their criminal proceedings in such a way that those interests were not unjustifiably imperilled. Against this background, principles of a fair trial also require that in appropriate cases, the interests of the defence are balanced against those of witnesses or victims called upon to testify.[63]

The Court, it will be recalled, held that the compensatory procedural measures adopted by the Dutch courts were adequate to counterbalance any handicaps that reliance on the testimony of anonymous witnesses caused the defence. The accepted risks that flow from the non-disclosure of a witness's identity to the defendant were weighed, *inter alia*, against the threat of intimidation to those testifying against him. This adoption of a balancing-interest approach by the Court is of course all the more significant given the enactment of the Human Rights Act 1998.[64] Significantly, the 1998 Act enables vulnerable witnesses to raise Convention rights in support of a claim for assistance and protection.

The Court's decision in *Doorson* was to some extent foreshadowed by decisions of the European Commission of Human Rights in *Baegen v The Netherlands*[65] and *Finkensieper v The Netherlands*.[66] In both cases the

---

[60] See generally, Mackarel, M., Raitt, F. and Moody, S., *Briefing paper on legal issues and witness protection in criminal cases* (2001, Edinburgh: Scottish Executive Central Research Unit).

[61] See Ashworth, A., '(2) Article 6 and the fairness of trials' [1999] *Criminal Law Review* 261.

[62] *Doorson v The Netherlands* (1996) 22 EHRR 330.

[63] See Ashworth, A., 'Victims' Rights, Defendants' Rights and Criminal Procedure' in (eds.) Crawford, A. and Goodey, J., *Integrating a Victim Perspective within Criminal Justice* (2000, Hants: Ashgate) 185.

[64] Rock, P., 'Acknowledging victims' needs and rights' (1999) 35 *Criminal Justice Matters* 4.

[65] (1995) Application 16696/90.   [66] (1995) Application 19525/92.

psychological and emotional trauma that sexual offence complainants might suffer if compelled to give evidence in open court in the presence of an accused were accepted by the Commission to be legitimate considerations for national courts. In *Baegen* the complainant asked to remain anonymous as she claimed to have been threatened with reprisals by the man who had allegedly raped her should she speak about the attack. The complainant gave three statements to the police and was examined under oath by an examining magistrate but did not testify at trial. The defence were invited to submit additional questions to be answered at a further preliminary hearing but failed to do so.[67] The applicant was convicted of rape and claimed that he had been deprived of his right to a fair trial as the defence had been denied the opportunity of examining the complainant directly. The Commission declared the application admissible but expressed the opinion that there had been no violation of Article 6.[68] The Commission noted that the applicant's conviction did not rest solely on the statements of the complainant and that the complainant's fear of reprisals was considered well founded by the investigating judge.[69] The Commission also had regard to the 'special features of criminal proceedings concerning rape and other sexual offences'. Such proceedings are, it stated, often conceived of as an ordeal by the complainant, in particular when the latter is unwillingly confronted with the defendant. Moreover, in the assessment of the question whether or not in such proceedings an accused received a fair trial, account must be taken of the right to respect for the complainant's private life. Accordingly, the Commission accepted that in criminal proceedings concerning sexual abuse certain measures may be taken for the purpose of protecting the victim, provided that such measures can be reconciled with an adequate and effective exercise of the rights of the defence.[70]

In *Finkensieper* the applicant was convicted of rape and indecent assault of four of his former psychiatric patients. Three of the victims, J, T, and D were examined at a preliminary hearing by an examining magistrate and the applicant's lawyer. The fourth victim, C, made a statement to the police but later refused to appear before the examining magistrate. None of the complainants gave evidence in court. The applicant did not request that the Regional Court hear any witnesses but later requested that the Court of Appeal summon all four complainants to testify at trial. The Court of Appeal rejected these requests considering, *inter alia*, police reports that C would not comply if summoned to give evidence at trial due to psychological and emotional problems and that the defence had had adequate opportunity to question J, T, and D. In

---

[67] It was only later, in the course of the hearing before the Court of Appeal, that the applicant expressed a wish to hear the complainant.

[68] The case was subsequently struck out of the Court's list in accordance with Rule 51 para. 2 when the applicant failed to confirm that he wished to take part in proceedings.

[69] The Commission further observed that the applicant had failed to avail himself of an offer by the investigating judge to put written questions to the complainant.

[70] The case has not been pursued before the Court.

relation to the use of C's police statement the Commission expressed the opinion that the applicant had not been deprived of a fair trial within the meaning of Article 6. Notwithstanding that it would have been preferable to hear C in person, the Commission found, taking into account the sensitive nature of the case and the problems C apparently experienced, that the assessment of the Court of Appeal could not be regarded as arbitrary or unreasonable. The Commission was additionally influenced by the existence of other evidence in the case that supported C's statements.

Other significant developments at European level include the adoption of *Recommendation No. (85) 11 on the Position of the Victim in the Framework of Criminal Law and Procedure* in 1985.[71] The recommendation, which calls on member states to have more regard for the needs of victims at each stage of the criminal justice process, focuses on three main issues: information, compensation, and treatment and protection.[72] With regard to court proceedings, paragraphs F. 15 and G. 16 stipulate the need to protect victims from publicity that will unduly affect their private lives and dignity and also from intimidation and the risk of retaliation respectively. Of significance for witnesses generally is *Recommendation No. R (97) 13 on Intimidation of Witnesses and the Rights of the Defence*.[73] The recommendation calls on member states to give greater recognition to the rights of witnesses and the need to guard against intimidation and unnecessary distress at trial.[74] The responsibility placed on witnesses, the accompanying memorandum states, gives rise to a corresponding duty on the criminal justice system to protect their interests. In an important passage it notes that:

To give testimony, if so required by the criminal justice, is above all and has been for a long time, a civic duty for everyone, unless the person is privileged. Compliance with such a legal obligation by witnesses should in principle be unconditional. In the context of certain types of criminality, e.g. organised crime and violence in the family, one cannot ignore the risk run by witnesses of exposing themselves to retaliation by the offender or his associates. Criminal justice must therefore be sensitive to the specific needs of such persons whose evidence is often essential to uncover the truth. The duty to give testimony

---

[71] Adopted by the Committee of Ministers of the Council of Europe in June 1985. The recommendation contains 16 guidelines for the police, prosecution services, and the courts. See also *Recommendation (87) 21 on Assistance to Victims and Prevention of Victimisation*. In a Resolution adopted by the Council of European Union (23 November 1995, 95/C 327/04) on the protection of witnesses in the fight against international organized crime, the European Union called on its member states to guarantee the appropriate protection of witnesses. See also Council Resolution 97/C 10/01 of 20 December 1996, on individuals who co-operate with the judicial process in the fight against international organized crime.

[72] A recent large-scale comparative study of the position of the victim of crime in 22 European criminal justice systems reports that most systems are not even close to meeting the requirements, although victim-centred reforms have been introduced in most jurisdictions since 1985. See generally Brienen, M. and Hoegen, E., *Victims of crime in 22 European criminal justice systems: The implementation of Recommendation (85) 11 of the Council of Europe on the position of the victim in the framework of criminal law and procedure* (2000, Nijmegen, The Netherlands: Wolf Legal Productions).   [73] Adopted by the Committee of Ministers in September 1997.

[74] *Recommendation No. R (97) 13 on Intimidation of Witnesses and the Rights of the Defence*.

implies the responsibility of the State to guarantee that witnesses can comply with it without the above consequences. What can be interpreted as a State responsibility may also be seen as a right for witnesses: laws should clearly establish that the status of witnesses comprises these two aspects at the same time, i.e. duty to give testimony and the right to carry out this duty without any interference, harm or risk whatsoever.[75]

Measures such as screens, live television links, and video-taped evidence may be necessary, the recommendation states, to spare witnesses unnecessary strain and distress and to avoid inappropriate influences on the search for the 'truth', including the witness's willingness to give evidence. Particular regard is made to alleged victims of intra-familial crime, especially children, women, and the elderly, who are described as vulnerable to intimidation by defendants at trial. Paragraph 25 of the recommendation provides that vulnerable witnesses should, whenever possible, be examined at the earliest stage of criminal proceedings, as soon as possible after the facts have been reported. If appropriate, statements made at the pre-trial stage should be recorded by video to avoid face-to-face confrontation and unnecessary repetitive examinations that may cause trauma.

Most recently, the Portuguese Presidency of the Council of Ministers submitted a draft Framework Decision on the standing of victims in criminal proceedings.[76] The framework decision, which remains subject to approval by EU member states, would provide outline rights for victims for the first time across the EU.[77] In relation to victim-witnesses who testify at trial, the document states that member states shall take the necessary measures to ensure that victims are treated with respect for the dignity of the individual and shall recognize the rights and legitimate interests of victims at all stages of procedure. It also states that appropriate measures shall be taken for victims who are particularly vulnerable on account of their age, sex, or other circumstances. Article 8 of the draft framework decision specifically provides that where there is a need to protect victims from the effects of giving evidence in open court, as may arise on account of a victim's age or the nature of the offence or for other reasons, member states shall ensure that victims are allowed to testify in camera or by way of a video conference or video recording or other appropriate means, without prejudice to Article 6 of the European Convention on Human Rights.

1. International Developments

The concept of balance has also been crucial in the development of international victim policy. In this regard the *Declaration of Basic Principles of Justice for Victims of Crime and Abuse of Power*, adopted by the General Assembly of

---

[75] Accompanying explanatory memorandum, para. 46.

[76] Initiative of the Portuguese Republic with a view to adopting a Council Framework Decision on the standing of victims in criminal proceedings, OJ 2000 C243/4.

[77] The government claims that these proposed requirements are already being met: Home Office: *A Review of the Victim's Charter* (2001, London: HMSO).

the United Nations in 1985, was a landmark.[78] The Declaration recommends measures to be taken on behalf of victims of crime at international, regional, and national levels to improve access to justice, fair treatment, restitution, compensation, and assistance.[79] Among these are 'measures to minimise inconvenience to victims, protect their privacy, when necessary, and ensure their safety, as well as that of their families and witnesses on their behalf, from intimidation and retaliation'.[80] The primary reference point for international law relating to the protection of witnesses at trial is, however, the International Criminal Tribunal for the Former Yugoslavia ('ICTY').[81] The procedural and evidential apparatus of the ICTY has been described as 'exceptional to the extent that [it is] more "victim friendly" than most parallel domestic criminal codes'.[82] Article 22 of the Tribunal's governing statute provides that '[t]he International Tribunal shall provide in its rules of procedure and evidence for the protection of victims and witnesses'.[83] Article 20 stipulates that 'the Trial Chamber shall ensure that a trial is fair and expeditious and that proceedings are conducted in accordance with the rules of procedure and evidence, with full respect for the rights of the accused and due regard for the protection of victims and witnesses'. The right of an accused to a fair trial is thus to be balanced against the safety of testifying witnesses.[84] These obligations are fleshed out in the Rules of Procedure and Evidence.[85] The main provisions are contained in rule 75 which provides that a judge or Chamber may order appropriate measures to ensure the privacy and protection of victims and witnesses. These include measures to prevent disclosure to the public or the media of the identity or whereabouts of a witness, the use of one-way closed-circuit television, and the exclusion of the public and the press from all or part of the proceedings. Rule 75(c) provides that the judge or

---

[78] GA Res. 40/35 1985.

[79] See United Nations, *Handbook On Justice For Victims: On the use and application of the United Nations Declaration of Basic Principles of Justice for Victims of Crime and Abuse of Power* (1999, New York: United Nations ODCCP).

[80] United Nations, *Declaration of Basic Principles of Justice for Victims of Crime and Abuse of Power* (1985) para. 6(d).

[81] The International Tribunal was established by the Security Council in the first half of 1993 as a measure to maintain or restore international peace and security pursuant to Chapter VII of the Charter of the United Nations. Resolution 827, containing the Statute of the International Tribunal, was adopted in May 1993, giving the International Tribunal jurisdiction 'to prosecute persons responsible for serious violations of international humanitarian law committed in the territory of the former Yugoslavia since 1991', in accordance with the provisions of the Statute.

[82] Aolain, F. N., 'Radical Rules: The Effects of Evidential and Procedural Rules on the Regulation of Sexual Violence in War' (1997) 60 *Albany Law Review* 892. See also Lakatos, A., 'Evaluating the Rules of Procedure and Evidence for the International Tribunal in the Former Yugoslavia: Balancing Witnesses' Needs Against Defendants' Rights' (1995) 46 *Hastings Law Journal* 909.

[83] See generally Chinkin, C., 'Amicus Curiae Brief on Protective Measures for Victims and Witnesses' (1996) 7(1) *Criminal Law Forum* 179.

[84] For a critical evaluation see Sherman, A., 'Sympathy for The Devil: Examining a Defendant's Right to Confront before the International War Crimes Tribunal' (1996) 10 *Emory International Law Review* 833.

[85] These came into force on 14 March 1994 and are shared by the International Criminal Tribunal for Rwanda.

Chamber shall whenever necessary control the manner of questioning to avoid any harassment or intimidation.[86] A victims' and witnesses' unit, charged with recommending protective measures and providing counselling and support, was created as provided in rule 34. These evidentiary and procedural rules were developed in response to a situation involving gross violations of humanitarian law, committed on a massive scale. Nevertheless, they are significant in their recognition of witnesses' rights, setting international standards which may be expected to filter gradually into domestic court-rooms.

The Rome Statute for the International Criminal Court is couched in terms similar to those of the ICTY. Article 68 provides that the Court shall take appropriate measures to protect the safety, physical and psychological well being, dignity, and privacy of victims and witnesses. Rule 87 of the draft text of the Rules of Procedure and Evidence sets out the protective measures available to witnesses; these include, *inter alia*, the conducting of proceedings in camera and the presentation of evidence by electronic and other means.[87]

Finally, obligations towards victim-witnesses who are vulnerable by virtue of incapacity or age may be implied from the *United Nations Declaration on the Rights of Disabled Persons*[88] and the *United Nations Convention on the Rights of the Child* respectively. Article 3 of the latter provides that the primary consideration in all actions concerning children, including those undertaken by courts of law, shall be the interests of the child.[89]

E. SUMMARY

The significance attached within adversarial trial systems to direct and public confrontation has proved a potent obstacle to improving the treatment of vulnerable and intimidated witnesses. The claims made for confrontation, as distinct from cross-examination, have been shown in this and previous Chapters to be largely overstated. The fears of defence lawyers regarding the 'prejudicial' impact of protective procedures also appear to have been exaggerated. The special measures provisions of the Youth Justice and Criminal Evidence Act 1999,

---

[86] In consideration of the unique concerns of victims of sexual assault, a special rule for the admittance of evidence in cases of sexual assault was included in the Rules of the International Tribunal. Rule 96 provides that corroboration of the victim's testimony is not required and consent is not allowed as a defence if the victim has been subject to physical or psychological constraints. Finally, the victim's prior sexual conduct is inadmissible. See Fitzgerald, K., 'Problems of Prosecution and Adjudication of Rape and Other Sexual Assaults under International Law' (1997) 8 *European Journal of International Law* 638.

[87] Finalized draft text of the Rules of Procedure and Evidence of the International Criminal Court, available at http://www.un.org/law/icc/.

[88] Proclaimed by General Assembly Resolution 3447 (XXX) of 9 December 1975.

[89] UN GA Res. 44/25 1989. Article 39 states that 'States Parties shall take all appropriate measures to promote physical and psychological recovery and social reintegration of a child victim of any form of neglect, exploitation, or abuse'. See also *United Nations Standard Minimum Rules for the Administration of Juvenile Justice* ('The Beijing Rules'), UN GA Res. 40/33 1985.

examined above, do not constitute a significant erosion of the rights of defendants, as opponents have claimed. Rather they represent a belated attempt to strike a more appropriate balance between the interests of defendants and those of witnesses and the wider public.[90] All parties have an interest in ensuring that the trial is an effective forum for testing evidence. The undisputed right of defendants to challenge contrary evidence must be safeguarded, but impediments to witnesses giving the best evidence they are capable of giving must be removed as far as they are compatible with that right.

F. Vulnerable Defendants

Although this book is primarily concerned with vulnerable witnesses it is noteworthy that certain arguments regarding the adverse effects of orality apply with equal force to defendants disadvantaged by age or incapacity. However, defendants are ineligible for special measures protection under the Youth Justice and Criminal Evidence Act 1999. The interdepartmental working group considered but ultimately rejected their inclusion within the recommended definition of vulnerable or intimidated persons, reasoning that a defendant has a right to legal representation and can elect not to give evidence, whereas ordinary witnesses may be compelled to do so.[91] The working group also considered that screens, live links, and video-recorded testimony were designed to shield a witness from the defendant and would therefore be inapt. Both arguments are highly unconvincing. They completely overlook the risk of adverse inference that attaches to a defendant's failure to testify[92] and the insulation which special measures afford from a potentially intimidating court-room environment. Moreover, the use of video-recorded testimony is principally designed to capture an accurate record of evidence while events are still relatively fresh and thereby to avoid, or at least minimize, the risks of diminished or distorted recall.

In a recent report the Law Reform Commission of New South Wales acknowledged that defendants with an intellectual disability may be disadvantaged at

---

[90] Paul Boateng, Minister of State for the Home Office, House of Commons Standing Committee E: *Hansard*, 17 June 1999.

[91] Home Office, *Speaking Up For Justice: Report of the Interdepartmental Working Group on the treatment of Vulnerable or Intimidated Witnesses in the Criminal Justice System* (1998, London: Home Office) para. 3.28.

[92] Criminal Justice and Public Order Act 1994, s. 35, as amended by Crime and Disorder Act 1998, s. 35. The Criminal Justice and Public Order Act 1994, s. 35(1)(b), precludes the drawing of inferences where 'it appears to the court that the physical or mental condition of the accused makes it undesirable for him to give evidence'. The meaning of this provision was considered by the Court of Appeal in *Friend* where it was stated that 'it will only be in very rare cases that a judge will have to consider whether it is undesirable for an accused to give evidence on account of his mental condition'. In this case the accused was 15 years old but had a mental age of 9, a low IQ, and was 'within the handicapped bracket'. The Court of Appeal held that the trial judge had not erred in directing the jury that they could draw adverse inferences from the accused's failure to testify: *R v Friend* [1997] 2 Cr App R 231.

trial even if legally represented.[93] The Commission concluded that some defendants would be denied the full opportunity to present and challenge evidence as due process requirements dictated unless special arrangements including screens and live television links were made available, in appropriate circumstances, to accused persons as well as vulnerable witnesses.[94] The difficulties which young defendants may experience within the adversarial process were recently rehearsed at length in the cases of *T v UK* and *V v UK*.[95] The rulings relate to the trial of the two-eleven-year old boys convicted of the murder and abduction of two-year-old James Bulger. The trial of the young defendants took place in an adult Crown Court, preceded and accompanied by massive national publicity. During the trial, which lasted over three weeks, the defendants were required to sit in a raised dock in the centre of the court-room in the full view of the press benches and public gallery, which were invariably full. The trial was conducted with the formality of an adult criminal trial, with judge and counsel donning formal court attire. Some modifications to trial procedure were made, for example the court sat for shorter periods with regular breaks and social workers were allowed to sit next to the defendants.

Before the European Court of Human Rights, lawyers for Venables and Thompson argued, *inter alia*, that the cumulative effect of the age of criminal responsibility,[96] and the accusatorial, public nature of the trial amounted to a breach of their right under Article 3 not to be subjected to inhuman or degrading treatment or punishment. It was further claimed that the boys had been denied a fair trial in breach of Article 6 as they were unable to follow the proceedings, participate effectively, or take decisions in their own best interests because of the nature of the trial process.[97] Psychiatrists gave evidence that the nine-month interval between events and trial meant that vital psychological care and therapeutic help had been delayed which was bound to be deleterious for children as young as ten or eleven years old.[98] There was also evidence that the defendants were presenting symptoms of post-traumatic stress at the time of the trial which may have limited further their ability to understand or participate.

The Strasbourg Court was not convinced that the particular features of the trial process had caused 'suffering beyond that which would inevitably have been engendered by any attempt by the authorities to deal with them following

---

[93] Law Reform Commission NSW, *Report 80 People with an Intellectual Disability and the Criminal Justice System* (1996, Sydney: Law Reform Commission NSW) para. 7.5

[94] Ibid. para. 7.13   [95] [2000] Crim LR 187.

[96] The age of criminal responsibility in England and Wales is 10, which is low in comparison to most countries in Western Europe. See Bandalli, S., 'Abolition of the Presumption of Doli Incapax and the Criminalisation of Children' (1998) 37(2) *Howard Journal* 114; Cavandino, P., 'Goodbye doli, must we leave you?' (1997) 9(2) *Child and Family Law Quarterly* 165.

[97] In February 1998, 4 boys aged 10 and 11 years old appeared at the Old Bailey accused of the rape and indecent assault of a 9-year-old girl. The defendants were all acquitted but the case prompted an outcry from children's organizations, who claimed that the court was an highly inappropriate venue for such a hearing. 'Shake up urged after boys cleared in sex trial' *The Guardian*, 6 February 1998.

[98] Cavadino, P., 'Children who kill: A European perspective' (1996) *New Law Journal* 1325.

the commission of their crime' and therefore found no violation of Article 3. However, the Court did consider that the applicants were unable to participate effectively in the criminal proceedings against them, and were in consequence denied a fair hearing, in breach of Article 6. The Court stated, that the formality and ritual of the Crown Court must at times have seemed 'incomprehensible and intimidating for a child of eleven'.[99] The Court opined that the raised dock, in particular, would have increased any sense of discomfort during the trial as it exposed the boys to press and public scrutiny.[100] Representation by experienced counsel was in these circumstances insufficient to ensure a fair trial:

... although the applicant's legal representatives were seated, as the Government put it, within 'whispering distance', it is highly unlikely that the applicant would have felt sufficiently uninhibited, in the tense courtroom and under public scrutiny, to have consulted them during the trial or, indeed, that, given his immaturity and his disturbed emotional state, he would have been capable outside the courtroom of co-operating with his lawyers and giving them information for the purposes of his defence.

The Court considered that in respect of young children charged with grave offences attracting high levels of media and public interest, it might be necessary to conduct hearings in private, so as to reduce, as far as possible, feelings of intimidation and inhibition.

In response to the Court rulings, the Lord Chief Justice issued a practice direction applying to trials in the Crown Court.[101] The practice direction states that the trial process itself should not expose young defendants to avoidable intimidation, humiliation, or distress and that all possible steps should be taken to assist young defendants to understand and participate in the proceedings. Appropriate steps include allowing a young defendant to sit, if he or she wishes, with family members; taking frequent and regular breaks; removing robes and wigs; ensuring that the trial is conducted in language appropriate to the defendant's age, and restricting attendance at the trial to a small number. However, such measures have rightly been deemed inadequate to meet the needs of child witnesses testifying in criminal proceedings, and will not satisfy the needs of young defendants nor those with a significant learning disability or mental disorder. Making special measures such as television links and video-taped testimony available to defendants would go some way towards ensuring effective participation. However, there is much force in the argument that no child should be tried in adult courts, regardless of the offence charged and the modifying measures adopted.

---

[99] The Commission described the public trial process in an adult court as a 'severely intimidating procedure'.

[100] The dock was raised to enable the defendants to see what was going on.

[101] Practice Direction by the Lord Chief Justice of England and Wales, 'Trial of Children and Young Persons in the Crown Court' (February 2000).

V.
Cross-examination and the Vulnerable Witness

Within common law jurisdictions cross-examination has traditionally been extolled as 'the best security against incomplete, distorted or false evidence'[1] and 'almost apotheosized for its role in truth discovery'.[2] However, it is increasingly acknowledged that the techniques of cross-examination are as well suited to obfuscation, intimidation, and coercion as to the effective testing of evidence.[3] In its report, *Speaking up for Justice*, the Home Office working group recommended that the Lord Chief Justice be invited to consider issuing a Practice Direction giving guidance to barristers and judges on the need to disallow unnecessarily aggressive and inappropriate cross-examination.[4] In so doing, it tacitly acknowledged that cross-examination is for many vulnerable witnesses an intimidating and humiliating ordeal. The working group further accepted that children and those with learning disabilities are caused particular problems by adversarial examination, which can result in them giving unreliable evidence.[5] Furthermore, the failure of legislation adequately to curb the use of sexual history evidence was identified by the group as a factor contributing to a disturbingly high attrition rate in rape cases.[6]

Drawing upon a substantial international literature, this Chapter opens with an overview of the problems confronting vulnerable witnesses during cross-examination. In particular, it describes the various strategies that defence lawyers commonly employ to upset, unsettle, confuse, confound, and otherwise intimidate witnesses in order to negate or discredit their testimony or to bring into question their personal credibility. For ease of exposition these are examined under the headings of cross-examination as to credit, inappropriate language, coercive questioning, and intimidation tactics. Having described *how* vulnerable witnesses are treated during cross-examination this Chapter then

---

[1] Wrottesley, F. J., *The Examination of Witnesses in Court* (1931, London: Sweet and Maxwell) 64. [2] Damaska, M., *Evidence Law Adrift* (1997, New Haven: Yale University Press) 79.

[3] As Frank remarked, 'The lawyer considers it his duty to create a false impression, if he can, of any witness who gives . . . [unfavourable] testimony. If such a witness happens to be timid, frightened by the unfamiliarity of court-room ways, the lawyer in his cross-examination, plays on that weakness, in order to confuse the witness and make it appear that he is concealing significant facts': Frank, J., *Courts on Trial: Myth and Reality in American Justice* (1963, Massachusetts: Antheneum) 82.

[4] Home Office, *Speaking Up For Justice: Report of the Interdepartmental Working Group on the Treatment of Vulnerable or Intimidated Witnesses in the Criminal Justice System* (1998, London: Home Office) para. 8.53.   [5] Ibid. para. 8.50.

[6] Ibid. para. 9.56.

explores *why* cross-examination takes the form it so often does. Surprisingly, this question has received relatively little attention. What explanations there are typically focus narrowly on the particular attributes of the witness in question or the peculiar characteristics of offences. Witness- and offence-specific factors have accordingly been advanced as the key determinants of the conduct of cross-examination. This tendency to examine categories of witness in isolation has led to a flawed understanding of their treatment as the wider context has been neglected. The systemic incentives driving cross-examination and the structural and attitudinal barriers to effective regulation of court-room questioning within an adversarial system of trial have been largely overlooked. So too the ideology of advocacy and the associate advocate's ethos. By examining these systemic factors a broader theoretical framework for understanding the treatment of witnesses during cross-examination can be developed.

A. THE GREATEST LEGAL ENGINE?[7]

1. Cross-examination as to Credit

Cross-examination has a number of aims. It is used constructively to strengthen a cross-examiner's case by eliciting favourable evidence, and destructively to weaken or destroy harmful evidence given by a witness in order to defeat the opponent's case.[8] Cross-examination as to credit falls within the latter category and its object, put simply, is to impugn the credibility of the witness so as to persuade the fact-finder that it would be unsafe to rely on anything the witness said in chief.[9] Frequently, this results in what many regard as the degradation of witnesses through unduly intrusive questioning on apparently irrelevant matters and the introduction of evidence whose probative evidence is outweighed by its potentially prejudicial effect.

Rape Trials

In the context of cross-examination as to credit, criticism has centred almost exclusively on the treatment of complainants in rape trials and, in particular, on the implementation of the Sexual Offences (Amendment) Act 1976, section 2. Studies have revealed the extent to which complainants continue to be quizzed about their past sexual history with persons other than the defendant despite the passing of this legislation. Adler, for example, found that applications for

---

[7] Wigmore famously described cross-examination as 'beyond doubt the greatest legal engine ever invented for the discovery of truth': Wigmore, J. H., *Evidence* vol.5 (1974, Boston, Mass.: Chadbourn revision) 32.

[8] Stone, M., *The Proof of Facts in Criminal Trials* (1984, Edinburgh: Green) 99.

[9] 'When a cross-examiner attacks the moral standing of a witness he often does so not only with a view to showing that the witness's word carries less truth-value but also to suggest that the morality and humanity of the witness is so inferior that no verdict can be based on his testimony': Zuckerman, A. A. S., *Principles of Criminal Evidence* (1989, Oxford: Clarendon) 248.

the admission of sexual history evidence were made in 40 per cent of the fifty rape trials she studied at the Old Bailey, and that 75 per cent of these were allowed.[10] More recently, Lees found that over half the women in her study who had been raped by acquaintances were asked about previous sexual experience with men other than the defendant.[11] In a number of cases questions about sexual history were asked without any application having been made. A similar position has been described by Brown *et al.* in Scotland, and by various commentators across common law jurisdictions.[12]

Although sexual history evidence has been the site of most feminist research, studies have in recent years disclosed the extent to which complainants in general are subject to wider attacks on their characters and personal lives. Citing cross-examination as the worst aspect of giving evidence in a rape trial, many complainants have described their treatment in court in terms of further abuse: 'I had put my trust and faith in the legal system and afterwards I felt like I had been abused again but this time by the legal system itself'.[13] In a study conducted by the UK organization Victim Support, women characterized the process of cross-examination as 'patronising', 'humiliating', and 'worse than the rape' accused defence barristers of asking intrusive and inappropriate questions about their private lives.[14] Describing her treatment in court as 'traumatic', one victim complained that she had been asked insinuating questions about her behaviour, her friends, and her social life since the offence.[15] The study was based on in-depth interviews with a small sample of rape complainants who had been in contact with a local Victim Support scheme and on questionnaires completed by Victim Support schemes and witness services. Forty-one per cent of witness services who took part in the study reported that women experienced problems with the nature of questioning during cross-examination, including feeling it was character assassination and feeling re-victimized by the defence barrister.[16]

Women responding to a survey conducted by Lees also complained that they had been asked irrelevant and unfair questions (72 per cent) during cross-examination and the majority (82 per cent) reported feeling that they were on trial and not the defendant.[17] The study was based upon the transcripts of

---

[10] Adler, Z., *Rape on Trial* (1987, London: Routledge and Kegan Paul); Adler, Z., 'The Relevance of Sexual History Evidence in Rape: Problems of Subjective Interpretation' [1985] *Criminal Law Review* 769.

[11] Lees, S., *Carnal Knowledge: Rape on Trial* (1996, London: Hamish Hamilton) 31. See also McColgan, A., 'Common Law and the Relevance of Sexual History Evidence' (1996) 16 *Oxford Journal of Legal Studies* 275; Temkin, J., 'Sexual History Evidence: The Ravishment of Section 2' [1993] *Criminal Law Review* 3.

[12] Brown, B., Burman, M. and Jamieson, L., *Sex Crimes on Trial: The Use of Sexual Evidence in Scottish Courts* (1993, Edinburgh: Edinburgh University Press).

[13] Dublin Rape Crisis Centre, *The Legal Process and Victims of Rape* (1998, Dublin: Dublin Rape Crisis Centre) 150.

[14] Victim Support, *Women, Rape and the Criminal Justice System* (1996, London: Victim Support) 39.

[15] Ibid. 41.

[16] Ibid.   [17] Lees, S., *Carnal Knowledge: Rape on Trial* (1996, London: Hamish Hamilton).

thirty-one rape trials and 116 questionnaires completed by victims of rape. Lees reports that women were asked not only about their sexual past but about their living arrangements, financial situation, marital status, past drug-taking, and use of alcohol. 'In more than half the cases where consent was in issue, questioning included whether the complainant was divorced, was an unmarried mother, had a habit of drinking with strangers or drank to excess.'[18] Women were also asked what they felt to be inappropriate questions about their behaviour before an alleged assault and about their dress. For example, complainants were asked whether they were in the habit of going to night clubs alone, invited to describe the underwear, shoes, and make-up they were wearing and to indicate the length and tightness of their skirts. One woman was even asked to hold her underwear up in court in order to prove that it was, as she claimed, not made of transparent material.[19] In other cases, painful and upsetting incidents in a complainant's past were dredged up by defence lawyers in an attempt to suggest emotional or psychological instability. Women were asked about past abortions, their use of tranquillisers, and in one case a complainant was asked about the death of her father from AIDS.[20] Such questioning was often used to suggest that emotional upset had distorted a complainant's memory of events or had prompted her to make a false allegation.[21]

Research in other common law jurisdictions provides many further examples of complainants being 'put on trial'.[22] For example, in a recent study by Heenan and McKelvie, conducted in Victoria, almost all the complainants interviewed described feeling 'extremely traumatised' while being cross-examined by defence counsel. Many women reported being subjected to endless questioning around matters that had apparently little to do with the issues in the trial. According to the researchers, complainants were routinely portrayed by defence barristers as persons of low intelligence or of low morality who were inherently untrustworthy. In one case 'almost every conceivable aspect of the complainant's life was canvassed before the jury over an eleven-hour period'. The complainant was asked whether she was having sexual dreams around the time of the alleged assault; how long she had known the man she married; whether she had experienced postnatal depression after the birth of her baby; when she had left her husband and when she had begun a relationship with another man; the history of her menstrual periods; and whether she was living with a gay

---

[18] Ibid. 134.   [19] Ibid. 140.

[20] Adler reports how evidence of a suicide attempt made by a complainant was introduced by defence counsel in one case despite the fact that it preceded the alleged rape by two years: see n. 10 above.

[21] Research suggests that defence tactics in cases of male and female rape are characterized by significant similarities: Rumney, P., 'Male Rape in the Courtroom: Issues and Concerns' [2001] *Criminal Law Review* 205.

[22] Heenan, M., McKelvie, H., *Evaluation of the Crimes (Rape) Act 1991* (1997, Melbourne: Department of Justice), 201. See also Department for Women, *Heroines of Fortitude: The Experiences of Women in Court as Victims of Sexual Assault* (1996, Sydney: Department for Women).

woman at the time the allegations were made.[23] The researchers identified a number of recurrent themes that were raised during cross-examination which included the complainant's drinking on the day of the offence, the complainant's emotional and psychological stability, and the complainant's clothing. In one trial the defence suggested that the complainant's hormonal balance had been affected by an abortion she had undergone on the day of the incident and that the emotional disturbance had prompted her to make a false allegation against her ex-boyfriend. In another case, the jury learned that the complainant had recently terminated a pregnancy, had split up with her boyfriend, and had financial difficulties.[24] With regards to dress, one woman was quizzed about her 'vagina length mini skirt' in court while another was asked why she had not thought to wear other sorts of clothes that would have made her less 'easy to get at'.[25]

As well as denigrating the character of complainants, research into the conduct of sexual offence trials has revealed the extent to which defence lawyers exploit the many cultural myths and prejudices that continue to surround rape allegations in order to discredit their stories.[26] In child sexual abuse cases, for example, a common defence strategy is to focus on the supposed tendency of children to fantasize and fabricate while stressing the alleged ease with which children can be influenced to make false allegations by adults or other children.[27] Brennan, for example, reports a case in which a child aged seven years was asked 121 questions about her propensity to make up stories.[28] These themes are pursued in the absence of empirical support and in the face of evidence indicating that children, including the very young, can resist suggestion well. According to Spencer and Flin:

Children and adults tell lies but there is no evidence to support the contention that children are more likely to lie than adults. In fact the opinion of psychiatrists and psychologists counter this notion . . . one might almost extend the argument and suggest that children are actually more truthful than adults. Certainly the research on children's beliefs about court implies that children may be more cautious about lying in the witness box than adult witnesses.[29]

In a similar vein adult rape complainants are frequently confronted with outlandish reasons for lying as defence lawyers appeal to the pervasive 'myth' that

---

[23] Heenan *et al.*, n. 22 above, 215.   [24] Ibid. 196.   [25] Ibid. 193.

[26] Torrey, M., 'When Will We Be Believed? Rape Myths and the Idea of a Fair Trial in Rape Prosecutions' (1991) 24 *University of California, Davis Law Review*, 1013.

[27] 'My Dad's lawyer kept asking me the same question and kept muddling me up. I know it's his job but the way he was shouting at me "You are a liar: your Mum told you to make it all up". I just kept on crying' (12-year-old girl): Murray, K., *Live television link: An evaluation of its use by child witnesses in Scottish criminal trials* (1995, Edinburgh: Scottish Office) 72.

[28] Brennan, M., 'The Battle for Credibility: Themes in the Cross-examination of Child Victim Witnesses' (1994) 7(19) *International Journal for the Semiotics of Law* 51, 58. See also Brennan, M., 'The discourse of denial: Cross-examining child victim witnesses' (1995) 23 *Journal of Pragmatics* 71.

[29] Spencer, J. R. and Flin, R., *Evidence of Children: The Law and the Psychology* (1993, London: Blackstone) 329.

sexual offences attract a disproportionate number of false allegations.[30] Although there is no evidence that people lie about sexual assault any more than people lie about other offences, a generalized mistrust of sexual assault complainants often pervades defence questioning.

A second common defence tactic observed in sexual offence cases is to challenge complainants about any time lapse between the alleged assault and disclosure.[31] In Davis *et al.*'s recent study, for example, defence counsel relied on a delay of one hour to submit to the jury that a fifteen-year-old complainant had fabricated an allegation of sexual assault.[32] It is now known that victims of sexual violence frequently delay reporting an offence for a variety of reasons, including fear of reprisals, embarrassment, fear of not being believed, fear of the court process, and shame. In the case of child sexual abuse many offenders use threats of violence or bribery to secure a child's silence or endeavour to make them share responsibility for the abuse. Moreover, an offender may have sexualized his or her relationship with a child gradually over time, persuading the victim at first that their actions were not sexual. In many cases delay will therefore simply reflect the dynamics of a sexually abusive relationship.[33] By encouraging the jury to equate promptness with veracity defence lawyers deliberately misrepresent the reality of sexual abuse. The same may be said of the noted proclivity of defence lawyers to labour the absence of visible signs of physical resistance. Research indicates that struggle is unlikely in many cases involving young children and that adults are often too frightened or shocked to attempt to physically repel an assailant.[34]

Questioning such as that described above evokes what Adler and others have termed the concept of the 'ideal rape'. A rape most approximating to the stereotype is one where the victim is sexually inexperienced and has a 'respectable' lifestyle, whose assailant was a stranger, and whose company she had not willingly found herself in. Moreover, the victim will have fought back, been physically hurt, and afterwards promptly reported the offence.[35] This stereotype is based on antiquated notions of sexual morality and 'appropriate' female behaviour and conflicts with much that is now known about the nature of sexual assault and the response of individuals to traumatic events. Accordingly, the determined efforts of defence lawyers to stress nonconformity are likely to result, not only in a complainant's humiliation, but also in the distortion of the

---

[30] False complaints of rape and sexual assault are of course sometimes made. See Durston, G., 'Cross-examination of rape complainants: Ongoing tensions between conflicting priorities in the criminal justice system' (1998) 62 *Journal of Criminal Law* 91.

[31] See Baird, V., *Rape in Court* (1999, London: Society of Labour Lawyers) 33.

[32] Davis, G., Hoyano, L., Keenan, C., Maitland, L. and Morgan, R., *An Assessment of the Admissibility and Sufficiency of Evidence in Child Abuse Prosecutions* (1999, London: Home Office) 65.

[33] See Davies, E., Henderson, E. and Seymour, F. W., 'In the interests of justice? The cross-examination of child complainants of sexual abuse in criminal proceedings' (1997) 4(2) *Psychiatry, Psychology and the Law* 217, 219.   [34] Ibid. 226.

[35] Adler n. 10 above, 119.

real issues in a case. For example, the propensity of defence lawyers to present the everyday behaviour of sexual offence complainants before an alleged attack as outlandish, imprudent, or provocative provides a skewed impression of existing cultural and social mores and is thus likely to deflect a jury from the facts in issue. As Temkin notes:

In rape trials, codes of behaviour, which have lost their force, are presented as taken for granted norms so that women, who will frequently fall foul of them, are condemned. Today women work, play, drink and travel with men who are not their partners and visit their homes. Failing to note this or to suggest otherwise is to misrepresent the circumstances of everyday living and consequently allocate blame where none is due.[36]

Other Trial Contexts

A common assumption in much of the literature on rape is that complainants in rape cases are treated differently from complainants of non-sexual offences. It is assumed, for example, that the types of questions routinely put to rape complainants would be considered unacceptable in other trial contexts. However, there is mounting evidence that witnesses other than rape complainants find cross-examination as to credit a gruelling ordeal. Rock's study of proceedings at Wood Green Crown Court, for example, revealed that other crime victims, and prosecution witnesses in general, often feel humiliated, degraded, and frustrated by the process of cross-examination. According to Rock, many witnesses reacted viscerally to cross-examination describing their treatment as being 'traduced' and 'put on trial', and often left the witness box angrily and in tears: 'They made me feel like a criminal! It's the last time I'll come to court.'[37] Rock reports how 'as a matter of course, and in the most ordinary trial, gravely wounding allegations would be put to witnesses'.[38] Complainants in general were automatically challenged about their 'veracity, disinterestedness, integrity, knowledgeability, way of life, reputation and associations'.[39] In one case observed by Rock, the complainant in an assault trial was described by defence counsel in his closing speech as 'a spiteful, bitchy woman with a drink problem'. In another trial, the complainant was cast as a deceitful, conniving, drug-pushing lesbian. Rock's observations of criminal trials led him to characterize witnesses as people whose very moral status were in contention who came to court to be 'vilified and shamed'.

Brereton has critically examined the prevailing assumption that rape complainants are singled out for special treatment in the court-room.[40] Brereton's analysis was based upon a comparative study of forty rape trials and forty-four

[36] Temkin, J., 'Prosecuting and defending rape: Perspectives from the Bar' (2000) 27(2) *Journal of Law and Society* 219, 244.

[37] Interviews were conducted with both lay and professional court users: Rock, P., *The Social World of the English Crown Court* (1993, Oxford: Clarendon), 35.   [38] Ibid. 88.

[39] Ibid. 70.

[40] Brereton, D., 'How Different are Rape Trials? A Comparison of the Cross-examination of Complainants in Rape and Assault Trials' (1997) 37 *British Journal of Criminology* 242.

serious assault trials conducted in Victoria, Australia between 1989 and 1991. In the typical rape case examined in the study the complainant was a woman, the defendant was previously known to the complainant, the alleged rape occurred in private without witnesses, and a claim of consent was the main line of defence. In the typical serious assault trial the complainant was male, the defendant was unknown to the complainant, the alleged offence took place in public in front of witnesses, and the main defence raised was that of self-defence.[41] Brereton compared the various cross-examination strategies utilized in both trial contexts. Unsurprisingly, Brereton found that rape complainants were questioned more frequently about their sexual relations with people other than the defendant.[42] In terms of general character, however, substantial similarities were found in the discrediting strategies employed. Similar proportions of rape and assault complainants were questioned about their drinking behaviour, drug-taking habits, and emotional and mental stability. Significantly, assault complainants were more likely to be questioned about a previous criminal record, although this was often of little apparent relevance to the case in hand. Similar proportions of rape and assault complainants were asked questions that imputed a motive for lying, and evidence of delay in reporting a defence was used by defence counsel in both trial contexts to suggest fabrication. Overall, Brereton found that the general form and structure of cross-examination questioning was remarkably similar. Most of the tactics used by defence counsel appeared, he concludes, to have been standard 'tools of the trade' for lawyers, rather than unique to the setting of rape trials.[43] Brereton's findings are supported by those of an earlier study conducted by McBarnet. Drawing on observation of 105 criminal cases in Scottish courts, McBarnet claimed that crimes against the person merely exacerbate the vulnerability of all witnesses to discrediting cross-examination.[44]

2. Inappropriate Language

Language has been identified as the 'primary manipulative tool' at the disposal of lawyers in court.[45] In the context of cross-examination, it is a tool often abused to gain advantage over immature and comparably unsophisticated language users. It is widely acknowledged that children and the learning disabled are disadvantaged during cross-examination by the use of language and interrogative techniques that make little reference to their developmental characteristics and linguistic capacity. Studies indicate, for example, that few, if any, modifications to the format and language of cross-examination are made when

---

[41] Brereton, D., 'How Different are Rape Trials? A Comparison of the Cross-examination of Complainants in Rape and Assault Trials' (1997) 37 *British Journal of Criminology* 250.

[42] Rape complainants were also questioned for longer. According to Brereton, this was primarily a function of the greater complexity of rape trials: ibid. 258.   [43] Ibid. 259.

[44] McBarnet, D., 'Victim in the Witness Box: Confronting Victimology's Stereotype' (1983) 7 *Contemporary Crises* 293, 294.

[45] See Eades, D., *Language in Evidence* (1995, Sydney: University of New South Wales Press).

the witness is a child.[46] An evaluative study of the live link in England and Wales found, for example, that 46 per cent of defence barristers exhibited only partial or limited accommodation to the child's linguistic style.[47] Similarly in Scotland, Murray reports that cross-examiners could rarely resist exploiting the immaturity of child witnesses and that very young children met with relentless and intrusive questioning.[48] In a 1994 study Davies *et al.* found that 17 per cent of defence barristers consistently used language that was inappropriate to the age of the child.[49]

Socio-linguistic studies of the conduct of criminal trials have identified specific age-inappropriate discursive devices typically used in the cross-examination of child witnesses. The Brennans' well documented study of lawyers' questioning of children, for example, identified a non-exhaustive list of thirteen language devices and questioning styles which confuse child witnesses and systematically help to destroy their credibility.[50] The study was based upon twenty-six transcripts of criminal trials conducted in New South Wales. Among the questioning techniques identified as causing particular difficulties were those containing multiple propositions,[51] nominalization,[52] embedded clauses,[53] and questions containing complex negative constructions.[54] The use of each device has been demonstrated to reduce comprehension and to impair the ability of child witnesses to respond accurately and fully to court-room questions. Multifaceted questions containing a number of propositions are, for example, problematic as they make no provision for the child witness who may quite conceivably agree with some of the propositions contained in any one question and emphatically disagree with others. Brennan and Brennan conclude that children with adequate verbal skills and clear, sustainable and substantial stories to tell

---

[46] See Walker, A. G., *Handbook on Questioning Children: A Linguistic Perspective* (1994, Washington: American Bar Association); Walker, A. G., 'Questioning Young Children in Court: A Linguistic Case Study' (1993) 17 *Law and Human Behaviour* 59. Walker's linguistic analysis of court-room transcripts revealed 3 areas of difficulty when lawyers question children: age-inappropriate vocabulary, complex syntactic constructions, and general ambiguity.

[47] See Davies, G. and Noon, E., *An Evaluation of the Live Link for Child Witnesses* (1991, London: Home Office).

[48] Murray, K., *Live television link: An evaluation of its use by child witnesses in Scottish criminal trials* (1995, Edinburgh: Scottish Office). See also Flin, R., Bull, R., Boon, J. and Knox, A., 'Child Witnesses in Scottish Criminal Trials' (1993) 2 *International Review of Victimology* 319.

[49] Davies, G., Wilson, C., Mitchell, R. A. and Milsom, J., *Videotaping Children's Evidence: An Evaluation* (1995, London: Home Office).

[50] Brennan, M. and Brennan, R. E., *Strange Language: Child Victims under Cross-examination* (1988, Wagga Wagga, NSW: Riverina Murray Institute of Higher Education).

[51] Example: 'Q. And did your mother ever say to you that if somebody asks you the questions I am asking you, you should say that we didn't say what was going to be said?' (transcript: question to a 10-year-old): ibid. 67.

[52] 'Nominalisation refers to the language process where an action is objectified so that neither the agent nor the recipient are mentioned. There is a great deal lost in the translation': ibid. 65.

[53] 'Embeddings themselves increase the stress on the respondent in court. If the child witness is confronted with questions containing a number of embedded pieces of information it is likely that comprehension will decrease and deteriorate as the number of embeddings increase': ibid. 76.

[54] Example: 'Q. And do you remember another occasion your father, or your stepfather, asked if you were playing sport, did you not say no?': ibid. 64.

are unable, due to their sense of self and command of language, to negotiate the rigours of cross-examination. The extant procedures focus not, they argue, on the establishment of truth 'but rather on the assertion of power . . . the power to confuse'.[55]

Other studies have criticized the adult centrism of traditional cross-examination techniques and have identified further 'child unfriendly' components, including the technique of juxtaposing unrelated topics, the use of complex sentence structures,[56] and the use of difficult and specific vocabulary. Research by Myers *et al.*, for example, found that many technical legal terms are lost on young children, including words such as allegation, minor, competent, hearsay, charges, defendant, and jury.[57] These studies reveal the extent to which the legalese of the court-room is often beyond the ordinary experience of young witnesses. According to one leading English commentator children in criminal trials 'are afforded little sensitivity, dignity or respect, even less the chance to present their account of events in a straightforward or meaningful way'.[58]

To compound matters, studies indicate that children rarely communicate their incomprehension when confronted with linguistically complex questions.[59] They may, of course, be unaware that they have misunderstood a question; alternatively, 'children may realize their failure to comprehend, but resist indicating this failure out of social desirability concerns.'[60] In the simplest form, children may want to avoid the overt embarrassment of appearing 'stupid' or may believe that their failure to understand a question is their own, not the examiner's fault.

Relatively little research has been conducted on how best to examine people with learning disabilities. Studies indicate that '[i]mpaired intellectual functioning, even when not amounting to mental handicap, can influence the ability of witnesses to understand questions, articulate their answers, and appreciate the implications of their answers'.[61] Troublesome language devices include

---

[55] Brennan and Brennan, n. 50 above, 4.

[56] See Carson, D., 'Regulating the examination of children' (1995) 4(1) *Expert Evidence*, 2; Perry, N. W., McAuliff, B. D., Tam, P., Claycomb, L., Dostal, C. and Flanagan, C., 'When Lawyers Question Children Is Justice Served?' (1995) 19 *Law and Human Behaviour* 609.

[57] Myers, J., Saywitz, K. and Goodman, G., 'Psychological research on children as witnesses: Practical implications for forensic interviews and courtroom testimony' (1996) 28 *Pacific Law Journal* 3, 54. See also Saywitz, K., 'Children's Conceptions of the Legal System: "Court is a Place to Play Basketball"' in (eds.) Ceci, S. J., Ross, D. F. and Toglia, M. P., *Perspectives on Children's Testimony* (1989, New York: Springer Verlag).

[58] Westcott, H., 'Children's experiences of being examined and cross-examined: The opportunity to be heard?' (1995) 4(1) *Expert Evidence* 13, 14. See also Kranat, V. and Westcott, H., 'Under fire: Lawyers questioning children in criminal courts' (1994) 3(1) *Expert Evidence* 16.

[59] See Saywitz, K., Synder, L. and Nathanson, R., 'Facilitating the communicative competence of the child witness' (1999) 3(1) *Applied Developmental Science* 58.

[60] Carter, C. A., Bottoms, B. L. and Levine, M., 'Linguistic and Socioemotional Influences on the Accuracy of Children's Reports' (1996) 20(3) *Law and Human Behaviour* 350.

[61] Gudjonsson, G. H., 'Testimony from persons with mental disorder' in (eds.) Heaton-Armstrong, A., Shepherd, E. and Wolchover, D., *Analysing Witness Testimony* (1999, London: Blackstone) 70.

multifaceted questions, complex grammatical constructions, the use of double negatives, and advanced vocabulary.[62] According to Ericson *et al.*, limitations in short-term memory capacity mean that learning disabled witnesses tend to have difficulty following long sentences.[63] When asked multiple questions simultaneously, the witness is likely to respond to only one question, due to an inability to process and retain multiple questions in short-term memory. However, which question is being answered may not be obvious to the examiner and the court, leading to confusion and frustration for all parties. A reduced understanding of abstract words and ideas can also result in difficulties, particularly with questions relating to concepts of time and sequence. Significantly, Ericson *et al.* note that witnesses with learning disabilities may have difficulty appreciating the adversarial nature of the court-room, and are likely not to understand that there may be a particular legal agenda or intent behind certain lines of questioning.

A case-study of trials and interviews with individuals and their carers led Sanders *et al.* to conclude that the law generally fails to recognize that learning disabled witnesses are caused particular problems by adversarial examination.[64] The researchers report little appreciation or understanding of learning disability, and that defence lawyers had difficulty making themselves understood by witnesses. Witnesses expressed frustration at the use of language which they felt had seriously undermined their performance in the witness box: 'Every time he [the defence barrister] said something to me I had to agree. He got me where he wanted me. The reason I agreed with everything he said was because I didn't understand what he was saying, which was all making me worse' (twenty-two-year-old man with a mild learning disability).[65] A twenty-year-old woman with a mild disability complained: 'They kept jamming my words up . . . his [the defendant's] side were the worst . . . they kept confusing me.'[66]

The Law Reform Commission of New South Wales, which conducted a five-year inquiry into the treatment of people with an intellectual disability in the criminal justice system, concluded in their report that questions containing many concepts and double negatives as well as questions which were leading, lengthy, or spoken rapidly cause learning disabled witnesses particular difficulties.[67] MENCAP has also recently expressed concern that the use of complex legal terms causes many people with learning disabilities to become confused and anxious in court. The organization has called for awareness training for all

[62] See Dent, H., 'An experimental study of the effectiveness of different techniques of questioning mentally handicapped witnesses' (1986) 25 *British Journal of Clinical Psychology* 13.

[63] Ericson, K., Perlman, N. and Isaacs, B., 'Witness competency, communication issues and people with developmental disabilities' (1994) 22 *Developmental Disabilities Bulletin* 101; Milne, R. and Bull, R., *Investigative Interviewing Psychology and Practice* (1999, Chichester: Wiley) 119.

[64] Sanders, A., Creaton, J., Bird, S. and Weber, L., *Victims with Learning Disabilities Negotiating the Criminal Justice System* (1997, Oxford: Centre for Criminological Research, University of Oxford) 75. See also Sanders, A., Creaton, J., Bird, S. and Weber, L., *Witnesses with Learning Disabilities*, Home Office Research Findings 44 (1996, London: HMSO).

[65] Sanders *et al.* (1997) n. 64 above, 75.　　　　　　　　　　　　　　　[66] Ibid. 75.

[67] Law Reform Commission NSW, *Report 80 People with an Intellectual Disability and the Criminal Justice System* (1996, Sydney: Law Reform Commission NSW).

barristers on learning disability following a survey of forty-nine barristers which found that 96 per cent had not received initial training on learning disability and that only 8 per cent of barristers had received such training since qualifying at the Bar.[68]

The use of complex syntax and vocabulary can of course also create difficulties for the 'average' adult witness. In a study conducted by Kebbell and Johnson the impact of 'confusing questions', such as those containing double negatives and multiple propositions, on 'ordinary' adult witness accuracy was examined.[69] Thirty-eight participants viewed a five-minute video-taped film depicting the physical assault of a woman and were individually questioned about the incident one week later. Half the participants were asked for information using fifty-six confusing questions; the remaining half were asked for the same information using simply phrased equivalents.[70] Analysis showed that questions were answered significantly more accurately in the simplified condition than the confusing condition. While acknowledging the limited generalizability of their findings to actual forensic settings, the researchers expressed concern that evidence distorted by lawyers' questions might well result in miscarriages of justice.

3. 'Coercive Questioning'

Cross-examination is characterized by the use of coercive, close-ended, and leading questions. Advocates prefer these types of questions 'because they enable them to control the topic choice, topic focus, and to construct the desired reality'.[71] A brief examination of advocacy texts reveals the importance typically attached to retaining strict editorial control over witnesses during cross-examination.[72] Advocates are warned that if a witness is allowed a degree of narrative freedom he or she may give evidence which is harmful to the cross-examiner's case or may miss out important points and stray into irrelevant details.[73] Accordingly, a familiar maxim of advocacy texts is that wherever possible an advocate should not ask a question to which he or she does not know the answer. In a similar vein, advocates are advised to avoid open-ended 'why'

---

[68] MENCAP, *Barriers to Justice: A MENCAP study into how the criminal justice system treats people with learning disabilities* (1997, London: MENCAP) 9.

[69] Kebbell, M. and Johnson, D., 'Lawyers' Questioning: The Effects of Confusing Questions on Witness Confidence and Accuracy' (2000) 24(6) *Law and Human Behaviour* 629.

[70] See the previous experiment conducted by Perry *et al.* using children: Perry, N. W., McAuliff, B. D., Tam, P., Claycomb, L., Dostal, C. and Flanagan, C., 'When Lawyers Question Children Is Justice Served?' (1995) 19 *Law and Human Behaviour* 609.

[71] Maley, Y. and Fahey, R., 'Presenting the Evidence: Constructions of Reality in Court' (1991) 4(10) *International Journal for the Semiotics of Law* 3, 7.

[72] Levy, for example, informs aspiring advocates that if there is only one commandment for cross-examination it should be 'Thou shalt control the witness': Levy, E., *Examination of Witnesses in Criminal Cases* (1991, Canada: Thompson Professional Publishing) 203.

[73] Stone, M., *Cross-examination in Criminal Trials* (1995, London: Butterworths) 309; Munkman, J. H., *The Technique of Advocacy* (1986, London: Sweet and Maxwell).

and 'how' questions. As Evans observes: 'Almost anything is responsive to a question that asks How? or Why? Those words are to be avoided like the plague in cross-examination.'[74]

Psychological research has identified a potential for the distortion of oral evidence in the use of controlling questioning techniques.[75] Interrogative suggestibility research has highlighted the danger of acquiescent responding, which indicates that the more a questioner suggests a particular answer, the less reliable the answer is likely to be. 'Acquiescence' refers to a tendency of people, when in doubt, to answer questions in the affirmative, irrespective of content.[76] While all people are potentially influenced by question structure and wording, children and those with an intellectual disability are particularly susceptible to certain question formats.[77] Research suggests that less accurate reports are obtained from learning disabled witnesses when focused or closed questions are used than in response to more open question formats. 'Broadly speaking as questions become more and more specific . . . responses become less accurate.'[78] The fact that some individuals with learning disabilities are more suggestible and acquiescent than their peers in the general population means that leading questions have a greater impact on their accuracy. A recent report by the organization Voice states that people with learning disabilities are often compliant and find difficulty in putting forward their own views, particularly if they feel intimidated or confused by repetitive or hectoring questioning or by the surroundings in which they are asked. Instead, they will try to provide answers which they think will please others.[79] This problem is apparently exacerbated when the person making the suggestion is an authority figure, such as a defence lawyer. According to Milne and Bull, if a specific question is suggestive about or misleads towards an incorrect answer, people with learning disability may agree with it because they may believe that an authority figure has more valid knowledge than themselves. For learning disabled witnesses, therefore, acquiescing to the suggestion makes sense.[80] The susceptibility of learning disabled persons to suggestion by perceived authority figures is, according to Perlman *et al.*, not surprising given that many often have multiple workers in positions of authority

---

[74] Evans, K., *Golden Rules of Advocacy* (1993, London: Blackstone) 108.

[75] See Spencer, J. and Flin, R., *The Evidence of Children: The Law and the Psychology* (1993, London: Blackstone), 271.

[76] See Clare, I. C. H. and Gudjonsson, G. H., 'Interrogative suggestibility, confabulation, and acquiescence in people with mild learning disabilities (mental handicap): Implications for reliability during police interrogations' (1993) 32 *British Journal of Clinical Psychology* 295.

[77] Siegel, C. K., Budd, E. C., Spanhel, C. L. and Schroenrock, C. J., 'Asking questions of retarded persons: A comparison of yes-no and either/or formats' (1981) *Applied Research in Mental Retardation* 347. See also Mortimer, A. and Shepherd, E., 'The Frailty of Children's Testimony' in (eds.) Heaton-Armstrong, A. *et al.*, n. 61 above, 46.

[78] Kebbell, M. and Hatton, C., 'People with retardation as witnesses in court: A review' (1999) 37(3) *Mental Retardation* 180. See also Dent, H., 'An experimental study of the effectiveness of different techniques of interviewing mentally handicapped child witnesses' (1986) 24 *Journal of Clinical Psychology* 13.   [79] VOICE, *Competent to tell the truth* (1998, Derby: Voice UK) 27.

[80] Milne, R. and Bull, R., *Investigative interviewing: Psychology and practice* (1999, Chichester: Wiley) 102.

over them and are frequently subject to training programmes designed to enhance their compliance with the expectations of authority figures.[81]

Children have also been shown to be susceptible to leading questions, providing less accurate information when they are employed in interviews.[82] Particularly distorting are questions tightly framed to elicit merely a 'yes' or 'no' response.[83] This is precisely the question format that advocacy manuals encourage advocates to adopt during cross-examination. Levy, for example, advises that leading questions should be framed to elicit a continuing series of 'yes' or 'no' answers as far as possible.[84] Such questions are often used to force a series of credibility-damaging 'I don't know' responses from a confounded witness.

Of course, strategically framed questions are not the only means by which advocates achieve linguistic dominance in court-room exchanges.[85] Vigorous objections, warnings, reminders, repetition of questions, and the insistence on proper answers are all devices used to attain and maintain editorial control. These preventative techniques are not only 'abrupt, frustrating and degrading to the witness'[86] but also dramatically reduce scope for clarification, explanation, and elucidation. For example, there is no provision, as there is in everyday conversations, for a witness 'to express their concerns, their possible lack of comprehension about the questions, or to negotiate in any way the content or direction of the line of questioning'.[87] Witnesses have described feeling 'silenced' by such trial tactics. A rape complainant interviewed in a study by the Dublin Rape Crisis Centre, for example, commented: 'I didn't like him at all . . . I'd try and explain it in my own way and he'd say sort of like "but no what I'm asking is . . . just say yes or no" . . . he only let me explain so much and then he'd cut me off . . . like he just wanted to hear what he wanted to hear . . . and he never really gave me a chance to say what I wanted to say.'[88]

---

[81] Perlman, N., Ericson, K., Esses, V. and Isaacs, B., 'The Developmentally Handicapped Witness: Competence as a Function of Question Format' (1994) 18(2) *Law and Human Behaviour* 186.

[82] Mortimer *et al.*, n. 77 above, 48; Bull, R., 'Interviewing Children in Legal Contexts' in (eds.) Bull, R. and Carson, D., *Handbook of Psychology in Legal Contexts* (1995, Chichester: Wiley) 242.

[83] See Bull, R., 'Interviewing People with Communicative Disabilities' in (eds.) Bull, R. and Carson, D., n. 82 above, 247; Peterson, C., Dowden, C. and Tobin, J., 'Interviewing preschoolers: Comparisons of yes/no and wh- questions' (1999) 23(5) *Law and Human Behaviour* 539.

[84] Levy, n. 72 above, 203.

[85] The importance of question form in achieving linguistic dominance has been demonstrated in numerous studies. See Atkinson, J. and Drew, P., *Order in Court* (1979, London: Macmillan); Matoesian, G., *Reproducing Rape* (1993, Cambridge: Polity Press); Danet, B. and Bogoch, B., 'Fixed Fight or Free for All? An Empirical Study of Combativeness in the Adversary System of Justice' (1980) 7 *British Journal of Law and Society* 36; O'Barr, W. M., *Language, power and strategy in the courtroom* (1982, New York: Academic Press).

[86] McBarnet, D., 'Victim in the Witness Box: Confronting Victimology's Stereotype' (1983) 7 *Contemporary Crises* 293, 299.   [87] Brennan *et al.*, n. 50 above, 59.

[88] Dublin Rape Crisis Centre, *The Legal Process and Victims of Rape* (1998, Dublin: Dublin Rape Crisis Centre) 202.

4. Intimidation Tactics

According to a recent Justice report: 'Some cross-examination is so lengthy, or so intimidatory, that it falls well outside what any person should be asked to endure. Nor does it serve the interests of justice: what witnesses may say during such an ordeal is likely to be just as unreliable as what defendants say after similar prolonged, intimidatory interrogation in a police station.'[89]

It is often claimed by defence lawyers that a hostile, intimidating approach is nowadays rarely adopted during cross-examination as it risks jury alienation, especially when a witness is perceived as vulnerable. This was the stance maintained by barristers recently interviewed by Temkin. One barrister remarked: 'I mean the jury would practically lynch you if you tried that now. The climate has shifted. It's not acceptable.'[90] This claim is, however, sharply at odds with the reported experiences of many vulnerable witnesses. Rape complainants interviewed in a Victim Support survey, for example, accused defence barristers of being unduly aggressive during cross-examination[91] and have elsewhere described defence lawyers as 'frightening', 'belligerent', and as 'waging a personal attack against them'.[92] Child witnesses surveyed have similarly reportedly described defence lawyers as 'hostile', 'mean', and 'unfair'.[93] In O'Grady's study, for example, many children felt that they had been unfairly treated, particularly in cross-examination. 'Some viewed cross-examination as an attack on their honesty by someone who they felt was attempting to confuse them, was unfair, and not a very nice person.'[94] Accusations of bullying and harassment were also made by prosecution witnesses interviewed by Rock.[95] Rock himself observed that advocates would frequently simulate a sternness of manner during cross-examination and goad witnesses in court.[96]

As Wigmore noted, an intimidating manner 'may so coerce or disconcert the witness that his answers do not represent his actual knowledge on the subject' and 'unfairly lead him to such demeanour or utterances that the impression

---

[89] Justice, *Victims in Criminal Justice, Report of the Committee on the Role of the Victim in Criminal Justice* (1998, London: Justice) 82.

[90] Temkin, n. 36 above, 229. In the same study some barristers pointed the finger at some of their older male colleagues while denying that they themselves ever practised harassment: 'I'm afraid it tends to be male barristers of advanced middle age. They can be very unpleasant.'

[91] Victim Support, n. 14 above, 56.

[92] Heenan, *et al.*, n. 22 above, 201. As one woman complained: 'Oh . . . he was antagonistic, he was offensive, theatrical . . . he didn't treat me with any respect': 202.

[93] O'Grady C., *Child Witnesses and Jury Trials: An Evaluation of the Use of Closed Circuit Television and Removable Screens in Western Australia* (1996, Perth: Western Australia Ministry of Justice) 82.

[94] Ibid. vi. Specific comments from an 11-year-old witnesses included: 'It was very unfair. . . . She kept saying the same question over and over.' 'She was very unfair because she was trying to trick me.' 'He tried to make me look stupid.' 'He treated me like dirt.'   [95] Rock, n. 37 above, 176.

[96] Ibid. 29. Rock, similarly describes how cross-examination routinely contains 'a passage in which counsel puts on a mocking or stern face and presses the witness hard as if trying to drive him or her to anger': Rock, P., 'Witnesses and Space in a Crown Court' (1991) 31 *British Journal of Criminology* 268.

produced by his statements does not do justice to its real testimonial value'.[97] While potentially distressing for any witness, the use of intimidating trial tactics can have particularly damaging results when the witness under examination is a child or person with a learning disability.[98] The ability of a witness to respond accurately to questions may well be curtailed, valuable information may be lost to the court, and the perceived credibility of the witness may be unjustly diminished as a result. Sanders *et al.* report that people with learning disabilities can be particularly sensitive to negative emotion and may respond to what they perceive as aggression by attempting to appease the questioner leading to heightened suggestibility and contradictory testimony.[99]

Tone of voice, speech rate, emphasis, eye contact, physical gesture, and facial expression are all devices which can be used to unsettle or unnerve a witness. The sheer volume of questions can also present problems. In one case studied by the Brennans the cross-examiner asked an eleven-year-old witness over 530 questions in one day.[100] An array of conversational ploys are also used to intimidate and thereby undermine opposing witnesses. Commonly observed trial tactics include repeating the same question many times, asking questions in rapid succession, and continuing a line of questioning despite its rejection by a witness.[101] In advocacy texts rapid fire questioning is presented as a legitimate technique which denies an untruthful witness the time to fabricate proper answers.[102] The technique is potentially damaging as it precludes adequate transition time. Repeated questioning has also been shown to result in undue deviations in testimony, since the repeated question leads especially immature or intellectually disabled witnesses to assume their initial response was not the 'right' answer.[103] Other notable devices include pre-emptive interruption and the juxtaposing of unrelated topics and questioning styles. Again in advocacy texts the 'skip around' technique is presented as a method which may be legitimately employed to confuse a dishonest witness. Levy, for example, recommends use of the technique when questioning a child witness whom counsel suspects of having memorized his or her testimony.[104] More widely recognized is the tendency of cross-examiners to latch onto trivial inconsistencies and present them as indicators of unreliability and lack of truthfulness. Related to this is the time-worn device of demanding precise recollection of seemingly obscure facts in the

---

[97] Wigmore, J. H., *A Treatise on the Anglo-American System of Evidence in Trials at Common Law* 3rd edn. (1940, Boston: Little, Brown) vol. 5.

[98] Carter, C. A., Bottoms, B. L. and Levine, M., 'Linguistic and Socio-emotional Influences on the Accuracy of Children's Reports' (1996) 20(3) *Law and Human Behaviour* 350.

[99] Sanders *et al.*, n. 64 above, 76. See also Greenstock, J. and Pipe, M., 'Interviewing children about past events: The influence of peer support and misleading questions' (1996) 20(1) *Child Abuse and Neglect* 69, 78.   [100] Brennan *et al.*, n. 50 above, 87.

[101] A 16-year old witness with a mild disability interviewed by Sanders *et al.* explained: 'I found it difficult . . . not asking me straight out, and asking the same things again and again. It made it difficult because they didn't seem to believe what we were saying. It was a nasty voice . . . that he used when talking to me': Sanders *et al.*, n. 64 above, 76.   [102] Levy, n. 72 above, 227.

[103] See Tully, B. and Cahill, D., *Police interviewing of the mentally handicapped: An experimental study* (1984, London: Police Federation).   [104] Levy, n. 72 above, 235.

presumed hope of eliciting a succession of damaging 'I don't remember' responses from a witness. As Weinreb writes: 'So far as he can, counsel "shakes" an opposing witness's testimony by revealing if not indeed creating minor inconsistencies, insisting on precision about trivia and then either lamenting the imprecision or pouncing on another inconsistency, and making the witness behave nervously and otherwise look unreliable.'[105]

Psychological research suggests that witnesses are undeservedly discredited in these circumstances because an inability to recall peripheral detail does not necessarily imply inaccurate or incomplete recall of significant salient information. Indeed, some studies suggest that a witness's memory for peripheral detail may be inversely related to memory for more central information.[106] Children and people with learning disabilities who can experience particular difficulty remembering peripheral detail are particularly easy targets for such trial tactics.[107] There is also some evidence to suggest that those who have witnessed or experienced traumatic events may have difficulty recalling peripheral detail but nevertheless retain an accurate recollection of the central action. The noted tendency of advocates in sexual assault trials to quiz complainants at length about ostensibly minor inconsistencies between their trial testimony and previous statements is thus likely, psychological research suggests, to undermine their credibility unjustly.

B. A Theory of Improper Cross-examination

Having surveyed the array of devices in the cross-examiner's armoury this Chapter now turns to the neglected question of why cross-examination takes the form it so often does. As stated, existing explanations for the treatment of vulnerable witnesses in court almost invariably present witness- or offence-specific factors as major determinants of the conduct of cross-examination. In other words, explanations focus heavily upon those factors that distinguish a specific category of witness or a particular offence from other witnesses and trial contexts. For example, rape literature has placed great emphasis on the cultural myths that continue to surround rape allegations,[108] the use of sexual history evidence, and the attitudes of defence barristers towards sexual offence complainants.[109] Victimological analyses of the cross-examination of children and people with learning disabilities have similarly centred largely on lawyers'

---

[105] Weinreb, L. L., *The Denial of Justice* (1977, London: Free Press) 102. According to Levy, catching a witness in a contradiction on what may be a minor point is a useful way of throwing a witness off balance and gaining an early advantage with a jury: n. 72 above, 218.

[106] See Goodman, G. and Helgeson, V., 'Child Sexual Assault: Children's Memory and the Law' (1985) 40 *Miami Law Review* 181, 189.

[107] See Kebbell, M. and Hatton, C., 'People with retardation as witnesses in court: A review' (1999) 37(3) *Mental Retardation* 179, 184.

[108] Taslitz, A., 'Patriarchal Stories: Cultural Rape Narratives in the Courtroom' (1996) 5 *Southern California Review of Law and Women's Studies* 387.   [109] Temkin, n. 36 above.

lack of knowledge, experience, and understanding of the particular communicative needs of these witnesses. However, such explanations provide a partial and somewhat misleading analysis of the problems confronting vulnerable witnesses during cross-examination. Essentially, they explain *how* rather than *why* witnesses are routinely humiliated, confused, and intimidated in court. 'Too much of an emphasis on visible problems rather than the deeper structures that help create them has distorted both understanding and diagnosis.'[110]

For a more complete understanding it is necessary to examine cross-examination within the wider context of trial adversariness. The basic theoretical structure of the adversarial trial and its underpinning assumptions must figure centrally in any analysis, because much of what happens during cross-examination is a function of systemic factors that operate across criminal trials. For too long these deeper structural issues have been ignored. The remainder of this Chapter is devoted to the nature of cross-examination as shaped by adversarial norms and the structural barriers inherent in the trial process for the effective regulation of defence questioning.

1. The Nature of Cross-examination

At the simplest level, criminal proceedings within an adversary system are conceived as a contest or 'fight', with advocates assuming primary responsibility for evidence presentation in accordance with the principle of party control or party autonomy. Advocates are not charged with any active fact-finding role but seek rather to persuade the judge or jury to accept their version of events. Accordingly, advocates are '. . . attitudinally and ethically committed to winning the contest rather than to some other goal, such as discovery of truth or fairness to the opposing side'.[111] This standpoint has spawned a decidedly gladiatorial view of court-room advocacy, as evidenced in the metaphors lawyers select to describe litigation. Cross-examination is compared to a physical fight between advocate and witness with frequent references to 'verbal pugilism',[112] 'forensic duels', and 'verbal combat'.[113] Advocacy manuals meanwhile speak candidly of 'butchering',[114] 'breaking',[115] and 'destroying' opposing witnesses.[116] Sherr, for example, advises advocates that 'quite often the most devastating cross-examination can be a fairly short build up rather like in boxing with one blow

---

[110] McBarnet, D., 'Victim in the Witness Box: Confronting Victimology's Stereotype' (1983) 7 *Contemporary Crises*, 293, 303.

[111] Goodpaster, G., 'On the Theory of American Adversary Criminal Trial' (1987) 78 *Journal of Criminal Law and Criminology* 120.

[112] Lord Devlin describes 'verbal pugilism' as a defining feature of adversarial proceedings: Devlin, P., *The Judge* (1979, Oxford: Oxford University Press) 54.

[113] 'Resort to the law is a form of civilised warfare, the advocate the modern representative of the medieval champion': Du Cann, R., *The Art of the Advocate* (1993, London: Penguin) 61.

[114] Evans, K., *The Golden Rules of Advocacy* (1993, London Blackstone) 97.

[115] Wellman, F. L., *The Art of Cross-examination* 4th edn. (1997, New York: Simon and Shuster), 39.   [116] Evans, n. 114 above, 97.

to the body followed by a quick blow to the chin'.[117] Thornburg notes: 'War provides a rich source domain for trial metaphors, providing words for process and participants and communicating the message that a hostile and competitive attitude is an important characteristic of the adversary system'.[118]

'Broughamesque' Defending

The contest model has also fostered a particular conception of the defence lawyer's role. It is a model that has been described as 'Broughamesque' in reference to Lord Brougham's often quoted admonition following Queen Caroline's Case. In response to criticisms of his threats to defend the Queen by revealing King George IV's adultery and secret marriage to a Catholic, Lord Brougham reportedly retorted that:

> an advocate, by the sacred duty which he owes his client, knows, in the discharge of that office, but one person in all the world, that client and none other. To save that client by all expedient means,—to protect that client at all hazards and costs to all others, and among others to himself,—is the highest and most unquestioned of his duties; and he must not regard the alarm, the torment, the destruction which he may bring upon any other.[119]

According to this conception of adversarial advocacy, it is the defence lawyer's duty to advance his or her client's interests as vigorously as the law allows regardless of the effect on third parties. The implications of a Broughameque vision of defending for opposing witnesses are considered by Luban.[120] Using a rape case as an example, Luban describes how a defence lawyer is compelled to grill the complainant about the details of her behaviour and 'to characterize every detail vividly from the most salacious point of view attainable and present it with maximum innuendo', as well as playing 'to the juror's deeply rooted cultural fantasies about feminine sexual voracity and vengefulness.' All the while, without seeming like a bully, the advocate must, Luban asserts, 'humiliate and browbeat the prosecutrix, knowing that if she blows up she will seem less sympathetic, while if she pulls inside herself emotionally she loses credibility as a victim'.[121]

Pannick suggests that such a conception of the role of the advocate would not now be widely shared as an advocate has important responsibilities to the court as well as to his or her client.[122] However, interviews with practising barristers

---

[117] Sherr, A., *Legal Practice Handbook: Advocacy* (1993, London: Blackstone) 99.

[118] 'Parties arm themselves, draw battle lines, offer or refuse quarter, plan pre-emptive strikes, joust, cross swords, undertake frontal assaults, win by attrition, seek total annihilation of their enemies, marshal forces, attack and sandbag their opponents. They deliver blows, attack flanks, kill, fire opening salvos, skirmish and cry craven': Thornburg, E., 'Metaphors Matter: How Images of Battle, Sports and Sex Shape the Adversary System' (1995) 10 *Wisconsin Women's Law Journal* 13.

[119] Trial of Queen Caroline 8 (1821) *per* Lord Brougham, cited in Cairns, D., *Advocacy and the Making of the Adversarial Criminal Trial 1800–1865* (1998, Oxford: Oxford University Press) 139.

[120] Luban, D., 'Partisanship, Betrayal and Autonomy in the Lawyer-Client Relationship: A Reply to Stephen Ellman' (1990) 90 *Columbia Law Review* 1004.   [121] Ibid. 1029.

[122] Pannick, D., *Advocates* (1992, Oxford: Oxford University Press) 105.

indicate that many continue to subscribe to a single-minded view of a defence lawyer's duty and to favour Brougham style advocacy. Lawyers interviewed by Rock, for example, explained that professional effectiveness demanded indifference on the part of counsel to the welfare of opposing witnesses: '. . . to become overly nice about a witness's feelings, would impair performance and betray a client'.[123] It was taken for granted by counsel that cross-examination would be an uncomfortable, if not painful, experience for many witnesses, leading Rock to conclude that those 'who dwelt too much on the pain of the lay witness would not last long as effective advocates'.[124] As one lawyer interviewed admitted: 'It's a dreadful business. We do have to be brutal.'[125] Similarly, in interviews conducted by Brown *et al.* with Scottish legal practitioners, advocates unapologetically eschewed any responsibility for the witnesses they examined. One lawyer remarked: 'You try and get away with anything which you think that the jury will use in assessing the credibility of the complainer or the credibility of your client.'[126] Defence lawyers freely admitted, that they would do whatever they could to suggest that a complainant in a rape trial was of 'easy virtue' precisely because they believed that juries were swayed by such trial tactics.[127] Temkin recently interviewed barristers highly experienced in rape trials and reports that those interviewed were clear that their approach was robust to the point of ruthlessness.[128] One barrister explained that when she was defending it was 'no holds barred' while another bluntly stated 'If you are asking do I take account of the sensitivity of the complainant, the blunt answer is no because it's not my brief.'[129] According to Temkin, the barristers who participated in the study appeared blissfully unconstrained by notions of ethics, save the duty which they owed to their client.

In a real sense the adversary system has been allowed to become its own excuse. The degradation of prosecution witnesses is more or less presented by advocates as an unfortunate but unavoidable consequence of fulfilling the 'ethical' responsibilities of a defence lawyer within an adversarial system. In other words, the claim is that if 'advocates restrain their zeal because of moral compunctions, they are not fulfilling their assigned role in adversary proceeding'.[130] It is further maintained by leading exponents, including Freedman, that zealous advocacy bounded only by law is necessary to advance the autonomy and dignity of the criminal defendant.[131] This extends, Freedman maintains, to cross-examination designed to make an apparently truthful witness appear to be

---

[123] Rock n. 37 above, 174.   [124] Ibid. 174.

[125] Ibid. 174. The need to impress a solicitor or her clerk by putting up a stubborn fight on behalf of a client is of course a further motivating factor.

[126] Brown, B., Burman, M. and Jamieson, L., *Sex Crimes on Trial: The Use of Sexual Evidence in Scottish Courts* (1993, Edinburgh University Press) 108.   [127] Ibid. 206.

[128] Temkin, n. 36 above, 230.   [129] Ibid. 230.

[130] Luban, D, 'The Adversary System Excuse' in (ed.) Luban, D., *The Good Lawyer* (1983, Totowa, New Jersey: Rowman and Allanheld) 83, 90.

[131] Freedman, M., *Lawyers' Ethics in an Adversary System* (1975, Indianapolis: Bobbs Merrill) 43.

mistaken or lying. The ideology of advocacy as espoused by Freedman and others has of course been challenged sporadically over the years.[132] It nevertheless clearly continues to exert an all-important influence over advocates cross-examining in criminal trials and to shape the experience of those who find themselves momentarily in their control.[133]

2. The Inadequacy of Existing Constraints

The treatment of vulnerable witnesses during cross-examination can also be explained in terms of the inadequacy of existing restrictions imposed on improper questioning in criminal proceedings. Typically, ambivalent enforcement is blamed and little consideration is given to the actual utility of the restrictions themselves. However, this overlooks the structural and attitudinal barriers to the effective regulation of questioning which operate within an adversarial process. Once these are identified the inherent inadequacy of existing constraints becomes readily apparent.

The Role of the Trial Judge

Trial judges are under a common law duty to restrain unnecessary, protracted cross-examination.[134] This duty extends to preventing questioning of an unduly offensive, vexatious, or oppressive character.[135] In terms of cross-examination as to credit, the principles which govern a trial judge's discretion to disallow questions are set out in *Hobbs v Tinling*.[136] Sankey LJ held that a trial judge should exercise this discretion to prevent improper cross-examination if questioning relates to matters so remote as to have a negligible impact on the credibility of the witness.[137] If a question is relevant only to a witness's credit then the finality rule applies: answers to questions dealing with collateral matters must be treated as final.[138]

It is commonly assumed that, if properly exercised, the duty of the trial judge to protect witnesses from improper cross-examination constitutes an adequate safeguard. This assumption is evident in Lord Hailsham's assertion that there would be fewer calls for the reform of rape trials if trial judges exercised greater control, or 'a tighter rein', over defending counsel.[139] It is also manifest in the

---

[132] Blake and Ashworth recently called for a reappraisal of the ethical boundaries of vigorous advocacy that takes due account of the needs and rights of witnesses: Blake, M. and Ashworth, A., 'Some Ethical Issues in Prosecuting and Defending Criminal Cases' [1998] *Criminal Law Review* 16.

[133] Unbridled partisanship is, moreover, presented as the best defence against oppression or overreaching by the state. According to this view the defence advocate is a 'wild card injected into the proceedings by the State and intended by the State to function as its own nemesis': Luban, D., *Lawyers and Justice: An Ethical Study* (1988, Princeton, New Jersey: Princeton University Press) 62.

[134] See *Mechanical and General Inventions Co Ltd* and *Lehwess v Austin and Austin Motor Co Ltd* [1935] AC 346; *R v Kalia* [1975] Crim LR 181.

[135] See *Wong Kam-ming v R* [1980] AC 247, 260.   [136] [1929] 2 KB 1, 51.

[137] *R v Sweet-Escott* (1971) 55 Cr App R 56.

[138] *Harris v Tippett* (1811) 2 Camp 637; *AG v Hitchcock* (1847) 1 Exch 9.1; *Somers* [1999] Crim LR 744.   [139] Lord Hailsham, HL Deb. vol. 375 col. 1773, 22 October (1976).

recommendation of the Royal Commission on Criminal Justice that trial judges adopt a firmer stance in protecting witnesses from the excesses of counsel. The Runciman Commission recommended that trial judges should act firmly to control bullying and intimidatory tactics on the part of counsel[140] and should be particularly vigilant to check unfair and intimidatory cross-examination of witnesses who are likely to be distressed or vulnerable. However, this assumption is flawed because it fails, as explained below to give due recognition to the conflict that exists between the role of the criminal trial judge within an adversarial process and the trial judge's duty to restrain unnecessary and improper cross-examination.[141]

Limits on Judicial Intervention in Criminal Trials

Within the adversarial process the trial judge is assigned the role of umpire.[142] The principle of party autonomy dictates that the parties develop and present their respective cases to the jury, and the trial judge is expected to afford advocates considerable latitude in their presentational roles. The adversarial tradition of equating neutrality and passivity has further inspired an umpireal ideal that sees the trial judge as detached and somewhat aloof from the party contest. The classic statement encompassing this ideal was made by Lord Denning in *Jones v National Coal Board*:[143]

> The judge's part in all this is to hearken to the evidence, only himself asking questions of witnesses when it is necessary to clear up any point that has been overlooked or left obscure; to see that the advocates behave themselves seemly and to keep to the rules laid down by law; to exclude irrelevancies and discourage repetition, to make sure by wise intervention that he follows the points that the advocates are making and can assess their worth; and at the end to make up his mind where the truth lies. If he goes beyond this, he drops the mantle of the judge and assumes the robe of an advocate; and the change does not become him well.[144]

The truly passive judge umpire is, it is true to say, a 'creature of theory rather than practice'.[145] The English trial judge has an overriding duty to ensure the fairness of criminal proceedings. To this end he or she may call witnesses whom both parties neglect to call and engage in the examination and cross-examination of witnesses if the trial judge deems this necessary in the interests of justice.[146] However, if a trial judge is found to have impeded counsel unduly in the presentation of his or her version of events through intervention

---

[140] Home Office, *Royal Commission on Criminal Justice Report* (1993, London: HMSO) para. 182.   [141] Ellison, L., 'Cross-examination in Rape Trials' [1998] *Criminal Law Review* 605.

[142] See Damaska, M., 'Evidentiary Barriers to Conviction and Two Models of Criminal Procedure: A Comparative Study' (1973) 121 *University of Pennsylvania Law Review* 551, 563.

[143] [1957] 2 QB 55, 63. This was a civil case but is generally accepted to apply to criminal proceedings.

[144] 'In our system the Judge presides somewhat like a referee on the football field, blowing his whistle from time to time for an infringement but not actually kicking the ball himself save in very limited or exceptional circumstances:' Du Cann, n. 113 above, 3.

[145] McEwan, J., *Evidence and the Adversarial Process* (1998, Oxford: Hart) 13.

[146] *R v Cain* (1936) 25 Cr App R 204.

a conviction may be overturned.[147] As the Court of Appeal stated in the case of *Gunning*:[148] 'when a judge's interventions were on such a scale as to deprive the accused of the chance, to which he was entitled under the adversarial system, of developing his evidence under the lead and guidance of defending counsel, the trial must be regarded as a mistrial even in the absence of an allegation that the judge's questioning was hostile to the accused'.

At the same time, concerns that judicial intervention may unduly influence jurors, given the dominant position of the trial judge *vis-à-vis* the jury, mean that trial judges must be ever alive to the danger of being seen to advance the case of one side over the other.[149] In exercising his or her legitimate powers to curb inappropriate questioning the trial judge runs the risk of being deemed to have evinced actual or perceived bias. According to Pinard, for example, a trial judge's intervention on behalf of the prosecution may inflate the worth of the prosecution's case. There is a very real probability, he opines, that the jury would interpret the judge's intervention as vouching for the prosecution's evidence and thus cloud the jury's vision of the strength, or lack thereof, of the prosecution's evidence.[150] A similar view was expressed by the Court of Appeal in *Sharp*:[151]

[T]he judge may be in danger of seeming to enter the arena in the sense that he may appear partial to one side or the other. This may arise from the hostile tone of questioning or implied criticism of counsel who is conducting the examination or cross-examination, or if the judge is impressed by a witness, perhaps suggesting excuses or explanations for a witness's conduct which is open to attack by counsel for the opposite party.[152]

Furthermore, the adversarial process ill equips judges for effective intervention during cross-examination. Deliberately insulated from pre-trial processes and lacking detailed knowledge of counsel's instructions, the trial judge is not in a

---

[147] It is the quality and not the quantity of interventions that is significant. In *Matthews*, where the trial judge put 524 questions to counsel's 538, the Court of Appeal stated: 'On any basis the number of interventions and questions asked by this judge were extremely great, and seemed to be more than ought to have been necessary for him to fulfil his functions in supervising the conduct of the trial. However, it appeared that he did not commit the cardinal offence of diverting counsel from the line of the topic of his questions into other channels. In spite of the exceptional number of interventions there was no ground for thinking that the convictions were unsafe': *R v Matthews* (1983) 78 Cr App Rep 23.

[148] [1980] Crim LR 592. See also *R v Perks* [1973] Crim LR 388; *R v Hirock and Others* [1970] 1 QB 67; *R v Hamilton* [1969] Crim LR 486; *R v Whybrow The Times*, 14 February 1994.

[149] 'It is always open to the judge to probe, but the tradition is strong that he is an arbiter and not an inquisitor and that the coming to the aid of a party in distress might impair his impartiality': Devlin, P., *The Judge* (1979, Oxford: Oxford University Press) 62.

[150] Pinard, M., 'Limitations on judicial activism in criminal trials' (2000) 33 *Connecticut Law Review* 243, 285. See also Saltzburg, S., 'The unnecessarily expanding role of the American trial judge' (1978) 64 *Virginia Law Review* 1.   [151] (1994) 98 Cr App R. 144.

[152] A judge interviewed by Jackson and Doran is quoted as stating: 'You have to be very careful because I just don't know what your duties are exactly. If you have a Crown witness who's confused and making a mess of the Crown case because they're upset, emotional, whatever it may be, should you straighten them out or should you let the defence have the benefit of this? If you straighten it out, you're undoubtedly aiding the Crown case, you're taking sides, you're giving the Crown an advantage, and you're being seen to take sides': Jackson, J. and Doran, S., *Judge Without Jury: Diplock Trials in the Adversary System* (1995, Oxford: Clarendon Press) 71.

strong position to ascertain when intervention may be appropriate. The trial judge views the case, in Frankel's words, from the peak of Olympian ignorance. As a consequence, his intrusions will in too many cases result from partial or skewed insights: 'He may expose the secrets one side chooses to keep while never becoming aware of the other's. He runs a good chance of pursuing inspirations that better informed counsel have considered, explored, and abandoned after fuller study. He risks at a minimum the supplying of more confusion than guidance by his sporadic intrusions.'[153]

Overall, the English trial judge must exercise his or her discretion within tight structural constraints which militate against the adequate protection of vulnerable witnesses from irrelevant and inappropriate questioning. The combination of umpireal judge and party-controlled evidence presentation puts effective limits on the extent to which witnesses can be shielded from improper cross-examination. At the same time it must not be overlooked that many judges, having risen from the lawyer ranks, may be sympathetically disposed towards a conception of defence advocacy which rails against the pulling of punches.[154] Some trial judges clearly believe that few fetters may be legitimately imposed on cross-examination if the fair trial rights of defendants are to be respected. Heenan and McKelvie report that a number of judges interviewed perceived a conflict between offering vulnerable witnesses even minimal protection and their duty in ensuring the accused a fair trial.[155]

Code of Conduct of the Bar of England and Wales

The Code of Conduct of the Bar of England and Wales lays down guidelines for the conduct of cross-examination. According to the Code, a practising barrister must not 'make statements or ask questions which are merely scandalous or intended or calculated only to vilify, insult or annoy either a witness or some other person'.[156] It further states that a barrister 'must not suggest that a witness or other person is guilty of fraud or misconduct or attribute to another person the crime or conduct of which his lay client is accused unless such allegations go to a matter in issue (including the credibility of the witness) which is material

---

[153] Frankel, M., 'The Search for Truth: An Umpireal View' (1975) 123 *University of Pennsylvania Law Review* 1024. As Frankel notes: '[t]he ignorance and unpreparedness of the judge are intended axioms of the system'.

[154] According to Lord Justice Sedley, too many judges still subscribe to a gladiatorial view of cross-examination, inherited from their time at the Bar, according to which 'you let the parties take off their gloves and see who is left dead on the floor at the end of the trial': 'Judge attacks trial by combat in rape cases' *The Times*, 17 May 1999.

[155] As one judge remarked: 'I can sit there silent and not intervene even though I know the poor old witness is having a rotten time . . . A fair cross-examination can be very difficult indeed, and I can't do anything in those circumstances other than give them a break and not to be in too much of a hurry and to try and be sympathetic etc . . . and the universal courtroom panacea, "would you like a glass of water?" ': Heenan *et al.*, n. 22 above, 223.

[156] General Council of the Bar of England and Wales, *Code of Conduct of the Bar of England and Wales*, (1991, London: Bar Council), pt. 5, para. 610(e) cited in Archbold, *Pleadings, Evidence and Practice in Criminal Cases* (1997, London: Sweet and Maxwell) Appendix B -21.

to his lay client's case and which appear to him to be supported by reasonable grounds'.[157] The responsibilities of an advocate as an officer of the court are also emphasized within the Code which states that a 'practising barrister has an overriding duty to the court to ensure in the public interest that the proper and efficient administration of justice is achieved'. At the same time the Code provides that it is a defence lawyer's duty 'to promote and protect fearlessly and by all proper and lawful means his lay client's best interests'.[158]

As stated previously in this Chapter, many barristers perceive a conflict between their duty to a client and a responsibility towards opposing witnesses. In terms of the Code of Conduct, provisions counselling restraint in the cross-examination of opposing witnesses are perceived to conflict with the duty to provide a fearless defence. As a result the former are, as Blake and Ashworth describe, 'neutralised' and 'circumvented'.[159] This was evident in rape trials monitored by Lees where the Code was routinely breached by defence counsel. Moreover, on these occasions there was no intervention by either prosecution counsel or the trial judge.[160] Research into the experiences of other categories of witness indicates that the Code is equally ineffective in other trial contexts.[161]

C. Conclusion

This chapter has sought to provide an overview of the significant problems facing vulnerable witnesses during cross-examination and has suggested explanations for their treatment that identify systemic factors as key determinants.

Clear dangers attach to a failure to protect witnesses from harassment and inappropriate cross-examination in court. First, there is the real risk that improper questioning may distort the fact-finding process by distracting juries from the central issues in a case. Research indicates that unnecessarily lengthy investigation of a witness's character during cross-examination can, for example, interfere significantly with consideration of a defendant's guilt. A number of studies suggest that jurors are unduly swayed by character evidence.[162] Kalvin and Zeisel's often cited study of jury decision-making in rape trials, for example, revealed that jurors were greatly influenced by the character of complainants and were less inclined to convict once a complainant's sexual history was introduced.[163] Improper questioning can further undermine the fact-finding

---

[157] Ibid. para. 610(h).   [158] Ibid. para. 203(a)

[159] Blake, M. and Ashworth, A., 'Some Ethical Issues in Prosecuting and Defending Criminal Cases' [1998] *Criminal Law Review* 16, 32.

[160] Lees, n. 11 above, 249. Victim Support similarly reports that the Code fails to protect victims of rape from what they perceive to be a savage cross-examination: n. 14 above, 56.

[161] See Rock, n. 37 above.

[162] Pattenden, R., 'The Character of Victims and Third Parties in Criminal Proceedings Other than Rape Trials' [1986] *Criminal Law Review* 367, 377.

[163] Kalven, H. and Zeisel, H., *The American Jury* (1966, Boston: Little Brown). See also La Free, G., Reskin, B. F. and Vischer, C. A., 'Jurors' Responses to Victims' Behaviour and Legal Issues in

function of the criminal trial by undermining the credibility of witnesses without good ground. The use of overly complex language, demands for total recall of peripheral factual information, and direct appeals to outmoded stereotypes are just some of the ways in which vulnerable witnesses are unjustly discredited and jurors misled. Furthermore, the reliance placed by cross-examiners on techniques for controlling questioning creates a serious potential for evidence distortion, particularly in the case of children and those with learning disabilities. Leading questions which form the mainstay of cross-examination have, for example, been shown to result in acquiescent responses which jeopardize the evidential integrity of witness testimony.

There is also the risk that improper questioning will result in others being deterred from coming forward and reporting offences for fear of the ordeal they will undergo in the witness box. For example, it is generally accepted that the treatment of complainants in court is a factor contributing to the low reporting rate for rape. As McEwan observes: '[t]here is little incentive for rape victims to come forward when the system which is supposed to protect the public from crime serves them up in court like laboratory specimens on a microscope slide'.[164] As a result, those guilty of heinous crimes escape prosecution.

The need to protect witnesses from unnecessary distress and humiliation when giving evidence is increasingly recognized by the courts.[165] As seen in Chapter IV above, the European Court of Human Rights has made it clear that witnesses have a right to privacy that is to be safeguarded. The right of sexual offence complainants to protection of their private life during criminal proceedings has been specifically emphasized by the European Commission of Human Rights.[166] It is therefore conceivable that cross-examination which intrudes unnecessarily into the private life of a witness and dredges up incidents of marginal relevance from his or her past may amount to a violation of Article 8 of the European Convention on Human Rights.[167] Unduly aggressive and prurient questioning may also raise issues under Article 3. Alternative obligations under the *United Nations Convention on the Rights of the Child*[168] and

Sexual Assault Trials' (1985) 32 *Social Problems*, cited in Ward, C. A., *Attitudes Towards Rape* (1995, London: Sage) 103; Field, H. S. and Bienen, L. B., *Jurors and Rape* (1980, Lexington, Mass.: Lexington Books).

[164] McEwan, J., 'Documentary Hearsay Evidence: Refuge for the Vulnerable Witness?' [1989] *Criminal Law Review* 642.

[165] See Ashworth, A., 'Victims' Rights, Defendants' Rights and Criminal Procedure' in (eds.) Crawford, A., Goodey, J., *Integrating a Victim Perspective within Criminal Justice* (2000, Hants: Ashgate) 187.   [166] See discussion in Chapter IV above.

[167] *Recommendation No. R (85) 11 on the Position of the Victim in the Framework of Criminal Law and Procedure* also states that '[a]t all stages of the procedure, the victim should be questioned in a manner which gives due consideration to his personal situation, his rights and his dignity'.

[168] Article 3(1) provides that '[i]n all actions concerning children, whether undertaken by public or private social welfare institutions, courts of law, administrative authorities or legislative bodies, the best interests of the child shall be a primary consideration'. Article 39 is also relevant: '[s]tates parties shall take all appropriate measures to promote physical and psychological recovery and social reintegration of a child victim of any form of neglect, exploitation, or abuse.'

the *United Nations Declaration on the Rights of Disabled Persons*[169] set standards for the treatment of children and learning disabled persons respectively. So far attempts to meet the rights and legitimate expectations of vulnerable witnesses in the context of cross-examination have been severely limited. The following Chapter examines latest efforts, as contained in the Youth Justice and Criminal Evidence Act 1999.

[169] Proclaimed by GA Res. 3447 (XXX) of 9 December 1975.

VI.

Cross-examination and the Youth Justice and Criminal Evidence Act 1999

Cross-examination has been rightly described as a *modus vivendi* rather than merely a *modus operandi* of trial advocates within the adversary system.[1] As a device for testing the reliability of testimony it occupies an apparently unassailable position within the criminal trial process of England and Wales. Working groups established to examine ways of improving the treatment of witnesses at trial have in their terms of reference been effectively precluded from considering possible alternatives to cross-examination as currently conceived.[2] The issue of the appropriateness or otherwise of cross-examination as a mechanism for testing the veracity of vulnerable witnesses was not discussed in recent debates prompted by the publication of the *Speaking up for Justice* report.[3] Against this backdrop, the set of reform proposals set out in the Youth Justice and Criminal Evidence Act 1999 are in line with expectations. The Act targets specific groups of witnesses for greater protection and assistance while retaining full commitment to the principle of party control, which accords responsibility for evidence presentation and testing to the parties, with the court playing an essentially passive role. In other words, there is no real deviation from the traditional adversarial model.

Measures contained in the 1999 Act include new restrictions on the admissibility of evidence of prior sexual history in sexual offence cases, and further limitations on the right of defendants to conduct cross-examination in person. Both measures have proved highly controversial, the former being subject to recent challenge in the House of Lords. The Act also introduces intermediaries into the criminal process whose role will be to 'explain' complex questions to child witnesses and those with mental or physical disorders or a significant impairment of intelligence and social functioning. Though not directed solely at cross-examination, it is at this stage of the trial process that eligible witnesses are likely to require greatest assistance from an intermediary. The Act's

---

[1] McGough, L., *Child Witnesses: Fragile Voices in the American Legal System* (1994, New Haven: Yale University Press) 223.

[2] For example the Advisory Group on Video Evidence was informed by the then Home Secretary that proposals that did not allow for traditional cross-examination would be unacceptable: Home Office, *Report of the Advisory Group on Video Evidence* (1989, London: Home Office) para 2.22.

[3] Home Office, *Action For Justice: Implementing the Speaking Up for Justice Report* (1999, London: Home Office).

provisions parallel and in some respects exceed developments in other common law jurisdictions. This Chapter critically examines each of these measures and in so doing seeks to demonstrate the limitations of official responses so far to the treatment of vulnerable and intimidated witnesses during cross-examination.

A. RESTRICTING THE USE OF SEXUAL HISTORY EVIDENCE

'The use of sexual history evidence in rape trials causes distress to complainants, can affect the outcome of the case and contributes to the low conviction rate for this offence. It also acts as a deterrent to reporting incidents of what is, in any case, already an under reported crime.'[4] The Sexual Offences Amendment Act 1976 was introduced to restrict the admissibility of evidence of previous sexual experience. Section 2 provided that a complainant could only be questioned on her prior sexual history with men other than the defendant with the leave of the judge. Leave was to be granted only where the judge was satisfied that it would be unfair to the defendant to refuse to allow the evidence to be adduced or the question to be asked. Subsequent research has shown the legislation to be an ineffective shield against the illegitimate use of what is often highly prejudicial previous sexual experience evidence.[5] The interpretation of the provision by the courts has been such that sexual experience has been routinely deemed relevant to the issue of consent and therefore admissible.[6] The Home Office working group accepted in its report that section 2 was not achieving its purpose and that the use of sexual history evidence extended far beyond that demanded in the interests of relevance to the issues in the trial.

As feminist critics have identified, the key problem centres on the fact that a decision on relevance, 'whether formed by experience, common sense or logic is a decision particularly vulnerable to the application of private beliefs and, thus, stereotype and myth'.[7] Sexual offence prosecutions are surrounded by pervasive myths, prejudices, and cultural stereotypes most of which work against

---

[4] Easton, S., 'The use of sexual history in rape trials' in (eds.) Childs, M. and Ellison, L., *Feminist Perspectives on Evidence* (2000, London: Cavendish) 167.

[5] See Adler, Z., *Rape on Trial* (1987, London: Routledge and Kegan Paul); Adler, Z., 'The Relevance of Sexual History Evidence in Rape: Problems of Subjective Interpretation' (1985) *Criminal Law Review* 769; Lees, S., *Carnal Knowledge: Rape on Trial* (1996, London: Hamish Hamilton); Temkin, J., 'Sexual History Evidence: The Ravishment of Section 2' [1993] *Criminal Law Review* 3.

[6] See for example *R v Viola* [1982] 1 WLR 1138; *R v Brown* (1989) 89 Cr App R 97; *R v SMS* [1992] Crim LR 310.

[7] L'Heureux-Dube in her dissenting judgement in the Canadian case of *Seaboyer* [1991] 2 SCR 577. In this case the Supreme Court of Canada held that Canada's rape shield legislation was contrary to ss. 7 and 11(d) of the Canadian Charter of Rights and Freedoms as it breached defendant's right to a fair trial. As a result of the Supreme Court's ruling, the provisions restricting the admissibility of sexual history evidence were substantially amended in 1992: see McColgan, A., *Women under the Law* (2000, Essex: Longman) 221.

complainants. Decisions regarding the admissibility of sexual history evidence have owed much to all three.[8] As McColgan remarks:

If the judiciary were free of this cultural conditioning, the question of relevance could be left to the discretion of the judge without statutory regulation. The judge would be able, where there was a danger of jurors being improperly influenced by information regarding a complainant's sexual history, to exclude this evidence as insufficiently relevant to the issue of the defendant's guilt. Experience of the judicial approach to section 2 of the 1976 Act and, elsewhere, to other attempts by legislatures to restrict the admission of sexual history evidence by means of discretionary legislation, suggest that this approach is wholly inadequate.[9]

Given this background, calls for reform have unsurprisingly focused on constraining judicial discretion through tighter statutory regulation. Recommendations range from a prohibition on the use of sexual history evidence subject to specific limited exceptions[10] to prohibitions with more open-ended exceptions and a residual discretion to include evidence if necessary in the interests of justice.[11] In its report, *Speaking up for Justice*, the Home Office working group ruled out the possibility of removing a trial judge's discretion to admit evidence on previous sexual history altogether on the ground that there may be instances, albeit infrequent, in which such evidence would be relevant to the case.[12] The working group instead concluded that the law should be amended 'to provide a more structured approach to decision taking and to set out more clearly when evidence of previous sexual history can be admitted'.[13] The new rule of exclusion is now contained in section 41 of the Youth Justice and Criminal Evidence Act 1999.

1. Section 41

In sexual offence cases, section 41 of the YJCEA provides that the leave of the court is required before adducing evidence about or cross-examining on any sexual behaviour of a complainant. 'Sexual offence' is defined in section 62 to include rape, burglary with intent to rape, indecent assault, unlawful intercourse, forcible abduction, and other offences. 'Sexual behaviour' means 'any sexual behaviour or other sexual experience' and significantly includes sexual

---

[8] Chief among these is the misguided belief that a woman who has consented in the past to sex with other men is more likely to have consented on the occasion in dispute.

[9] McColgan, A., 'Common Law and the Relevance of Sexual History Evidence' (1996) 16 *Oxford Journal of Legal Studies* 275, 307.

[10] As in Michigan and New South Wales. See Kibble, N., 'The sexual history provisions: Charting a course between inflexible legislative rules and wholly untrammelled judicial discretion?' [2000] *Criminal Law Review* 274.   [11] As in the Federal approach: ibid. 280.

[12] Home Office, *Speaking Up For Justice: Report of the Interdepartmental Working Group on the Treatment of Vulnerable or Intimidated Witnesses in the Criminal Justice System* (1998, London: Home Office) para. 9.67.

[13] Ibid. para. 9.70. The Group favoured the Scottish approach contained in the Criminal Procedure (Scotland) Act 1995, ss. 274–5.

experience with the defendant.[14] Leave may be applied for by or on behalf of the accused. The reasons for granting or refusing leave and the extent of any leave given must be stated in open court but in the absence of the jury.[15] Before granting leave the court must be satisfied of the existence of the circumstances set out in subsections 41(3) or (5) *and* that refusal of leave might render a conclusion unsafe on a relevant issue. Subsection (3) specifies three grounds on which evidence or questioning may be allowed. First, the evidence or question must relate to a relevant issue in the case other than whether the complainant consented.[16] Under section 41(3)(b) leave may be given if the issue is consent and the sexual behaviour of the complainant to which the evidence or question relates is alleged to have taken place at or about the same time of the alleged offence.[17] Under section 41(3)(c) leave may be given if the issue is consent and the sexual behaviour of the complainant to which the evidence or question relates is so similar to the sexual behaviour of the complainant at or about the same time of the alleged offence that the similarity cannot reasonably be explained as a coincidence. As a further restriction, section 41(4) provides that no evidence or question shall be regarded as relating to a relevant issue in the case if it appears to the court that the main purpose is to impugn the credibility of the complainant as a witness. For the purposes of subsection (3), the evidence or question must also relate to specific instances of alleged sexual behaviour. Accordingly, no evidence of sexual reputation may be admitted under the exceptions.[18]

Section 42(1)(b) states that the term 'issue of consent' does not include any issue as to the belief of the accused that the complainant consented. Sections 41(3)(b) and (c) therefore do not apply when the *Morgan* defence of honest belief in consent is raised. Such evidence will not be regarded as relating to a relevant issue if the court considers that its main purpose is to impugn the credibility of the complainant, and must relate to specific instances of sexual behaviour. Section 41(5) applies if the evidence or question relates to evidence adduced by the prosecution about any sexual behaviour of the complainant and, in the opinion of the court, does not go beyond what is necessary to enable that evidence to be rebutted or explained by the accused. Again, the evidence or question must relate to specific instances of alleged sexual behaviour.[19] Evidence admitted under this exception is not subject to the exclusion in section 41(4) and thus may be called specifically to impugn the complainant's credibility. As stated above, before allowing any evidence of sexual behaviour to be introduced, the court must be satisfied that the jury or magistrate might make an unsafe decision if the evidence were not heard.

---

[14] S. 42(1)(c).   [15] S. 42(3).   [16] S. 41(3)(a).

[17] This section was originally drafted to include behaviour taking place within 24 hours. According to the Act's explanatory notes, it is expected that 'at or about the same time' will generally be interpreted no more widely than 24 hours before or after the offence.

[18] S. 41(6).   [19] S. 41(6).

The new provisions of the 1999 Act have proved highly controversial. Just one week after their introduction a key aspect of the legislation was challenged on the ground that it infringed the right of an accused to challenge the evidence against him. It was argued on behalf of a defendant that the provision thwarted his right to a fair trial as it prevented him adducing evidence that the complainant had had consensual sexual intercourse with him on occasions in the three weeks before the alleged rape. The defendant appealed specifically against a preliminary ruling that the defence was precluded by section 41 from adducing evidence of any previous sexual behaviour which had occurred between the complainant and the accused, unless the sexual behaviour had occurred at or about the same time as the alleged rape or was so similar that it might be said to be part of a pattern of sexual behaviour. The defence to be raised was, as in most rape cases, that of consent.[20] The trial judge took the view that the exclusionary part of his ruling *prima facie* offended the defendant's right to a fair trial under Article 6 of the European Convention of Human Rights and accordingly gave leave to appeal 'with enthusiasm'.

On appeal, counsel for the appellant argued that the trial judge had been wrong to exclude evidence about the defendant's relationship with the complainant on the ground that sexual intercourse when not remote in time, is and should be regarded as relevant to the issue of consent.[21] It would be wrong, counsel argued, for the jury to evaluate the evidence of what would appear to them to be a first sexual encounter, without knowing the background and history of the sexual relationship. The Court was referred to an article by Galvin in which it was stated that the probative value of such evidence rested on the nature of the complainant's specific mindset towards the accused, permitting an inference that the state of mind continued to the occasion in question.[22] The Crown countered that consent on a previous occasion, even in relation to the defendant, is not probative or relevant as to the issue of consent because consent to sexual behaviour is exercised independently on each occasion that it occurs.

Allowing the appeal, the appeal judges stated that they had no difficulty accepting that the previous sexual activity of the complainant had no relevance to credit and that sexual activity with persons other than the defendant generally had no relevance as to whether the complainant consented to sexual intercourse. However, they rejected the Crown's argument that recent sexual activity between the complainant and the defendant was irrelevant to consent. It was, the appeal judges opined, common sense that a person, whether male or female, who had previously had sexual intercourse with the defendant, particularly in

---

[20] The trial judge was not invited to consider whether evidence in relation to the complainant's prior sexual activity with the defendant was admissible under the 1999 Act in relation to the defence of belief in consent.

[21] *R v Y* (Sexual Offence: Complainant's Sexual History) *The Times*, 13 February 2001.

[22] Galvin, H., 'Shielding Rape Victims in the State and Federal Courts' (1986) 70 *Minnesota Law Review* 763, 807.

recent weeks or months, might on the occasion in dispute have been more likely to consent to sexual intercourse with the defendant than with a stranger or someone with whom no sexual familiarity had occurred. This approach stemmed, the appeal judges maintained, not from a sexist view of women, but from a reflection on human nature, regardless of sex. The trial process would, it was stated, be unduly distorted if the jury were precluded from knowing that the complainant and the defendant had recently taken part in sexual activity with each other, ruling out the possibility, on occasion, of a fair trial. The Court of Appeal granted leave to appeal to the House of Lords. The question of law to be established was whether a prior sexual relationship between defendant and complainant is relevant to the issue of consent so as to render the exclusion under section 41 of the Youth Justice and Criminal Evidence Act 1999 a contravention of the defendant's right to a fair trial.

In May 2001 the Law Lords dismissed an appeal by the Crown against the Court of Appeal ruling.[23] The blanket exclusion of prior sexual history between the complainant and the accused (subject to narrow categories of exemption) was held to be capable of preventing an accused person from putting forward relevant evidence which was critical to his defence. Although it was accepted that an isolated episode distant in time and circumstances would be irrelevant to the issue of consent, the fact that the complainant and the accused were at the time of the alleged rape lovers would, it was held, be relevant in circumstances wider than those catered for by the Act's provisions. In the words of Lord Steyn, to exclude such material would create the risk of disembodying the case before the jury and increase the danger of miscarriages of justice. The relevance of such evidence apparently rests in Lord Steyn's presumption that the activities in which one has engaged in the past influence the choice one makes on future occasions.

However, the House of Lords did not, as widely anticipated, declare the 1999 Act to be incompatible with the Human Rights Act 1998. The 'excessive breadth' of section 41 could, it was decided, be attenuated in accordance with the will of Parliament as reflected in section 3 of the 1998 Act by reading section 41(3)(c) as subject to an implied provision that evidence or questioning which is required to ensure a fair trial under Article 6 of the Convention should not be treated as inadmissible. Section 41(3)(c) of the 1999 Act was thus to be construed as admitting evidence relevant to the issue of consent where to exclude it would endanger the fairness of the trial under Article 6 of the Convention. The discretion which had been taken away from trial judges on this point was thus restored.

Given the way trial judges have exercised their discretion in the past, in the wake of *R v A* complainants can expect very little protection from questioning

---

about prior sexual experience with an accused when the defence of consent is raised. When the *Morgan* defence of mistaken but honest belief in consent is run, the more stringent conditions in 41(3)(b) and (c) do not apply. Sexual history evidence may be adduced unless the court is satisfied that the main purpose of this is to impugn the credibility of the complainant and that a refusal of leave might have the result of rendering the defendant's conviction unsafe. Once again complainants can look forward to very limited protection.[24]

Concerns have also been raised regarding the application of the provisions to sexual experience with men other than the accused. For example, it has been suggested that section 41(5) of the Act, allowing evidence by way of rebuttal or explanation, will open the gates to some very unpleasant and irrelevant questioning.[25] Neutral prosecution assertions, it is feared, will be construed as relating to a complainant's sexual behaviour, leading to the introduction of prejudicial sexual experience evidence. It is interesting to note that in Scotland the similarly worded 'explain or rebut' exception of the Criminal Procedure (Scotland) Act 1995 has been criticized for being so widely expressed and open to interpretation as to render the basic prohibition almost ineffective. A report published by the Scottish Executive, *Redressing the Balance*, provides the example of a case in which the Crown led evidence to the effect that the complainant was a lesbian.[26] The defence used this to bring in evidence to suggest that the complainant had a promiscuous and chaotic sexual lifestyle, and to play on any prejudices the judge or jury might have had about lesbians. At least it would appear from the wording of the 1999 Act that the prosecution must adduce some evidence before the defence can take advantage of the provision. This should prevent the defence from relying on implied assertions to introduce sexual experience evidence, as has happened spuriously in the past. As Adler found, sexual history evidence was often admitted under section 2 of the 1976 Act to rebut an implied assertion that a young complainant was a virgin, or to counter the possible inference that a complainant was unlikely to consent to sexual intercourse with a man of a different racial background.[27]

The absence of any requirement on judges to consider whether the probative value of evidence is outweighed by its prejudicial effect has also rightly attracted criticism.[28] Sexual history evidence which is logically relevant may cloud issues and prejudice a jury, in much the same way as details of an accused's previous convictions, which are generally excluded. The question should therefore be,

---

[24] The problem here rests with the substantive criminal law. Until the *Morgan* decision is abandoned complainants will, as McColgan notes, be subject to intrusive interrogation in order to lend an 'air of reality' to defence claims otherwise unsupportable in the circumstances of the case. McColgan, n. 9 above, 292. See generally Home Office, *Setting the boundaries: Reforming the law on sex offences* (2000, London: Home Office).

[25] McEwan, J., 'In defence of vulnerable witnesses: The Youth Justice and Criminal Evidence Act 1999' (2000) 4 *International Journal of Evidence and Proof* 29.

[26] Scottish Executive, *Redressing the Balance* (2000, Edinburgh: Scottish Executive).

[27] Adler, Z., 'Rape: The Intention of Parliament and the Practice of the Courts' (1982) *Modern Law Review* 664, 670. [28] Easton, n. 4 above, 186.

not whether the evidence is relevant, but whether it is sufficiently relevant to counter any potential prejudice flowing from its admission. The Canadian Criminal Code requires the court to assess the probative value of evidence against its possibly prejudicial or misleading effect. Section 276(2) basically prohibits the introduction of evidence of any sexual activity engaged in by the complainant, other than that forming the subject matter of the charge, unless the court is satisfied that the evidence: is of specific instances of sexual activity, is relevant to an issue in the trial, and has significant probative value which is not outweighed by the danger of prejudice to the proper administration of justice. In determining admissibility, the judge must take into account a range of factors, including the potential prejudice to the complainant's personal dignity and right of privacy.[29] There is much to recommend this approach. The Scottish Executive is currently considering proposals modelled closely on the Canadian model.[30]

Overall, the provisions do promise to afford complainants greater protection from illegitimate defence attempts to malign their character by focusing upon their prior sexual experience, at least with third parties. Nevertheless, it is difficult to disagree with Birch's assertion that the value of the sexual history provisions would have been enhanced if they had been the subject of a more comprehensive consultation exercise.[31]

B. Protection from Cross-examination by the Accused in Person

The second measure in the Youth Justice and Criminal Evidence Act 1999 affecting cross-examination deals with the identity of the cross-examiner. Defendants in criminal proceedings are generally entitled to represent themselves and to cross-examine prosecution witnesses in person. As an exception to this rule, section 34A of the Criminal Justice Act 1988 has prohibited unrepresented defendants from personally cross-examining child witnesses in cases of sex and violence.[32] The YJCEA extends and replaces this section[33] and introduces a welcome if belated mandatory prohibition on defendants charged with rape or other sexual offences from cross-examining complainants in person. Sections 36 and 37 of the Act give the court an additional discretionary power to prohibit an accused from cross-examining other witnesses in person if the court is satisfied that the quality of their evidence

---

[29] Other factors to be considered include the interests of justice, including the right of the accused to make a full answer and defence, and the need to remove from the fact-finding process any discriminatory belief or bias.   [30] Scottish Executive, n. 26 above.

[31] Birch, D., 'A Better Deal for Vulnerable Witnesses?' [2000] *Criminal Law Review* 223, 249.

[32] As amended by the Criminal Justice Act 1991.

[33] S. 35. Protection is extended to those involved in cases of kidnapping, false imprisonment, and abduction.

would be diminished by such a cross-examination and that it would not be contrary to the interests of justice to give a direction. In determining whether to give a direction the court must have regard, in particular, to any views expressed by the witness, the conduct of the accused, and any relationship between the accused and the witness.[34] Alleged victims of stalking, domestic violence,[35] and other intimidated witnesses are seen as obvious candidates for this special measure.[36] Any such direction will be binding unless and until the court considers that the direction should be discharged in the interests of justice. The court may discharge the order of its own motion or on the application of a party to the proceedings which can be made if there has been a material change in the circumstances since the order was made or last considered. The court must state in open court its reasons for making, refusing or discharging directions.

Where a prohibition on personal cross-examination applies, the accused will have an opportunity to arrange legal representation.[37] If none is arranged the court must appoint a qualified legal representative if it decides is necessary in the interests of justice to have the witness cross-examined.[38] Court-appointed legal representatives are to be paid from central funds.[39] Section 39 requires a trial judge to give any necessary warning to the jury to ensure that the defendant is not prejudiced by the drawing of inferences from the fact that he has been prevented from cross-examining the witness in person.

Of the restrictions introduced, the mandatory ban in sexual offence cases has proved the most controversial. Section 34 was inspired by a number of high-profile cases which highlighted the particular problems faced by rape complainants cross-examined by defendants exercising their right to conduct their own defence. In 1996 Ralston Edwards subjected Julia Mason to a cross-examination lasting thirty hours during which time he wore the clothes he was wearing during the attack.[40] Mason, who had to be prescribed tranquillizers during the trial, described Edward's cross-examination as 'furthering the act' of rape. In 1997 Milton Brown subjected his two victims to a 'merciless cross-examination' which lasted for five days.[41] Following the trial Judge Pontius

---

[34] S. 37.

[35] In 1999 the New Zealand Law Commission recommended an absolute bar on personal cross-examination by unrepresented defendants in the case of all complainants of domestic violence: New Zealand Law Commission, *Evidence Report 55 Volume 1: Reform of the Law* (1999, Wellington: New Zealand Law Commission) 110.

[36] The plight of victims of stalkers was highlighted by the case of Dennis Chambers who personally cross-examined a woman he was alleged to have stalked for 4 years: see *Daily Telegraph* 18 September 1996. [37] S. 38(2).

[38] Ss. 38(3) and 38(4). S. 38(5) provides that a person so appointed shall not be responsible to the accused. A court-appointed lawyer will have access to the courts and the prosecution's papers, statements made by a defendant to the police, and any medical evidence. [39] S. 40.

[40] See n. 36 above. In another case, a Japanese student who had been gang-raped by 6 men spent 12 days in the witness box.

[41] The working group expressed concern that publicity surrounding the *Edwards* (n. 40 above) and *Brown* (*R v Brown (Milton)*, [1998] 2 Cr App R 364) cases would influence other defendants to seek to cross-examine in person: Home Office, n. 12 above, para. 9.29.

stated that it was highly regrettable that the law allowed an unrepresented defendant 'virtually an unfettered right to personally question his victims in needlessly extended and agonising detail for the obvious purpose of intimidation and humiliation'. These remarks prompted Lord Chief Justice Bingham to offer guidance to judges on controlling protracted and irrelevant questioning where defendants had dispensed with their legal representatives. Refusing Brown leave to appeal, Lord Bingham stated that whilst a trial cannot be conducted on the assumption that the defendant is a rapist and the complainant a victim, a trial judge had a clear duty to do everything he could, consistently with giving the defendant a fair trial, to minimize the trauma suffered by other participants. If the defendant proved unwilling or unable to comply with the judge's instructions the judge should, if necessary to save the complainant from avoidable distress, stop further questioning by the defendant or take over the questioning of the complainant himself. Moreover, judges were assured that the Court of Appeal would be 'very slow indeed, in the absence of clear evidence of injustice, to disturb any resulting conviction'. The Lord Chief Justice acknowledged that the exercise of these powers would always call for the exercise of very careful judgment, as the judge must not only ensure that the defendant had a fair trial but also that the jury felt he had had a fair trial.

Clearly, the *Brown* guidelines were not in the government's view of sufficient reach to allay complainants' concerns which centred, it was rightly said, as much on the *risk* of being cross-examined by an alleged attacker as on the form which that cross-examination might take. An automatic mandatory ban was seen as the most effective way of providing complainants with reassurance and the necessary degree of certainty. As Minister of State Paul Boateng remarked:

It is only of limited use for judges to step in and stop abusive questioning once it has started: often the damage has already been done. The problem with unrepresented defendants cross-examining sexual offence complainants goes further than the questions they ask. The very fact that the complainant is being cross-examined by someone whom he or she alleges has raped or abused them is intimidating in itself. No one should underestimate the impact of having to face one's alleged attacker when one is in the witness box. The victim is accused by the person in the dock and is obliged to answer questions that are designed to humiliate, degrade and intimidate. That cannot be right.[42]

Challenging the mandatory nature of the ban prior to enactment, Lord Bingham commented in the House of Lords that there had been no further examples of abuse since the *Brown* guidance had been issued. In fact, there have been a number of subsequent cases in which complainants have endured humiliating personal cross-examination. In one such case a rape complainant was forced to attend court six times when her attacker, Camille Hourani, repeatedly changed his mind about questioning her. The complainant was eventually subjected to nearly a day in the witness box, during which the defendant 'tormented

---

[42] House of Commons Standing Committee E, 22 June 1999.

and bullied her, frequently reducing her to tears'.[43] In another disturbing case Patrick Andrew Simms subjected his victim to four days of cross-examination.[44]

Other opponents have presented the prohibition as an infringement of the rights of criminal defendants to challenge witnesses' evidence. Friedman, for example, maintains that the preparation and support of complainants is preferable to denying defendants a longstanding right to face-to-face examination.[45] However, the European Court of Human Rights has ruled that mandatory legal representation may be in the interests of justice and consistent with Article 6(3)(c).[46] The Court also made clear that the interests of witnesses are to be balanced against the fair trial rights of defendants.[47] The right of witnesses to be protected from unnecessary trauma and the public interest vested in convicting those guilty of sexual offences must thus be weighed against the detriment to an uncooperative defendant of having qualified counsel conduct questioning on his behalf.[48] Overall, the provision can be said to strike an appropriate balance between competing interests. Nonetheless, it is unfortunate that personal cross-examination should have dominated the debate. In focusing on the admittedly deplorable antics of a handful of defendants charged with rape, the intimidatory and intrusive tactics employed daily by defence lawyers in a range of trial contexts have escaped examination.

C. THE INTERMEDIARY

The third and final measure that will impact on cross-examination concerns the introduction of intermediaries into the criminal process. In *Speaking Up for Justice* the Home Office interdepartmental working group acknowledged the communication problems that young and learning disabled witnesses often experience in court.[49] To ameliorate their position the report recommended that courts should have a statutory power to require the use of a communicator or intermediary in criminal trials. According to the working group, the use of intermediaries would improve the quality of the evidence received, save court time, and diffuse the pressure of cross-examination on vulnerable witnesses.[50] Section 29 of the Youth Justice and Criminal Evidence Act 1999 implements the

---

[43] 'Verdict ends rape victim's court ordeal' *The Times*, 5 April 2000.

[44] 'Rapist given a life sentence' *The Times*, 7 October 2000. The case was active before the prohibition came into force in September 2000.

[45] Friedman, R., 'Thoughts from across the water on hearsay and confrontation' [1998] *Criminal Law Review* 697, 709.   [46] *Croissant v Germany* (1992) 16 EHRR 135.

[47] See Chapter IV.

[48] As Lord Williams of Mostyn remarked: 'we have a criminal justice system which in the eyes of many—sometimes I feel justifiably—resembles a game. It is not a game for the defendant to indicate that it is his bat and he is going home': HL Deb., vol. 597 col. 23, 8 February 1999.

[49] Home Office, n. 12 above, 57.

[50] The use of intermediaries was first proposed in 1989 by the Pigot Committee which recommended that the court should have discretion to order exceptionally that questions an advocate wishes to put to a child witness should be relayed through a person approved by the court who

working group's recommendation.[51] It provides that in cases involving children, or involving witnesses suffering from physical or mental disabilities or a significant impairment of intelligence and social functioning, a court may allow an approved intermediary to help the witness communicate with legal representatives and the court.[52] The function of the intermediary, briefly stated in the Act, is to communicate questions put to the witness and a witness's replies and to explain both so far as is necessary to enable both to be understood.[53] The judge and legal representatives must be able to see and hear any examination of the witness and to communicate with the intermediary.[54] The jury must also be able to see and hear the examination of the witness when an intermediary is used.[55] Intermediaries appearing in court will have to declare that they will perform their function faithfully[56] and will be subject to the Perjury Act.[57]

The bare bones of section 29 have yet to be fleshed out with rules of court making the precise scope of the intermediary role impossible to state. However, it is clear that the intermediary is to perform a relatively passive 'translator' function, 'reinterpreting' lawyers' complex language into a more developmentally appropriate and therefore accessible form as well as explaining a witness's answers, where necessary, for the benefit of the court. In this regard the intermediary procedure resembles similar schemes already operating in other common law jurisdictions. In South Africa the role of the intermediary was established in section 170A of the Criminal Procedure Act 1977.[58] The section provides that a court-appointed intermediary is to convey the 'general purport' of any question to the relevant witness.[59] In practice, this gives intermediaries limited leeway in

enjoys the child's confidence, such as a child psychiatrist or social worker. Preventing the loss of potentially crucial evidence was the primary perceived advantage of the scheme: Home Office, *Report of the Advisory Group on Video Evidence* (1989, London: Home Office) para. 2.32.

[51] The government aims to introduce this in the Crown Court by Autumn 2001. See Home Office, *Action For Justice: Implementing the Speaking Up for Justice Report* (1999, London: Home Office).

[52] Witnesses eligible on the grounds of fear or distress do not qualify: s. 18(1)(b).

[53] The use of an intermediary is not an entirely new measure. Evidence of a video-taped interview between a social worker and a disabled witness with severe speech difficulties was, for example, received in *R v Duffy* [1999] 1 Cr App R 307.   [54] S. 29(3)(a).

[55] S. 29(3)(b). Where intermediaries are used at a very early stage of an investigation or proceedings, and an application is subsequently made for a video recording of an interview in which they were involved to be admitted as evidence, that direction can be given despite the judge and legal representatives not having been present. But the intermediary who was involved must still gain the court's approval retrospectively before the recording can be admitted. See Home Office, *Explanatory Notes to Youth Justice and Criminal Evidence Act* (1999, London: Home Office).

[56] S. 29(5).   [57] S. 29(7)

[58] S. 170A was inserted by s. 3 of the Criminal Law Amendment Act 1991 and came into operation on 30 July 1993. The provision is based on recommendations of the South African Law Commission. See *Report of the South African Law Commission: The Protection of the Child Witness Project 71* (1991, Pretoria: South African Law Commission).

[59] S. 170(2)(b). In contrast to s. 29, eligibility under the South African legislation is dependent upon a finding that a witness under the age of 18 years would be exposed to 'undue' mental stress of suffering if required to testify in court. Where an intermediary is appointed no examination or cross-examination of a witness, except examination by the court, may take place in any manner other than through the intermediary. The child witness is placed in another room and does not hear the original questions put by the prosecutor or defence counsel; he or she only hears the prosecutor's

their reformulation of complex questions. 'By conveying "the general purport" of the question, the intermediary is not permitted to alter the question. He must convey the content and meaning of what was asked in a language and form understandable to the witness.'[60] The intermediary may not conduct his or her own independent questioning and can interfere only in response to a question put by one of the parties. As Merwe notes, the parties remain broadly in control as they can, through their questions, 'confine the witness *and* the intermediary to those aspects of the case which they wish to probe. And in this respect there has been no real deviation from the adversarial model.'[61] The success of the intermediary system in South Africa has yet to be authoritatively evaluated.

A similar procedure operates in Western Australia where the Evidence Act 1906 (WA) defines the intermediary role as communicating and explaining both the questions put to a child witness and his or her elicited response.[62] Here too, the intermediary or 'communicator' has been assigned a relatively restricted function that allows the advocates to retain effective control over the content and form, if not the *ipsissima verba* and pace, of cross-examination questions. According to one judge interviewed in a study commissioned by the Ministry of Justice: '[t]he communicator must only interpret and not lead the witness, or, in interpretation, alter the nature of the questions and answers.'[63]

Two primary concerns have so far been voiced following the announced introduction of intermediaries into criminal proceedings. First is the contention that the interposing of a third party between advocate and witness necessarily impairs the efficacy of cross-examination, thereby infringing the rights of criminal defendants to challenge evidence, as enshrined in Article 6 of the European Convention on Human Rights.[64] This claim must be assessed against the ample

---

or defence counsel's question as relayed by the intermediary to the witness, either in its original or an amended form.

[60] *Klink v Regional Court Magistrate NO and Others* [1996] 1 All SA 191 (SE).

[61] Van der Merwe, S., 'Cross-Examination of the (Sexually Abused) Child Witness in a Constitutionalized Adversarial Trial System: Is the South African Intermediary the Solution?' in (eds.) Nijboer, J. F. and Reijntjes, J. M., *Proceedings of the first World Conference on New Trends in Criminal Investigation and Evidence*, The Hague, The Netherlands, 1–5 December 1995, World Conference on New Trends in Criminal Investigation and Evidence (1997, The Netherlands: Koninklijke Vermande) 240. See also Louw, D. and Olivier, P., 'Listening to Children in South Africa' in (eds.) Bottoms, B. and Goodman, G., *International Perspectives on Child Abuse and Children's Testimony* (1996, London: Sage) 180.

[62] Evidence Act 1906 (WA) s. 106F(2). New Zealand legislation also currently provides for the limited use of an interpreter or intermediary in cases of sexual violence where the complainant is a child or mentally handicapped person. S. 23E(4) of the Evidence Act 1908 (NZ) provides that where a witness is to give evidence from out of court by closed-circuit television or from behind a screen by audio link, the judge may direct that questions be put to the witness through a person approved by the judge. This provision does not, however, allow the intermediary to rephrase questions or interpret the witness's answer.

[63] O'Grady, C., *Child Witnesses and Jury Trials: An Evaluation of the Use of Closed Circuit Television and Removable Screens in Western Australia* (1996, Perth: Western Australia Ministry of Justice) 107.

[64] See for example Doak, J., 'Confrontation in the courtroom: Shielding vulnerable witnesses from the adversarial showdown' (2000) 5(3) *Journal of Civil Liberties* 296, 317.

opportunity that the intermediary provisions afford for contemporaneous objection on the part of counsel whenever questions or testimony are considered to have been misinterpreted or unduly altered in translation. The cross-examination of a witness through an intermediary must take place in the presence of defence counsel. Moreover, the court retains the power to direct the intermediary to relay questions in their original form. Accordingly, use of an intermediary need neither bar the defence from any relevant inquiry nor inhibit the legitimate testing of a witness's credibility. In South Africa claims that questioning through an intermediary destroyed the effectiveness of cross-examination and was therefore unconstitutional were rejected by the South African Appeal Court in *Klink*.[65] Stating that the forceful cross-examination of a young person by skilled counsel may be more likely to 'obfuscate than reveal the truth', the court held that the use of an intermediary who could convey the 'general purport' of any question did not result in such unfairness to an accused that it impinged his fundamental rights. The presiding officer at trial would, the Court stated, be able to see to it that there was no prejudice to the accused. That judges had to be prepared to intervene, where necessary, to insist that the exact question rather than its import be conveyed to the witness in order to ensure the effectiveness of cross-examination was emphasized by the same Court in the later case of *Stefaans*.[66]

In terms of a defendant's right to challenge contrary evidence, Article 6(3)(d) of the Convention does not require that cross-examination be personally conducted by defendant's counsel. The interests of a defendant have been found to be met when questioning is relayed by a neutral third party in the presence of counsel provided the defendant has had adequate opportunity to challenge the evidence against him.[67] As Spencer remarks: '[t]o many ECHR judges the suggestion that this sort of arrangement is contrary to the Convention would be astonishing'.[68]

The second area of concern relates to the practical matter of finding persons suitably qualified for the task.[69] According to reports, the unavailability of qualified intermediaries has proved a problem in both Western Australia and South Africa. The identity of the intermediary is not specified in section 29, which merely states that a special measures direction may provide for any examination of the witness to be conducted 'by an interpreter or other person approved by the court' for this purpose.[70] In other jurisdictions social workers, psychologists,

---

[65] *Klink v Regional Court Magistrate NO and Others* [1996] 1 All SA 191 (SE).

[66] *Stefaans* [1999] (1) SACR 182.   [67] *Kostovski v The Netherlands* (1992) 14 EHRR 396.

[68] Spencer, J. R., 'The Memorandum: An international perspective' in (eds.) Westcott, H. and Jones, J., *Perspectives on the Memorandum. Policy, Practice and Research in Investigative Interviewing* (1997, Aldershot: Arena) 105.

[69] See Birch, D., 'A Better Deal for Vulnerable Witnesses?' [2000] *Criminal Law Review* 231.

[70] The explanatory notes accompanying the Act add that the intermediary will usually be a specialist who, through training, or perhaps through unique knowledge of the witness, can help a witness who has difficulty understanding questions or framing evidence coherently to communicate. An interdepartmental steering group has been set the task of drawing up proper guidelines setting out the intermediary's appropriate qualifications and training.

and child counsellors have typically filled the role. The government has stated that aptitude and familiarity with the particular disabilities or vulnerabilities of witnesses will be more important than any formal qualification.[71] However, intermediaries will require some knowledge of court procedure as well as language skills.[72] This and the need for a degree of detachment in performing the intermediary function appear to rule out those closely involved with a witness.[73] Procedures facilitating effective liaison between an appointed intermediary and those with experience of communicating with an eligible witness will have to be put in place. Witnesses with learning disabilities may, for example, exhibit speech behaviours which only their carers can explain. The Home Office is currently in the process of developing guidance: a code of practice for intermediaries is expected alongside guidelines detailing who can and should act as an intermediary.

1. More Empathic Communication?

Little attention has yet focused on the central question regarding the extent to which section 29 will achieve its declared aim of assisting eligible witnesses to give their best evidence in criminal proceedings. Young children will no doubt benefit from the assistance of an intermediary trained to accommodate their linguistic and cognitive needs. Those with learning difficulties and physical disabilities will similarly gain from having a person familiar with their capabilities communicate and explain lawyers' questions and their replies. In some cases the intermediary procedure will allow witnesses with severe communication problems to testify in criminal proceedings who would otherwise be denied the opportunity.[74] For these reasons the provision is very welcome. However, the limitations of the intermediary procedure become apparent when the full extent of the problems confronting vulnerable witnesses during cross-examination is considered. As the previous Chapter made clear, complex vocabulary and 'confusing' grammatical construction are not the only barriers to effective communication and to testimony that is both reliable and complete. The techniques for controlling questioning practised during cross-examination, and the use of improper discrediting tactics which cause considerable distress, represent equally potent impediments. It appears that intermediaries are to be in a position to temper only the former. The intermediary role has been narrowly

---

[71] House of Commons Standing Committee E, 22 June 1999.

[72] Bates, P., 'The Youth Justice and Criminal Evidence Act: The evidence of children and vulnerable adults' (1999) 11(3) *Child and Family Law Quarterly* 289.

[73] See Hoyano, L. C. H., 'Variations on a theme by Pigot: Special Measures directions for child witnesses' [2000] *Criminal Law Review* 250; McEwan, J., 'In defence of vulnerable witnesses: The Youth Justice and Criminal Evidence Act 1999' (2000) 4 *International Journal of Evidence and Proof* 29.

[74] S. 30 of the YJCEA provides for the use of aids to communication. The sort of device contemplated is a sign or symbol board. The measure is available only to witnesses eligible on the grounds of youth or incapacity under s. 16.

defined as that of 'translator'. The function has been compared to that of an interpreter for non-English speakers and, like court interpreters, intermediaries are to have a limited influence over the basic tenor of cross-examination.[75] There is no suggestion that the intermediary will be at liberty to intervene actively during cross-examination to challenge the use of interrogatory devices which are potentially misleading or suggestive and liable to elicit unreliable testimony. Minister of State Paul Boateng has stated that '[t]he Government are firmly of the view that the intermediary's function must be tightly restricted to communicating questions and answers between court and witness'.[76] This appears to preclude the possibility of intermediaries acting on their own initiative to highlight the evidential dangers of questioning which is unduly repetitive, protracted, or in some other sense inappropriate. This is a significant constraint on the level of protection that eligible witnesses will receive under section 29.

It may be argued that the adversary nature of the trial process effectively dictates a limited role for intermediaries. Granting intermediaries a wider participatory role in criminal proceedings would inevitably draw the trial judge into the role of an active manager of court-room exchanges. It is the trial judge's task to monitor mediated cross-examination and he or she must act as ultimate arbiter when disputes arise. Allowing intermediaries to perform anything but a narrow translator function would require judges to intervene more actively during the cross-examination of vulnerable witnesses than current structural constraints allow.[77] The provision, limited as it is, thus arguably goes as far as the traditional balance between party control and judicial passivity permits.

2. Vulnerable Defendants

It should be noted that defendants are exempted from the special measures provisions of the Youth Justice and Criminal Evidence Act 1999, including the assistance of intermediaries. The use of developmentally inappropriate language in the court-room may, however, equally disadvantage defendants who by virtue of age or incapacity have limited language ability. An inarticulate defendant who is fearful of testifying must also set the risks of a poor performance in the witness box against the risk of adverse inferences being drawn from his failure to give evidence.[78] The particular plight of learning disabled defendants was acknowledged in a recent report by Law Commission of New South Wales, which states:

---

[75] For criticism of the limited latitude afforded bilingual interpreters in criminal proceedings see Mikkelson, H., 'Towards a Redefinition of the Role of the Court Interpreter' (1998) 3(1) *Interpreting* 21; Morris, R., 'The gum syndrome: Predicaments in court interpreting' (1999) 6(1) *Forensic Linguistics* 8; Morris, R., 'The Interlingual Interpreter: Cypher or Intelligent Participant?' (1993) 6(18) *International Journal for the Semiotics of Law* 291.
[76] House of Commons Standing Committee E, 22 June 1999.
[77] Ellison, L., 'Cross-examination in Rape Trials' [1998] *Criminal Law Review* 605.
[78] The age limitation for inferences from failure to testify was repealed by the Crime and Disorder Act 1998, s. 35. See also *R v Friend* [1997] 2 Cr App R 231.

Cross-examination tests not only the truthfulness of a witness's evidence but also his or her capacity to understand legal language that is not always clear, abstract concepts, subtle nuances and, often as not, sentences that are long, complicated and convoluted. It is an intimidating experience for all defendants and pits an often inarticulate and uneducated defendant against a highly skilled lawyer. The fear that a defendant will not perform well in the witness box (whether or not his or her evidence is truthful) is a common reason for a defence lawyer to advise a defendant not to give evidence ... This may prejudice the defendant in the eyes of the jury who may think that the defendant has something to hide.[79]

The decision of the European Court of Human Rights in *T v UK* and *V v UK* may yet prompt amendment of the YJCEA.[80] Commenting on the treatment of the two eleven-year-old defendants in the case, the Court stated that it was essential that a child charged with an offence was dealt with in a manner which takes full account of his age, level of maturity, and intellectual and emotional capacities, and that steps are taken to promote his ability to understand and participate in the proceedings. The rulings caused the Lord Chief Justice to issue a Practice Direction stating that, as far as was practicable, the criminal trial of a young child should be conducted in language which a young child can understand.[81] However, this is unlikely to be widely considered adequate protection of the fair trial rights of young defendants and completely neglects the position of vulnerable adults.

D. Discussion

Having reviewed in the previous Chapter the various strategies advocates employ during cross-examination to discredit, confuse, and otherwise undermine opposing witnesses, it is clear that the majority of those tactics fall outside the scope of the YJCEA. Section 41, for example, deals with questions relating to a complainant's sexual behaviour in sexual offence cases. It is accepted that such questioning often adds unnecessarily to a complainant's distress and can deflect a jury from the central issues in a case. Nevertheless, complainants face equally damaging and intrusive assaults on their private lives when their mental and emotional stability, lifestyle, financial situation, clothing, make-up and general character are scrutinized in court.[82] Complainants are also

---

[79] Law Reform Commission NSW, *Report 80 People with an Intellectual Disability and the Criminal Justice System* (1996, Sydney: Law Reform Commission NSW) para. 7.27.

[80] [2000] Crim LR 187.

[81] *Practice Direction by the Lord Chief Justice of England and Wales, Trial of Children and Young Persons in the Crown Court* (February, 2000). See also The United Nations Standard Minimum Rules for the Administration of Juvenile Justice (The Beijing Rules) adopted by the General assembly of the United Nations in 1985 and The European Convention on the Rights of the Child adopted by the General Assembly in 1989, Article 40, The International Covenant on Civil and Political Rights, GA Res. 2200A (XXI) 1966 Article 14.

[82] It is worth noting that where tight restrictions have been imposed upon the admittance of evidence of sexual history, the focus of the defence in rape cases has typically shifted to a complainant's

discredited by cross-examiners on the basis of stereotypical perceptions as to how 'real' victims should react to their experience. Such questioning is not confined to sexual offence cases but (as recent research has shown) extends to other trial contexts with similarly damaging results. Section 29 is designed to facilitate more empathic communication in criminal proceedings. But, as explained above, the measure offers only limited protection against the developmentally inappropriate questioning techniques practised during cross-examination.

A number of common law jurisdictions have attempted to deal with the problem of improper cross-examination in broader terms. Some have introduced or proposed legislation disallowing improper questioning more generally as a means of promoting greater judicial control over the conduct of cross-examination. The Law Reform Commission of Queensland has recently recommended the adoption of provisions of existing Commonwealth[83] and New South Wales[84] legislation which basically enable the court to disallow a question put to a witness in cross-examination if the question is misleading, unduly annoying, harassing, intimidating, offensive, oppressive, or repetitive.[85] In assessing the propriety of questions the court is, under the terms of this legislation, required to consider the relevant characteristics of the witness, including age, personality, and any mental or physical disability. The Law Reform Commission of Queensland advocated the insertion of an additional provision giving the court specific power during the cross-examination of a child witness to disallow a question which, having regard to the child's age, level of understanding, and culture, is intimidating, overbearing, confusing, misleading, unduly repetitive, or phrased in inappropriate language.[86] Addressing cross-examination as to credit, the Queensland Taskforce on Women and the Criminal Code has further recommended the amendment of existing legislation[87] to give the court power to disallow a question if it would not 'materially impair confidence in the reliability of the evidence of a witness'. The purpose of this amendment would, the report states, be to ensure that cross-examination as to

medical, counselling, and psychiatric records: see Bronitt, S. and McSherry, B., 'The Use and Abuse of Counseling Records in Sexual Assault Trials: Reconstructing the "Rape Shield"?' (1997) 8(2) *Criminal Law Forum* 259.

[83] Evidence Act 1995 (Cth) 42(2)(d).

[84] Evidence Act 1995 (NSW) 41(1). S. 42 provides that the court may also disallow a leading question in cross-examination, or tell the witness not to answer it, if satisfied that the relevant facts would be better ascertained if leading questions were not used.

[85] Existing legislation only enables the court to disallow a question if it is indecent or scandalous or is intended only to insult or annoy, or is needlessly offensive in form: Evidence Act 1977 (Qld), s. 21. See Queensland Law Reform Commission, *The Receipt of Evidence by Queensland Courts: The Evidence of Children*, Report No. 55 Part 1 (2000, Brisbane: Queensland Law Reform Commission) 1.

[86] This is based on the Evidence Act 1939 (Northern Territory), s. 21B, which applies to children under the age of 16 and provides that a judge may disallow questions which are 'confusing, misleading or phrased in inappropriate language', having regard to the child's age, culture and level of understanding'. See Law Commission (New Zealand), *Evidence Report 55, vol. 1: Reform of the Law* (1999, Wellington: Law Commission (New Zealand)).

[87] Evidence Act 1977 (Qld), s. 29.

credit is focused on the reliability of the evidence of the witness, rather than credit for credit's sake.[88]

The New Zealand Law Commission has recently recommended the imposition of similar restrictions on the 'unfair' questioning of witnesses in court.[89] Section 85 of the proposed Evidence Code provides that the judge may disallow any question that he or she considers to be intimidating, improper, unfair, misleading, needlessly repetitive, or expressed in language too complicated for the witness to understand. In deciding whether to disallow questions the trial judge may take into account the age or maturity of the witness, any physical, intellectual, or psychiatric disability, the linguistic or cultural background of the witness, and the nature of the proceedings.[90]

These proposals arose partly in response to recent empirical research which revealed a marked reluctance on the part of trial judges to intervene actively during the cross-examination of witnesses. Studies in various Australian states, for example, pointed to a 'culture of judicial reticence' as far as curtailing improper questioning is concerned.[91] Similarly, in recent studies in England and Wales trial judges have been found to be slow to take the initiative during the cross-examination of child witnesses[92] and were apparently indisposed to prevent questioning which learning disabled witnesses regarded as bullying.[93] Judges have, of course, been criticized for some time across common law jurisdictions for failing to adopt a more interventionist stance in rape trials to curb inappropriate cross-examination as to credit.[94] However, the problem is not (as these proposals presuppose) one of insufficient judicial powers. To a substantial degree at least, the provisions described above merely duplicate powers already held by the courts.[95] The problem rests with the adversary nature of proceedings and the tension between the umpireal function ascribed to trial judges within an adversarial process and their duty to protect witnesses from improper cross-examination. As explained in the previous Chapter, the trial judge must in his or her guise as neutral referee avoid appearing to advance the case of either side and, in line with the principle of party autonomy, must allow counsel sufficient leeway to develop and present their respective cases to the jury. Denied a clear

---

[88] Office of Women's Policy, Department of Equity and Fair Trading (Qld) *Report of the Taskforce on Women and the Criminal Code* (2000, Brisbane: Office of Women's Policy) 319.

[89] New Zealand Law Commission, *Evidence Report 55 vol. 1: Reform of the Law* (1999, Wellington: New Zealand Law Commission). [90] S. 85(2).

[91] See Law Reform Commission of Western Australia, *Review of the Criminal and Civil Justice System Final Report* (1999, Perth: Law Reform Commission of Western Australia) ch. 21.

[92] Davis, G., Hoyano, L., Keenan, C., Maitland, L. and Morgan, R., *An Assessment of the Admissibility and Sufficiency of Evidence in Child Abuse Prosecutions* (1999, London: Home Office) 61.

[93] Sanders, A., Creaton, J., Bird, S. and Weber, L., *Victims with Learning Disabilities Negotiating the Criminal Justice System* (1997, Oxford: Centre for Criminological Research, University of Oxford) 78.

[94] See Lees, S., *Carnal Knowledge: Rape on Trial* (1996, London: Hamish Hamilton).

[95] *Mechanical and General Inventions Co Ltd and Lehwess v Austin and Austin Motor Co Ltd* [1935] AC 346; *R v Kalia* [1975] Crim LR 181; *Wong Kam-ming v R* [1980] AC 247, 260.

advance overview as to counsel's line of argument, the trial judge is also ill equipped to intervene and prevent questioning that may in retrospect be deemed insufficiently probative or misleading. As the South African Law Commission has acknowledged:

The presiding officer may limit or prohibit offensive, humiliating, misleading or tormenting cross-examination. In practice, however, the problem remains that the dividing line between this kind of cross-examination and admissible sharp and aggressive cross-examination is sometimes very vague and presiding officers are extremely cautious not to cross this line. If the limit is indeed exceeded this may well lead to nullification of the whole matter. Such a result is extremely undesirable.[96]

Legislation detailing the types of questions which judges may legitimately disallow might serve to remind judges of their protective role, but it will not overcome the structural barriers to effective judicial management of courtroom questioning inherent within the adversarial process. Indeed, common law jurisdictions with equivalent provisions in place report that they are rarely invoked.[97]

Clearly, more radical solutions are required. Unfortunately the Home Office interdepartmental working group did not venture beyond the bounds of the established trial framework to consider possible alternatives to cross-examination as currently conceived. This can only be regarded as a major missed opportunity.

E. Restoring Credibility

The remainder of this Chapter considers witness credibility. It is an issue neglected in the Youth Justice and Ciminal Evidence Act 1999, but is very often the pivot upon which criminal prosecutions turn. The purpose is to challenge the prevailing orthodoxy regarding the circumstances in which the credit of witnesses testifying in criminal proceedings may be enhanced.[98] The basic common law rule as stated in *Turner* is that 'evidence can be called to impugn the credibility of witnesses but not led in chief to bolster it up'.[99] Three principal justifications are advanced for the exclusion of supportive evidence. First, it is argued that such evidence is unlikely to be of appreciable assistance to the jury. Jurors, it is assumed, are generally adept at assessing the reliability of witnesses. Secondly, it is claimed that to admit evidence on credibility would be to usurp the

---

[96] *Report of the South African Law Commission: The Protection of the Child Witness Project 71* (1991, Pretoria: South African Law Commission) para. 2.10.

[97] See, for example, Office of Women's Policy, Department of Equity and Fair Trading (Qld) n. 88 above, 314.

[98] See Mewett, A. W., 'Credibility of Witnesses' (1995) 37 *Criminal Law Quarterly* 37.

[99] *R v Turner* [1975] QB 834, 842. See also *Lowery v The Queen* [1974] AC 85; *R v Ward* [1993] 2 All ER 577.

function of the jury.[100] Thirdly, it is feared that juries may attach too much significance to such evidence or be distracted from the main issues of a case.[101]

The presumption that witness credibility is one within the 'common experience' of jurors has been subject to criticism. For example, it is claimed that a lack of general knowledge and understanding of the capabilities of people with learning disabilities may give rise to unfounded doubts as to their credibility. Such witnesses in particular may display demeanour in court which makes a fact-finder less inclined to consider them truthful. As the Law Reform Commission of New South Wales recently noted, jurors may notice that a learning disabled witness 'has a short attention span, appears nervous and hesitant or possibly frustrated and angry. The witness may not look at the lawyer asking the questions . . . may wear a fixed smile or frown persistently or mumble answers to questions or possibly shout them out.'[102] The admission of 'corrective' evidence would help counter popular misconceptions and prejudice regarding those with intellectual disabilities. The current evidentiary regime provides limited scope for anticipatory rehabilitation. In the case of *Robinson*, for example, a fifteen-year-old complainant was alleged to have a mental capacity of a seven- or eight-year-old and to be within the bottom one per cent of children her age.[103] It was held on appeal that the expert testimony of an educational psychologist that the complainant was neither suggestible nor prone to fantasy was inadmissible in the absence of a defence allegation to the contrary in cross-examination. In general terms the court stated that 'the Crown cannot call a witness of fact and then, without more, call a psychologist or psychiatrist to give reasons why the jury should regard that witness as reliable'.[104] Surely the appropriate test should be whether the fact-finder would be substantially aided by the admission of such evidence?[105] In the case of witnesses with learning disabilities juries are liable to be guided by unhelpful stereotypes and erroneous assumptions in the absence of suitable assistance. Under current rules 'witnesses who are unlikely to perform "normally" are less likely to have their cases prosecuted; or when they do, their cases fail more often'.[106]

---

[100] Witness credibility may also be viewed as an 'ultimate issue' although the courts appear to moving towards abandonment of the ultimate issue rule in criminal cases.

[101] *R v Turner* [1975] QB 834.

[102] Law Reform Commission NSW, *Report 80 People with an Intellectual Disability and the Criminal Justice System* (1996, Sydney: Law Reform Commission NSW), para. 7.30. The Commission accordingly recommended that both the prosecution and defence should be able to lead expert evidence about the intellectual disability of one of their own witnesses.

[103] [1994] 3 All ER 346.

[104] *R v Robinson* [1994] 3 All ER 346, 352. See also *R v Kyselka* (1962) 133 CCC 103, Ont CA.

[105] MacKay, R. and Colman, A., 'Excluding Expert Evidence: A tale of ordinary folk and common experience' [1991] *Criminal Law Review* 800; MacKay, R. and Colman, A., 'Equivocal Rulings on Expert Psychological and Psychiatric Evidence: Turning a Muddle into a Nonsense' [1996] *Criminal Law Review* 88.

[106] Sanders, A., Creaton, J., Bird, S. and Weber, L., *Victims with Learning Disabilities Negotiating the Criminal Justice System* (1997, Oxford: Centre for Criminological Research, University of Oxford) 61.

A second area in which juries are likely to be materially aided in their deliberations by the admission of expert evidence is that of sexual offences. As mentioned in the preceding Chapter, victims of sexual offences often behave in ways that do not correspond with juror expectations. Common notions of timeliness and consistency, for example, may lead juries astray in assessing credibility. Research indicates that victims of sexual offences often delay disclosure, recant allegations, and revise their accounts over time. Studies also suggest that children's initial disclosures of sexual abuse tend to be tentative and partial, becoming fuller over time once they ascertain whether they are believed, supported, rejected, or punished.[107] Similarly, research indicates that women who have been raped:

... often present initial accounts that try to make things normal again. They try to smooth out social relations by minimising the harm of abuse, engaging in self blame, telling stories that offer alternative explanations of events so that the full consequences of the abuse do not have to be dealt with at the time, and disguising the brutality through descriptive distortions of events.[108]

In the absence of 'social framework' evidence regarding patterns of disclosure in sexual offence cases, juries may well attribute instances of narrative inconsistency to a lack of truthfulness. Corrective evidence is thus needed 'not because the subject is not a matter of common knowledge but rather because what is commonly "known" about is simply wrong'.[109]

Experience in other jurisdictions suggests a need for caution with regard to the admission of so-called 'syndrome' evidence in sexual offence cases. Reliance on psycho-pathological explanations has not always benefited complainants. Raitt and Zeedyk, for example, described how expert Rape Trauma Syndrome testimony generates new myths about women's behaviour and supplements the list of expectations about women.[110] The classification of the mental state of complainants as pathological can also, Raitt and Zeedyk maintain, diminish the credibility of rape complainants by opening complainants up to defence claims that they are mentally unstable and thus unreliable.

1. Alternative Strategies

Alternative strategies for combating popular misconceptions and myths which affect vulnerable witnesses include provisions for judicial warnings and suitable jury direction. Trial judges are currently restricted in the positive noises they can

---

[107] See Davies, E., Henderson, E. and Seymour, F. W., 'In the interests of justice? The cross-examination of child complainants of sexual abuse in criminal proceedings' (1997) 4(2) *Psychiatry, Psychology and the Law* 217.

[108] Schepple, K. L., 'Just the Facts, Ma'am: Sexualised Violence, Evidentiary Habits, and the Revision of Truths' (1992) 37 *New York School Law Review* 123, 139.

[109] Norris, J. and Edward, M., 'Myths, Hidden Facts and Common Sense: Expert Opinion Evidence and the Assessment of Credibility' (1995) 38 *Criminal Law Quarterly* 73, 83.

[110] Raitt, F. and Zeedyk, S., *The Implicit Relation of Psychology and Law, Women and Syndrome Evidence* (2000, London: Routledge) 99.

make about credibility when directing juries. The introduction of mandatory judicial warnings regarding the weight to be attached to demeanour evidence, for example, or delayed disclosure in sexual offence cases may help to prevent discriminatory inferences from being drawn. Legislation in Victoria provides that a trial judge must warn the jury that any delay in complaining does not necessarily indicate that the allegation is false and must inform the jury that there may be 'good reason' why a victim of sexual assault may hesitate in complaining about it.[111] Moves to introduce a similar provision in England and Wales have so far proved unsuccessful.[112]

Relaxing the hearsay rule would be another way of restoring the credibility of vulnerable witnesses. At present, out of court statements can be used negatively to undermine a witness's credibility where they differ from live oral testimony; but consistent statements have no evidential status and cannot add credit to a witness's account unless they come within limited exceptions.[113] According to Raitt, relaxing the hearsay rule to allow words spoken by victims to confidant(e)s to be repeated in court as evidence of the truth of the events recounted could compensate for the corroborative obstacles frequently encountered in sexual offence cases.[114] At present such statements may be admitted under the doctrine of recent complaint only as evidence of consistency and if made at the first reasonable opportunity.[115] Statements made weeks or months after an assault are excluded irrespective of their apparent reliability. Raitt cites the example of an adult survivor of child sexual abuse whose recovery leads her to join an incest survivors' group:

If she subsequently gains the courage to report the abuse to the authorities and a prosecution ensues, none of the content of what she previously disclosed to her group will be competent as evidence of the truth of her allegations, due to the operation of the hearsay rule. Since women are invariably more comfortable making disclosures of early child sexual abuse to another survivor, disclosures that may not be made until years after the event, the effect of the hearsay rule is to devalue both the significance of the disclosure and the relationship of trust.[116]

---

[111] Unfortunately, subsequent judicial developments have neutralized the potential beneficial impact of these reforms. See, for example, the High Court of Australia decision in *Crofts* (1996) 88 A Crim R 232.

[112] In 1996 Tessa Jowell MP proposed an amendment to the Criminal Procedure and Investigations Bill that would have introduced an equivalent provision, but it failed. Commons Hansard 12 June 1996 col. 355. The amendment read: 'Where on the trial of a person for a sexual offence evidence is given either by the prosecution or the defence or a question is asked of a witness which tends to suggest an absence of complaint in respect of the commission of the alleged offence by the person upon whom the offence is alleged to have been committed or to suggest delay by that person in making any such complaint, the trial judge shall: (a) give a warning to the jury to the effect that absence of complaint or delay in complaining does not necessarily indicate that the allegation that the offence was committed was false; and (b) inform the jury that there may be good reasons why a victim of a sexual offence may delay in making, or may refrain from making, a complaint about the offence.'   [113] See discussion in Chapter II above.

[114] Raitt, F., 'Gender Bias in the Hearsay Rule' in (eds.) Childs, M. and Ellison, L., *Feminist Perspectives on Evidence* (2000, London: Cavendish) 59.   [115] See discussion in Chapter II above.

[116] Raitt, n. 114 above, 66.

As Raitt notes, complainer and confidant would be present in court, providing an opportunity for cross-examination and thus removing the primary objection to hearsay evidence.

The option of removing the hearsay status of all previous consistent statements was recently considered but ultimately rejected by the Law Commission for England and Wales.[117] However, the Law Commission took the view that a previous statement by a witness should be admissible in specified circumstances not only to support the witness's credibility, but also as evidence of the truth of what it states. This would include statements adduced to rebut an allegation of recent invention, a prior identification or description of a person, object, or place, and recent complaints. In relation to the recent complaint doctrine, the Law Commission also recommended that it be extended to all other offences, but disappointingly elected to retain the temporal condition. Unfortunately, there appear to be no plans at present to act upon the Law Commission's limited proposals.

Finally, it may prove necessary to limit through legislation the negative noises which judges may permissibly make about certain categories of witness when directing juries. Prior to the Criminal Justice Act 1988 trial judges were obliged to give a corroboration warning advising the jury of the dangers of acting on the uncorroborated sworn evidence of child witnesses.[118] Trial judges were similarly required to give what was termed a 'full warning'[119] as to the dangers of convicting on the uncorroborated evidence of a complainant of a sexual offence until 1995.[120] These common law requirements have now been abolished but a trial judge has a residual discretion to administer a corroboration warning where he or she considers it warranted. Warnings should be issued only where there is an evidential basis for suggesting that the evidence of the witness may be unreliable, and not on the ground that the witness belongs to a specific category.[121] There is, however, evidence that old-style corroboration warnings are creeping back. Davis *et al.*, for example, report that police officers and CPS lawyers remain wary of prosecuting cases which rest entirely on the credibility of a child complainant because of the tendency of trial judges to administer indiscriminate corroboration warnings.[122] The researchers describe how in one case a trial judge directed the jury to seek corroboration because of an eleven-year-old complainant's 'age and disabilities and behaviour' notwithstanding a

---

[117] *Evidence in Criminal Proceedings: Hearsay and Related Topics* Consultation Paper No. 138 (1995, London: HMSO).   [118] Criminal Justice Act 1988, s. 34(2).

[119] The following statement of Salmon LJ is often cited as a typical example: '. . . human experience has shown in these courts that girls and women do sometimes tell an entirely false story which is very easy to fabricate, but extremely difficult to refute. Such stories are fabricated for all sorts of reasons, which I need not now enumerate, and sometimes for no reason at all': *R v Henry* (1968) 53 Cr App R 150 153.   [120] Criminal Justice and Public Order Act 1994, s. 32(1).

[121] *R v Makenjuola* [1995] 3 All ER 730.

[122] Davis, G., Hoyano, L., Keenan, C., Maitland, L. and Morgan, R., *An Assessment of the Admissibility and Sufficiency of Evidence in Child Abuse Prosecutions* (1999, London: Home Office) 68.

lack of evidence that the child suffered from any mental disability which could affect her capacity to give accurate testimony. Experience in Australia has also shown that removal of the requirement to warn does not necessarily reduce the frequency, or improve the tenor, of judicial comments when women testify about sexual assaults.[123] In spite of remedial legislation trial judges in Australia continue to give harsh corroboration warnings with the approval of the appellate courts.[124] Mack, for example, confirms that '[f]alse beliefs in negative stereotypes about women and sexual assault still result in unwarranted judicial attacks on the credibility of women'.[125] It may therefore be desirable to introduce legislation expressly prohibiting trial judges from negatively warning jurors to regard the evidence of any *category* of witness as inherently suspect.[126] Similar legislation has already been introduced in Victoria, where section 61 of the Crimes Act 1958 provides that a judge must not warn or suggest in any way to the jury that the law regards complainants in sexual cases as an unreliable class of witness.[127]

[123] In New South Wales the Crimes (Sexual Assault) Amendment Act 1981 abolished the requirement to give a corroboration warning in trials where the accused person was charged with sexual assault. However, a recent study of 92 trials reports that judges said it 'was dangerous to convict on complainant's evidence alone' in 40% of cases. Department for Women, *Heroines of Fortitude: The Experiences of Women in Court as Victims of Sexual Assault* (1996, Sydney: Department for Women) 188.

[124] In Canada so many judges continued to issue warnings after the abolition of the mandatory requirement that the government had to ban warnings entirely: McColgan, A., 'Common Law and the Relevance of Sexual History Evidence' (1996) 16 *Oxford Journal of Legal Studies* 275, 277.

[125] Mack, K., '"You should scrutinise her evidence with great care": Corroboration of women's testimony about sexual assault' in (ed.) Easteal, P., *Balancing the Scales: Rape, Law Reform and Australian Culture* (1998, Sydney: Federation Press) 59.

[126] The Law Commission did consider whether legislation should positively seek to prohibit warnings in these terms but concluded that it would be unnecessary to do so: *Criminal law: Corroboration of evidence in criminal trials* (1991, London: HMSO).

[127] Crimes Act 1958 (Vic) s. 61(1)(b).

VII.

A Comparative Perspective: The Dutch Trial Process

It is a popular contention that inquisitorial civil law systems hold inherent advantages for vulnerable and intimidated witnesses. The absence of cross-examination as such and the correspondingly subdued cut and thrust of trial proceedings are considered key benefits from a witness perspective. However, this assertion is rarely based on close comparative study of the treatment of witnesses within alternative systems. Analysis is instead confined to contrasting the 'distinguishing characteristics' of each classical model of proof and surmising their significance for testifying witnesses. Such an exercise is unlikely to yield convincing results. This Chapter aims to fill a gap in the literature by examining the experience of one specific category of witness within a single civil law jurisdiction. Specifically, it explores the experience of adult rape complainants within the Dutch criminal trial process.

Dutch criminal proceedings emphasize the preliminary investigative stage, and the accent is upon written evidence as opposed to oral testimony; thus they differ markedly from English criminal proceedings. The roles of key players within the Dutch process are also distinct, with lawyers notably playing a part subsidiary to that of the trial judge. Also distinct is the character of Dutch evidence law which is basically conceived as a set of decision-making rules and is little concerned with issues of admissibility. The examination of complainants at a preliminary hearing before an examining magistrate instead of oral interrogation at trial is perhaps the most striking feature of rape proceedings in the Netherlands. The examining magistrate has no counterpart in common law jurisdictions. These key features of the Dutch trial process have major implications for the treatment of rape complainants in the Netherlands.

In describing Dutch trial practice in rape cases, this Chapter draws upon semi-structured interviews conducted with two small groups of Dutch legal practitioners based in Amsterdam and The Hague. The first were examining magistrates who had conducted pre-trial hearings in rape cases. The second group were lawyers who had represented rape complainants in criminal proceedings and had attended pre-trial hearings.[1] Both groups can claim a special insight into the treatment of rape complainants in criminal proceedings in the

---

[1] In the Netherlands victims may be legally represented but the role played by their legal representatives is severely limited. A victim advocate is not permitted to participate actively at any stage of the criminal proceedings. The role of victim advocates is largely confined to providing complainants with support and information about the trial process.

Netherlands. Although the number of interviewees was small their comments nevertheless provide a useful account of first-hand experience.[2]

Throughout this Chapter the terms 'adversarial' and 'inquisitorial' are used to denote the criminal justice processes of England and Wales and the Netherlands respectively. The appropriateness of these labels for contemporary comparative study has been called into question. It has been argued that these terms are outdated, have confusing associations, and suggest a homogeneity across European continental legal systems which simply does not exist. It is certainly true that no system is an embodiment of either paradigmatic model, and that so-called continental systems vary widely in their approaches, as do the systems of England and Wales and, for example, the United States.[3] However, trial proceedings in England and Wales are still very much within the adversarial mould and the Dutch trial process remains firmly planted within an inquisitorial tradition. Jörg *et al.*, in a comparative examination of the nature of Dutch and English criminal procedure, argue that the criminal trial processes of England and Wales and the Netherlands 'may be regarded as typical examples of adversarial and inquisitorial systems respectively'.[4]

A. THE NATURE OF THE DUTCH TRIAL PROCESS

Fundamentally, Dutch criminal proceedings are conceived as an official inquiry rather than as a dispute between two opposing sides. The trust placed within adversarial systems on partisan pressures to bring facts to light is largely replaced by faith in the integrity and capacity of public officials to pursue the 'truth', unprompted by party allegiances. As Jörg *et al.* note: '[a]n inquisitorial system assumes that the truth can be, and must be, discovered in an investigative procedure, and, because it may be in the interests of the parties to conceal it, that the state is best equipped to carry out such investigations'.[5] The main emphasis of the Dutch criminal process is upon the pre-trial investigative stage of proceedings and not the trial itself. The decision of the trial court will be based largely on evidence gathered at this stage and recorded in the investigative file (*dossier*). In line with other inquisitorial systems, proof within the Dutch trial system is constituted episodically throughout the entire process and not merely at the post-investigation stage.[6] The pre-trial stage of the process is thus centred on ensur-

[2] 4 examining magistrates and 3 lawyers were interviewed.

[3] 'The old labels do not stick anymore. The systems have grown together and will continue to do so': Vogler, R., 'Learning from the Inquisitors' (1994) June *Legal Executive*, 29.

[4] Jörg, N., Field, S. and Brants, C., 'Are Inquisitorial and Adversarial Systems Converging?' in (eds.) Harding, C., Fennel, P., Jörg, N. and Swart, B., *Criminal Justice in Europe: A Comparative Study* (1995, Oxford: Clarendon Press) 43.   [5] Ibid.

[6] See for example Jackson, J. and Doran, S., *Judge Without Jury: Diplock Trials in the Adversary System* (1995, Oxford: Clarendon Press) 68.

ing that the dossier contains all germane evidence and is a sound basis for judgment at trial.[7] A summary of the possible contents of the dossier is provided by Field *et al.*:

(1) [T]he police file: this consists of a formal account of arrest, search and seizure, police detention, witnesses' statements, the appearance of counsel, (various) statements of the accused, police evidence from the scene of the crime, summary of the results of wire-tapping, and (where applicable), (2) the file of the investigating judge: a statement of the accused, and of witnesses interrogated by the investigating judge on request by the prosecutor or defence counsel; forensic expert evidence; social and psychiatric reports; results of wire-tapping and an inventory of seized objects. (3) [T]he pre-trial detention file: a formal account of all the decisions taken on such detention, together with statements by the defendant before the examining judge and possibly before the court in chambers when further extended detention is requested. (4) [A] file of pre-trial proceedings: wire-tapping orders, seizure of property orders, record of appeal against pre-trial detention orders and/or decisions on requests to discontinue the prosecution.[8]

A number of officials play a role in the construction of the dossier and their diverse influences are regarded as one of the key strengths of the process.[9] As director of the investigation, the public prosecutor (*officier van justitie*) is responsible for monitoring the evidentiary quality of the dossier. Institutional pressures operate upon prosecutors to ensure that both exculpatory and inculpatory lines of inquiry are pursued.[10] For example, if a prosecutor fails to act upon defence requests for further investigation, the trial judge may postpone a trial for such investigation to be conducted. For prosecutors this carries the stigma of failing to display proper judicial impartiality and of bureaucratic inefficiency. Where postponement leads to a lengthy delay in proceedings this may lead to a discharge. It is also relevant that public prosecutors in the Netherlands are regarded as judicial figures and train together with future members of the Bench.[11] Dutch public prosecutors reportedly perceive themselves in such terms and are keen to present themselves not as contending parties but as 'dignitaries of the court'.[12]

---

[7] Beerling, H. W. R., 'An Outline of Dutch Criminal Procedure' (1976) 5 *Anglo American Law Review* 50, 60.

[8] Field, S., Alldridge, P. and Jörg, N., 'Prosecutors, Examining Judges and the Control of Police Investigations' in (eds), Harding *et al.*, n. 4 above.

[9] See Leigh, L. H. and Hall Williams, J. E., *The Management of the Prosecution Process in Denmark, Sweden and the Netherlands* (1981, Leamington Spa: James Hall).

[10] See Field *et al.*, n. 8 above, 234.

[11] Although the two careers develop differently, and the Public Prosecutor's Department is seen as the administrative arm of the judiciary—and has accordingly to improve its managerial capabilities—it is to the benefit of a democratic and independent administration of justice that public prosecutors should think and operate in a judicial manner': Holthuis, H., 'The Role of the Public Prosecutor in the Netherlands' in NACRO, *International Comparisons in Criminal Justice: The London Seminars* (1993, London: NACRO) 17.

[12] See Van de Bunt, H. G., 'Officieren van Justitie: Verslag van een participerend observatieonderzoek' cited in Field *et al.*, n. 8 above, 236.

In serious cases, the prosecutor may request a pre-trial hearing (*gerechtelijk vooronderzoek*) before an examining magistrate (*rechter commissaris*).[13] The role of the examining magistrate is to institute an independent inquiry as an extension of the initial criminal investigation. At the hearing the examining magistrate will examine the accused and any witnesses, including the complainant, and interview any experts.[14] The concept of 'cross-examination' as formalized at common law is unknown to Dutch law. As a general rule the accused is questioned separately although a confrontation may be arranged at the discretion of the examining magistrate or at the request of the defence or the public prosecutor.[15] At the close of the hearing a record of what took place (*proces-verbal*) is added to the dossier.[16] The thoroughness of the investigation is once again safeguarded by institutional incentives to pursue relevant exculpatory evidence. The trial court refers a case back to an examining magistrate if defence concerns are not, in the opinion of the court, adequately addressed: 'And the embarrassment of repeated referral back for further investigation should not be underestimated. RCs want to be seen to be efficient in their processing of cases and judicial in their decision making. This provides a strong motive for them to show distance and impartiality in their day to day dealings with police and prosecutor.'[17]

As indicated, defence lawyers play a vital role in pointing out deficiencies in the investigative file, including allegations of impropriety, and if necessary requesting further investigation. Once the police have passed the investigative file to the public prosecutor the complete file must be made available to the defence. The defence therefore have early access to the statements of all witnesses. At pre-trial hearings the examining magistrate is the primary interrogator of the accused and any witnesses, but the defence lawyer may ask questions and is expected to draw the attention of the examining magistrate to any perceived evidentiary weaknesses in the file.

1. The Trial

The trial is essentially a forum for the evaluation of evidence contained in the dossier rather than a forum for oral argument.[18] Decisions can be made

---

[13] 181 CCP. The defence and the trial judge may also request an instruction if further investigation is deemed necessary. It is reported that actual criminal instruction, in which the examining magistrate gets personally involved in the investigation process and questions witnesses and the defendant, only takes place in about 3% of the cases which go to court. Field *et al.*, n. 8 above, 240.

[14] Neither the accused nor the defence lawyer has an absolute right to attend the examination of witnesses. The examining magistrate has a wide discretion to exclude defence lawyers, which extends to the examination of witnesses who will not appear in court.

[15] Lensing, H. and Rayar, L., 'Notes on Criminal Procedure in the Netherlands' [1992] *Criminal Law Review* 623, 629.

[16] Both the prosecutor and the defence counsel may request a reopening of the inquiry and, if refused, may apply to the district court.   [17] Field *et al.*, n. 8 above, 242.

[18] Nijboer, J. F., 'The Law of Evidence in Criminal Cases (The Netherlands)' in (ed.) Nijboer, J. F., *Forensic Expertise and the Law of Evidence* (1992, Amsterdam: Elsevier) 63.

on the basis of out of court statements and written documents gathered at the pre-trial stage of the process. The defendant generally appears in court and is examined, principally by the trial judge and then by the prosecution and the defence. Witnesses may be called to testify orally in court but in most cases the court will simply rely on their written statements.[19] 'In short, the trial is not seen as the occasion for an independent judicial investigation, nor the occasion for the finding of the truth presented by conflicting witnesses. Rather it is the occasion at which it is demonstrated that the truth has been found elsewhere by prosecuting officials.'[20] The evaluative nature of the trial means that proceedings tend to be of a much shorter duration than criminal trials in England and Wales.[21] For example, according to Fionda a typical rape case lasts one hour in the Netherlands.[22] A neat description of the course of the trial is provided by Osner *et al.*:

The trial procedure is conducted by the presiding judge who first asks the defendant his name, address, etc. The prosecutor then reads the indictment or a summary of it. Then there is the 'investigation into the facts'. The court inquires primarily on the basis of the written evidence included in the dossier. The witnesses, if any, and then the accused are then questioned by the presiding judge. The Public Prosecutor and the defence lawyer are allowed to ask supplementary questions. However, there is no system of cross-examination and re-examination to test the veracity of witnesses. The written evidence is read aloud. After the investigation into the facts, the prosecutor and the defence make closing speeches. The defence always has the last word. The court then gives its verdict.[23]

With a few exceptions, proceedings are held in public.[24] Significantly, Dutch criminal courts are required to explain their reasoning in reaching verdicts in written decisions (*vonnis*) and to articulate precise reasons for the acceptance of evidence contained in the dossier.[25]

As Osner *et al.*'s description implies, it is the judge who dominates trial proceedings, assuming an active inquiring role. Whereas the English trial judge relies largely upon evidence presented by the parties, the trial judge in the Netherlands is not expected to sit and await proof but to move on his or her own

[19] The public prosecutor is charged with summoning witnesses. The trial judge also has the power to summon witnesses to court. A witness called to court must take an oath or pledge to speak the truth: Hulsman L. H. C. and Nijboer, J. F., 'Criminal Justice System' in (eds.) Chorus, J. M. J., Fokkema, D. C., Hondius, H. and Lisser, E., *An Introduction to Dutch Law for Foreign Lawyers* (1993, Kluwer: Law Tax Publications) 348.
[20] Rossett, A., 'Trial and Discretion in Dutch Criminal Justice' (1972) 19 *UCLA Law Review* 353, 376. According to Vogler, the trial is 'merely the final procedural act of a lengthy and continuous judicial investigation conducted largely in private': see n. 3 above, 28.
[21] In one study it was estimated that Dutch trials typically last one-tenth as long as English trials: Fionda, J., *Public Prosecutors and Discretion: A Comparative Study* (1995, Oxford: Clarendon Press) 96.
[22] Ibid.
[23] Osner, N., Quinn, A. and Crown, G., *Criminal Justice Systems in Other Jurisdictions* (1993, London: HMSO) 152. See also Tak, P., *Criminal Justice Systems in Europe: The Netherlands* (1993, Kluwer: HEUNI).
[24] 273 CCP.
[25] Nijboer, n. 18 above, 64.

initiative with the help of the prosecution and defence.[26] For example, the trial judge is the primary interrogator of the accused and any witnesses called to trial. [27] The advocates play a subsidiary role, asking questions only after the trial judge has completed his or her examination. As well as directing the investigation at trial the judge also decides the guilt or innocence of the accused. The Dutch criminal justice system has no trial by jury.[28] According to Njiboer, there has been very little discussion or debate about whether the very active role of the judge in Dutch proceedings violates the standards of impartiality implicit in the notion of a fair trial.[29] This stands in sharp contrast to the position in adversarial proceedings where judicial intervention in the examination of witnesses is widely regarded as a threat to impartiality.[30]

2. Rules of Evidence

The reliance placed in Dutch criminal proceedings on written out of court statements is attributable to a ruling of the Supreme Court (*Hoge Raad*) in 1926.[31] The current Code of Criminal Procedure (*Wetboek van Strafvordering*) which was introduced in the same year envisaged a procedure with an emphasis upon oral evidence and direct confrontation from which hearsay evidence would be largely excluded. The drafters of the Code imagined a trial process that would reflect key aspects of the adversarial model. In ruling hearsay evidence admissible regardless of whether a witness was available to be called, the Supreme Court ensured that the traditional emphasis on written evidence and the preliminary investigative stage of Dutch criminal proceedings remained in place. Dutch evidence law is therefore generally unconcerned with issues of admissibility. According to Nijboer, the Dutch evidence rules can be fairly summarized in eight principles:

(1) The rules of evidence in their strictness only apply to the decision whether or not it has been proved that the defendant committed the alleged crime. (2) Only five means of proof are authorized by the legislation to be used as legal proof, these include: observation by the court itself, confessions/statements made by the defendant, statements made by witnesses, statements made by experts, and written materials. (3) The court's verdict has to be based on information discussed during the trial. (4) The Code never compels the court to convict the defendant. (5) The Code sometimes compels the court not to acquit the defendant. (6) A statement by a witness, a single piece of written evidence, or the confession of the defendant on its own can never be full proof: corroborative

---

[26] Rossett, n. 20 above, 371.

[27] Commenting on the contrasting role of the trial judge in inquisitorial proceedings, Vogler states: 'In its essence, the inquisitorial method of fact-finding is based upon the almost unlimited power of the judge to obtain and evaluate evidence. Whereas, in an adversarial system, the evidence is called by the parties and the judge sits as neutral umpire, in inquisitorial process the roles are reversed. It is the judge who calls and examines the evidence and it is the lawyers who are there largely to ensure that the proceedings are fair': Vogler, n. 3 above, 28.

[28] The jury system was abolished in 1813.   [29] Nijboer, n. 25 above, 165.

[30] See Chapter V above.   [31] HR 20 December 1926, NJ 1927 85.

evidence is required. (7) The decision of the court must be argued extensively in written form. (8) Rules of general experience and generally known facts do not need any special proof. The fact that the court is obliged to give precise written reasons for its decision means that the Supreme Court may review the decision and ensure that it was based upon legally accepted means of proof.[32]

The rules of evidence are thus conceived not as rules regulating presentation but as a set of decision-making rules.[33] In contrast to the complex exclusionary rules that characterize adversarial proceedings, the Dutch law of evidence is essentially concerned with rules which prescribe what evidence may form the basis of a decision.

The approach to hearsay evidence and issues of admissibility generally no doubt owes much to the fact that professional judges replace juries in the Netherlands. Great faith is placed in the capacity of judges to weigh evidence and make critical evaluations of potentially prejudicial or unreliable information. A basic assumption of the Dutch trial process is that any weaknesses in evidence can be compensated for by judicial care in its assessment. It is further assumed that exclusionary presentational rules would unduly impede the court in its 'quest for the truth'. Within the adversarial tradition distrust regarding the capacity of jurors to attach the appropriate probative weight to potentially unreliable evidence has traditionally shored up the hearsay rule. The use of out of court statements can also be attributed to a fundamentally different attitude towards live oral testimony. The 'testing conditions' said to promote truthful and considered testimony in adversarial style proceedings are specifically afforded far less weight.[34] Relatively little importance has, for example, traditionally attached to a physical confrontation between defendant and witness within the Dutch criminal process.[35] The same can be said of the public scrutiny of witnesses at trial and the officality of the courtroom. Moreover, far less importance has conventionally attached to the opportunity afforded to the fact-finder to observe the demeanour of a witness. To a significant degree: '[t]he Dutch system relies on the skill and competence of the professional judge to decide on the basis of cold files'.[36] Accordingly, hearsay witness statements attract far less suspicion from the outset.

---

[32] Nijboer, J. F., 'Protection of Victims in Rape and Sexual Abuse Cases in the Netherlands' in (ed.) Nijboer, J. F., *Proof and Criminal Justice Systems Comparative Essays* (1995, Frankfurt: Peter Lang) 99. See also Nijboer, J. F., 'The Requirement of a Fair Process and the Law of Evidence in Dutch Criminal Proceedings' in (ed.) Nijboer, J. F., n. 25 above.

[33] See Nijboer, J. F., 'Common Law Tradition in Evidence Scholarship Observed from a Continental Perspective' (1993) 41 *American Journal of Comparative Law* 299.

[34] See discussion in Chapter II above.

[35] Swart, B. and Young, J., 'The European Convention on Human Rights and Criminal Justice in the Netherlands and the United Kingdom' in (eds.) Harding *et al.*, n. 4 above, 71.

[36] Beijer, A., Cobley, C. and Klip, A., 'Witness Evidence, Article 6 of the European Convention on Human Rights and the Principle of Open Justice' in (eds.) Harding *et al.*, n. 4 above, 299.

3. Implications for Rape Complainants

Dutch trial practice holds a number of advantages for rape complainants.[37] These stem directly from the inquisitorial nature of criminal proceedings and specifically from the general tolerance of hearsay evidence.[38] The principal advantage of the Dutch system for complainants is that they are rarely required to testify at trial. Instead they give evidence at a pre-trial hearing before an examining magistrate. Such hearings take place in the relatively informal environment of the office of the examining magistrate and in private. The complainant answers questions while seated at an ordinary desk, rather than from the isolation of the witness box. The only persons present are the examining magistrate, the defence lawyer, and, at the examining magistrate's discretion, a support person (*hulpverlener*) to lend the complainant 'moral support'.[39] Complainants in the Netherlands are thus spared the acute embarrassment of giving evidence in public and the ordeal of facing the accused directly. A face-to-face confrontation between complainant and accused may be arranged at the discretion of the examining magistrate. There are no figures available on the frequency with which such confrontations are staged. Dutch practitioners interviewed by this author were asked whether they understood this to be common practice. All agreed that confrontation was generally avoided as it caused complainants considerable distress and resulted in no discernible gain for defendants as their legal representatives would be present and would relay any information. Significantly, the practitioners perceived no intrinsic value in a face-to-face encounter. It was generally felt that the interests of the complainant could be respected without unfairness to the accused. In adversarial systems the sentiment attached to a physical encounter between accused and accuser has traditionally proved an effective obstacle to the acceptance of alternative methods such as screens and television links, even in cases involving young children.

While pre-trial hearings are generally held in rape cases it is open to the defence to request that a complainant appear in court.[40] The public prosecutor may refuse such a request where it can be reasonably assumed that the defendant will not be hampered in his defence by so ruling.[41] The defendant may appeal to the court to overrule the decision of the public prosecutor. The court will summon the witness unless it finds that the non-appearance of the witness cannot reasonably damage the defence of the accused.[42] Nijboer maintains that the courts are typically reluctant to compel rape complainants to testify at

---

[37] For an examination of the comparative treatment of victims in American and German courtrooms see Pizzi, W., 'Crime victims in German courtrooms: A comparative perspective on American problems' (1996) 32 *Stanford Journal of International Law* 37.

[38] See Ellison, L., 'The Protection of Vulnerable Witnesses in Court: An Anglo-Dutch Comparison' (1999) 3(1) *International Journal of Evidence and Proof* 29.

[39] In relation to sexual offence complainants this is laid down in the 1999 Directive on the Treatment of Victims of Sexual Offences, available at http://www.victimology.nl/.   [40] 263 CCP.

[41] 280(4) CCP.   [42] 280(4) CCP.

trial.[43] This was confirmed by the Dutch practitioners I interviewed, who reported that as a general rule rape complainants were kept out of the court-room. It was explained that where the defence had had an opportunity to examine a complainant at a pre-trial hearing there must be special reasons for a rape complainant to be called as a witness at the trial. According to the practition-ers, the distress caused to complainants by a court appearance was an influen-tial factor in any decision made by the court. The practitioners also expressed the view that the interests of defendants were in no way prejudiced where such requests were denied. The defence have an opportunity to put questions to a complainant at the pre-trial hearing and therefore had little to gain, it was felt, from questioning the complainant a second time in court.

Where rape complainants are required to give evidence in court they may do so via a live television link, thus avoiding direct confrontation with the accused.[44] Alternatively, if a personal confrontation between the defendant and the witness is thought to be 'too painful', the examination of the complainant can take place in the absence of the defendant.[45] To safeguard the interests of the accused, his or her lawyer is present throughout and is allowed to question the witness and contradict information provided. If the defendant is excluded in order to avoid confrontation he or she is allowed back into the court-room and instructed immediately after the examination of the witness and is then able to contest any statement made. Alternatively, an excluded defendant may follow events through a live television link and suggest additional questions contem-poraneously.[46] In serious cases the court may prevent an accused from person-ally questioning a witness and may generally disallow certain questions put by defence counsel.[47] According to Brienen and Hoegen, the courts intervene read-ily to protect witnesses, but in general, defence counsel do not ask questions that are harmful or degrading. The courts do not particularly appreciate such defence strategies, they claim, and therefore such questions are not in the inter-est of their client.[48] According to Damaska, this is typical of Continental pro-cedural systems: 'Anglo-American observers of the court scene are regularly struck by the rarity and the subdued nature of the challenges to the witnesses' credibility. If such a challenge occurs, it mainly focuses on the witness's reliabil-ity with respect to the facts to which he has been disposed and seldom escalates into a general attack on his character or reputation for truthfulness.'[49]

---

[43] Nijboer, n. 32 above, 105.

[44] The trial judge also has the power to order an accused to leave the court-room while a witness is giving evidence: 292 CCP.　　　　　　　　　　　　　　　　[45] Nijboer, n. 32 above, 43

[46] Nijboer n. 32 above, 103.　　　　[47] 288 CCP.

[48] Brienen, M. and Hoegen, E., *Victims of crime in 22 European criminal justice systems: the implementation of Recommendation (85) 11 of the Council of Europe on the position of the victim in the framework of criminal law and procedure* (2000, Nijmegen: Wolf Legal Productions) 701.

[49] Damaska, M., *Evidence Law Adrift* (1997, New Haven; London: Yale University Press) 80. But see Pizzi's account of the robust interrogation of witnesses in German criminal trials: n. 37 above, 37.

Furthermore, as an exception to the principle of publicity the court may hold proceedings in camera if this is deemed to be in the interests of fair proceedings or to protect the privacy of the defendant, minors, or any other participant in the process.[50] Any party involved in the trial proceedings may request that the court hold the trial wholly or partly behind closed doors.

A further possible advantage of Dutch practice for rape complainants centres on the relative freedom witnesses enjoy when testifying. In adversarial-style proceedings witnesses give evidence responsively to advocates' questions, first in examination in chief and then in cross-examination. The nature of examination in chief is greatly influenced by considerations concerning the persuasiveness of court-room stories. In taking a witness step by step through his or her evidence the prosecution will, for example, seek to elicit a version of .events which 'fits' with the prosecution case, thus maximizing overall narrative consistency and thus, it is thought, believability. Through the use of various discursive devices the witness's testimony is actively shaped to meet the strategic concerns associated with oppositional presentation of evidence. Witness testimony is of course additionally constrained within adversarial criminal proceedings by a complex body of exclusionary evidentiary rules. The resultant manipulation of a witness's evidence can prove extremely frustrating and confusing for witnesses who arrive at court expecting to tell *their* stories.

In contrast, in the Netherlands the examining magistrate will at a preliminary hearing invite a complainant to testify in narrative form. As a 'neutral' inquisitor, the examining magistrate's principal concern is the completeness of the dossier; he or she is accordingly concerned with neither issues of admissibility nor the effectiveness or otherwise of the complainant's oral performance. To confine witnesses through the use of controlled questioning and pre-emptive interruption is arguably inconsistent with the examining magistrate's duty to conduct a thorough investigation.[51] More importantly, the structural and evidential barriers which preclude free testimonial narration within the adversarial process are largely absent from the Dutch system. Nonetheless, it should not be imagined that all Dutch complainants are granted complete narrative freedom at pre-trial hearings.[52] According to the Dutch practitioners interviewed by this author, some complainants are invited to give their version of events from beginning to end in their own words; however, others are simply asked to verify their police statements and to elaborate on selective points. Practice, it was maintained, varied significantly between examining magistrates.

---

[50] 121 CCP.

[51] 'Whereas the modern inquisitorial model combines questioning by the judge with relative freedom for witnesses to tell their stories in open-ended narrative style, the adversary model requires tight control of questioning so that claims are generally expressed as answers to very specific questions': Danet, B., 'Language in the Legal Process' (1980) 14 *Law and Society Review* 514.

[52] See Stuart, H. V., 'Towards a Civilised Law Against Sexual Violence'(1990, unpublished paper); Van Driem, G., 'Waarom Slachtoffers van Seksueel Geweld het Strafproces Moeten Mijden' in (ed.) Soetenhorst de Savorin Lohman, J., *Slachtoffers van misdrijven ontwikkelingen in hulperverlening recht en beleid* (1989, Arnhem: Gouda Quint).

4. The Nature of Questioning

In terms of the questioning of rape complainants in the Netherlands the picture that emerges is one which will be more familiar to common law observers. As stated, rape complainants are, as a general rule, examined at a pre-trial hearing by an examining magistrate and by a defence lawyer. The treatment of complainants at such hearings has been the subject of sustained criticism in the Netherlands. Defence lawyers stand specifically accused of engaging in improper questioning, and examining magistrates have been criticized for their allegedly inadequate protection of complainants.[53] In many ways, concerns expressed parallel those raised by researchers in England and Wales and other common law jurisdictions, though interviews with Dutch practitioners did point to some intriguing contrasts. Unsurprisingly perhaps, the examining magistrates interviewed by this author were less critical than the lawyers who had represented women in rape cases.

The Dutch lawyers interviewed were keen to voice their objections to what they described as the secondary victimization of rape complainants in criminal proceedings. Defence lawyers were accused of asking irrelevant, offensive questions and of invoking outmoded stereotypes as well as engaging in what was termed 'victim blaming'. This supports claims made by Van Driem, for example, that questioning often focuses on the 'culpability' of the complainant and the propriety of *her* behaviour before, during, and after an alleged assault.[54] Defendants, Van Driem contends, are typically portrayed as the 'true' victims of rape, as responsibility is effectively shifted through defence questioning to complainants. In line with research findings in England and Wales and elsewhere, key common themes in defence questioning were identified. These included the complainant's clothing, evidence of physical resistance or the absence thereof, delays in reporting, motivations for lying, and the consumption of drugs or alcohol prior to the alleged rape.[55] Where complainant and accused had had a prior sexual relationship, the lawyers I interviewed maintained that questioning was often of an unduly intrusive nature. However, when questioned on the subject of the use of sexual history evidence and character evidence more generally in rape cases, the lawyers stated that the position had improved in recent years. The complainant's previous sexual experience with men other than the accused was, they claimed, less central to the conduct of rape cases than had been the case a decade previously. The same was true of evidence relating to a complainant's lifestyle.

---

[53] Van Driem, n. 52 above.

[54] Ibid. See also Doomen, J., *Heb Je Soms Aanleiding Gegeven, Handeleiding voor Slachtoffers van Verkrachting bij de Confrontie met Politie en Justitie* (1978, Amsterdam: Feministische Uitgeverij Sara).

[55] See Leuw, E., 'De Behandlung van Verkrachtinszaken voor de Rechtbank' (1985) *Tijdschrift voor Criminologie* 212.

When asked about the role of the examining magistrate, the lawyers all claimed to have attended hearings where examining magistrates had failed to protect complainants from what they regarded as irrelevant and inappropriate questioning. Generally, it was felt that practice varied significantly between individual practitioners. It was suggested that defence lawyers should be required to submit any questions prior to a hearing to enable examining magistrates to rule on acceptability. Under current arrangements examining magistrates could only inform complainants that they were not obliged to answer 'improper' questions and this, they argued, constituted inadequate protection.[56] The need for legal representation for all rape complainants was also strongly advanced. Moreover, it was argued that 'victim advocates' should have a legal right to attend the pre-trial hearing[57] and the right to intervene during defence questioning.[58]

There are no rules within the Dutch process specifically governing the examination of rape complainants.[59] The only limits on defence questioning at preliminary hearings are those imposed by examining magistrates. The examining magistrates I interviewed all accepted that they had a positive duty to protect vulnerable complainants from improper questioning and claimed to intervene actively to restrain defence lawyers who went 'too far' or were 'too offensive'. There may be no 'legal rules', one practitioner explained, but there were 'ethical rules' and these were enforced. The principal consideration was, it was stated, the relevance of the question asked. As such it was conceded that different examining magistrates would have differing views as to what constituted improper questioning, so that the protection afforded to rape complainants could vary considerably. When asked whether further limitations upon defence questioning were required, all refuted the need for further shielding measures.

The examining magistrates were invited to comment on the use of sexual history evidence in rape cases and the extent to which the private lives of complainants came under scrutiny. In response the practitioners maintained that the sexual reputation or history of complainants no longer played a significant role in rape cases. Moreover, they were keen to emphasize that a complainant's character was a peripheral matter and that questioning would be directed to more central issues in the case. In assessing credibility, they claimed that more attention would be paid to any inconsistencies in a complainant's account than to her lifestyle and general character.

---

[56] Compulsory training for examining magistrates was also recommended, as well as training courses for lawyers to raise awareness of the effects of rape and to encourage the employment of greater sensitivity in the questioning of rape complainants.

[57] The attendance of victim advocates is a matter of discretion for the examining magistrate.

[58] Lawyers representing rape complainants act largely as support persons as they are not permitted to intervene actively in the process. The examining magistrates interviewed were generally hostile to the suggestion of an enhanced role for victims' lawyers.

[59] The lack of obstacles when presenting the complainant's prior sexual conduct must, Nijboer asserts, be considered against the background of a society that does not have a lot of trouble with 'liberal' sexual behaviour in general: see n. 32 above, 123.

The small number of interviews conducted of course precludes the drawing of any firm conclusions about the questioning of rape complainants within the Dutch criminal justice system. However, the reduced emphasis on character evidence claimed by the practitioners corresponds with certain aspects of the Dutch trial process. First, the nature of advocacy is likely to be different in a system that is much more an investigation than a contest and where 'neutral' inquisitors assume primary responsibility for witness examination. One would not expect the 'no holds barred' approach that distinguishes cross-examination. Moreover, the examining magistrate is in a better position than the English trial judge to assess the appropriateness of defence questions as he or she has full access to the dossier prior to the hearing. This may in itself deter overly intrusive examination. The replacement of the jury by career judges may also be considered relevant.

B. A BREAK WITH TRADITION?

The general tolerance of hearsay evidence in Dutch criminal proceedings has clear advantages for rape complainants and other vulnerable and intimidated witnesses. However, some years ago Dutch commentators were predicting a shift in practice towards trials with an accent on direct confrontation and the oral interrogation of witnesses.[60] The ruling of the European Court of Human Rights in *Kostovski v The Netherlands* sparked the debate. It will be recalled from Chapter IV above, that Kostovski's conviction was based to a decisive extent on the statements of two anonymous witnesses. The defence was denied the opportunity of examining either witness directly and questioning was restricted in scope in order to safeguard the witnesses' anonymity. The examining magistrate in the case was also not informed of the identity of the witness he examined. In these circumstances, the Court held that Kostovski had not received a fair trial.[61] This ruling, together with that of the European Commission in *Cardot v France*,[62] heralded, according to some commentators, 'the beginning of the end of the Dutch tradition of doing justice on the documents of the case, having heard the accused'.[63] Article 6, it was argued, embodied an 'adversarial bias' that had been overlooked by contracting states from civil law

---

[60] See, for example, Groenhuijsen, M. S., 'Artikel 6 EVRM en de dagelijkse rechtspraktijk Inleiding en perspectief', cited in Henket, M., 'European Human Rights and the Pragmatics of Criminal Adjudication: The Case of Cardot v France' (1992) 15 *International Journal for the Semiotics of Law* 249, 266.

[61] Following the *Kostovski* judgment ((1992) 14 EHRR 396) new provisions were introduced into the Dutch Code of Criminal Procedure regarding the protection of witnesses: Witness Protection Act 1994. This provided that an anonymous statement could only be used in evidence if it had been taken down by an investigating judge who knew the identity of the witness, who had expressed his opinion as regards the reasons for the witness's desire to remain anonymous and the witness's reliability, and who had provided the defence with ample opportunity to question the witness.

[62] *Cardot v France* (1990) Application 11069/84.

[63] Stolwijk, S. A. M., 'Wachten op Cardot' (1991) 21 *Delikt en Delinkwent* 109.

traditions, including the Netherlands.[64] The 'Anglo-Saxon character' of the Convention had become, it was noted, increasingly apparent as principles had developed into detailed rules.[65] At the time, Nijboer remarked: 'There is a fair chance that countries like France and the Netherlands will be "forced" by the European Court on Human Rights in Strasbourg to change the practice of the trial, especially as regards the role of direct examination of witnesses and other aspects of an open, "contradictoire", oral and public style.'[66]

The rulings did prompt the Dutch government to introduce additional procedural safeguards to protect the rights of defendants to challenge anonymous testimony.[67] Whether these arrangements are adequate remains open to debate.[68] Fortunately for rape complainants, some years later the shift in practice in Dutch trial procedure is said to have been slight. Beijer and Van Hoorn, for example, report that the influence of the Strasbourg Court on the case-law of the Dutch Supreme Court has not been so strong as to cause a break with existing trial traditions.[69]

C. CONCLUSION

Inspiration for procedural reform is frequently drawn from trial arrangements as practised in civil law jurisdictions. However, it is unrealistic to expect that procedural rules can be isolated and imported directly into domestic law. As Damaska notes, the impact and meaning of procedural regulation often turns on what he refers to as external conditions, most directly on the institutional context in which justice is administered in a particular country.[70] An imported

---

[64] Henket, n. 60 above, 264.

[65] 'These provisions are basically founded upon a kind of "adversarial" model, with an emphasis on the independent role of the parties': Nijboer, J. F., 'Common Law Tradition in Evidence Scholarship Observed from a Continental Perspective' (1993) 41 *American Journal of Comparative Law* 299, 311.   [66] Ibid. 304.

[67] Intimidated witnesses who fear for their personal safety and indicate that they are unwilling to testify at trial for this reason may still be granted complete anonymity. The case must involve a serious offence and the examining magistrate must be satisfied that the witness has been intimidated and will not testify without the guarantee of anonymity. Under the terms of the Witness Protection Act 1994, a request for anonymity may be made by the public prosecutor, the defence, or the witness himself and will be granted or refused by the examining magistrate who will be aware of the witness's identity. The views of the respective parties on the issue of anonymity will be sought prior to any determination. Importantly, the Code of Criminal Procedure stipulates that a defendant may not be convicted solely on the basis of an anonymous witness statement. Beijer, A. and Van Hoorn, A. M., 'Report on anonymous witnesses in the Netherlands' in (ed.) Hondius, E. M., *Report on the Fifteenth International Congress of Comparative Law* (1998, Antwerpen, Groningen: Intersentia Rechtswetenschappen) 523.

[68] See *Doorson v The Netherlands* (1996) 22 EHRR 330; *Van Mechelen v The Netherlands* (1997) 25 EHRR 547. Beijer and Van Hoorn report that the anonymity provisions are used sparingly as public prosecutors are reluctant to make requests unless the witness's evidence is crucial and the anonymity of the witness can be guaranteed: ibid. 536.   [69] Ibid. 525.

[70] Damaska, M., 'The uncertain fate of evidentiary transplants: Anglo-American and continental experiments' (1997) 45 *American Journal of Comparative Law* 839. See also Edwards, H. T.,

practice can, he warns, alter its character in interaction with the new environment and while some of the consequences can be a pleasant surprise, others can be very disappointing.

Those contemplating to combine common law and civil law approaches to fact-finding should be especially sensitive to the potential costs of normative shortcuts to procedural reform; institutional differences between the two Western families capable of affecting the fact-finding style are quite considerable.[71]

The Dutch system of fact-finding relies to a large extent on co-operation and relationships of trust between criminal justice personnel and, as stated above, upon the effectiveness of institutional incentives which have no parallel within the criminal process of England and Wales. The system is also based on very different political and epistemological assumptions and rooted in a distinct legal culture.[72] These realities would present formidable barriers to the successful emulation of civil law evidentiary arrangements should this be deemed desirable. This is not to say that valuable lessons cannot be learnt from the comparative study of non-adversarial systems of trial. Such analysis can provide a valuable new perspective and useful insights into old problems, such as the difficulties facing vulnerable and intimidated witnesses, which may assist in the crafting of indigenous solutions. It is submitted that the Home Office interdepartmental working group would have been specifically advised, in identifying measures to improve the position of vulnerable and intimidated witnesses, to examine more closely the experience of witnesses in the Netherlands and other 'inquisitorial' jurisdictions. Unfortunately limited comparative analysis appears to have taken place.

'Comments on Mirjan Damaska's of evidentiary transplants' (1997) 45 *American Journal of Comparative Law* 853.

[71] Damaska, n. 70 above.

[72] The extent to which legal cultures are converging, thereby reducing barriers to successful transplantation of 'alien' procedural elements, is a matter of debate. See Chase, O., 'Legal Process and National Culture' (1997) 5 *Cardozo Journal of International and Comparative Law* 1; Jackson, J., 'Playing the Culture Card in Resisting Cross-Jurisdictional Transplants' (1997) 5 *Cardozo Journal of International and Comparative Law* 51.

VIII.
Conclusions

When witnesses are unable to give the best evidence they are capable of giving, the only interests served are those of guilty defendants, whether the witnesses be for the prosecution or the defence. The Youth Justice and Criminal Evidence Act 1999 laudably aims to assist vulnerable and intimidated witnesses to give more complete, coherent, and accurate testimony in criminal proceedings and to strike a better balance between the various interests of those who enter the criminal process as defendants, complainants, and witnesses. The extent to which the measures introduced can be expected to achieve these dual objectives has been the focus of this book. What has emerged, *inter alia*, from preceding Chapters are the limitations of an accommodation approach to the problems facing vulnerable and intimidated witnesses. The measures which deviate least from the adversarial model and cling to conventional methods of fact-finding, albeit in modified form, have been shown to be the least effective both in terms of alleviating the stress associated with giving evidence and for securing access to the best evidence potentially available.

The establishment of the Home Office working group represented a valuable opportunity to re-examine traditional features of the adversarial criminal trial and to re-assess the validity of some of its key assumptions in the light of the experiences of vulnerable and intimidated witnesses. Lamentably, the nettle was not grasped. The basic constraints of the established trial framework were accepted by the working group from the outset. While recognizing, for example, that many of the difficulties faced by vulnerable witnesses stem from an insistence upon direct oral evidence, the working group did not seriously question the English courts' commitment to orality in criminal proceedings. Instead the working group proposed a range of measures some of which shored up an attachment to live oral evidence.[1] In advocating the wider use of screens and television links the working group was apparently persuaded that the best evidence a witness was capable of giving could be captured in *vive voce* testimony. The weight of research reviewed in this book suggests that this holds true for a minority of vulnerable and intimidated witnesses. For the majority, trial delay and accumulated stress are likely to diminish the accuracy and efficiency of recall and impair the proficiency with which past events are communicated even where live links and courtroom-modifying measures are deployed. Moreover, psychological research has cast doubt on the validity of basic assumptions of

---

[1] Home Office, *Speaking Up For Justice: Report of the Interdepartmental Working Group on the Treatment of Vulnerable or Intimidated Witnesses in the Criminal Justice System* (1998, London: Home Office).

adversarial theory regarding the optimal testing of informational sources. The faith placed specifically in public scrutiny, face-to-face confrontation, and the court-room environment as deterrents to false testimony lacks empirical validation. The available evidence indicates that these 'evidentiary safeguards' in fact impair the ability of truthful witnesses who might otherwise perform well in the role to provide the court with a full and reliable account. This is supported by the documented accounts of witnesses themselves who describe the difficulty of relaying events in the physical presence of the accused and an audience of strangers many months after they occurred. At the same time, witnesses are put through what many describe as a harrowing ordeal on the strength of orthodox legal assumptions that are at best untested.

Video-taping witnesses' entire testimony in advance of trial emerges as the measure most likely to provide courts with the best evidence and to meet the needs of vulnerable and intimidated witnesses. The compromise scheme that has been in operation was rightly met with disappointment when initially announced a decade ago. The primary perceived weakness of the scheme centred on the proviso that cross-examination be conducted live. This meant that child witnesses in cases of sexual and physical abuse were still required to endure lengthy pre-trial delays and the stress of attending court, and were also plunged directly into hostile cross-examination. The separation of examination in chief and cross-examination has subsequently been shown to have negative implications for both the welfare of child witnesses and the quality of evidence to which the court is confined. One might therefore have expected the working group to reject the half-Pigot model outright and to recommend that a video-taped pre-trial interview be considered the natural precursor of video-taped pre-trial cross-examination and re-examination. The working group did go so far as to recommend the introduction of pre-trial cross-examination but stated that it should be available for use in appropriate cases where the witness has had their statement recorded on video and could particularly benefit from cross-examination outside the court-room. This presupposes that some witnesses would benefit from the video-taping of a pre-trial interview but would not necessarily benefit in equal measure from pre-trial cross-examination. The available evidence does not support this view. Unfortunately, under the terms of the YJCEA vulnerable adult witnesses are likely to find themselves in the same unhappy position as originally endured by child complainants of physical and sexual abuse. All the indications so far are that pre-trial cross-examination will remain very much the exception rather than the rule, and that the oral nature of criminal trials will be preserved.

More recent research has raised additional concerns regarding the evidential use of video-recorded evidence under the adopted statutory regime. The Criminal Justice Act 1991 introduced a novel form of evidence into the criminal process, very different in character to trial testimony. Despite these differences, the assumption was made that the former could be an effective substitute for the latter to the extent that supplementary questioning would be required only in limited circumstances. Studies have since called into question the transposability of these two types of evidence. Research suggests that video-recorded evidence of memorandum interviews can compare unfavourably with testimony extracted by counsel in key respects. During examination in chief the trial advocate is guided by strategic concerns and strives to elicit a structurally coherent narrative that 'fits' with the overall theory of the case. Having prior knowledge of the basic facts, counsel can guard against both damaging omission and detrimental elaboration. The techniques of advocacy are employed to ensure that favourable evidence is given due prominence and less favourable evidence is minimized, or at least presented in the best possible light. In crafting a credible narrative, sequence, intonation, pace, interruption, repetition, and juxtaposition are all used to effect. Police officers conducting memorandum interviews are generally unable to exercise the same degree of presentational control over pretrial disclosures given the investigative nature of such interviews and inevitably find it more difficult to negotiate the boundaries of acceptable questioning techniques. As a result, studies suggest that memorandum interviews can produce incomplete, inadmissible, and sometimes incoherent accounts that place greater demands on the concentration of jurors. This raises major questions which one would have expected the working group to address. Unfortunately, the working group reported before a major study on the admissibility and sufficiency of evidence in child abuse prosecutions highlighting key areas of difficulty was published.[2] Without the benefit of its findings the working group elected to recommend an extension of the established statutory scheme, with apparently little consideration of alternative procedural models for the advance video recording of witness testimony. It is particularly disappointing that they did not canvass the possible merits of staging a preliminary hearing along the lines of that originally proposed by the Pigot Committee, as is the practice, for example, in Western Australia and in various guises in a number of non-adversarial jurisdictions.

The limitations of an accommodation approach to the problems facing vulnerable and intimidated witnesses are most apparent when applied to cross-examination. Widely regarded as the aspect of trial proceedings that witnesses find most difficult, even traumatic, cross-examination is also capable, as explained in Chapter V above, of compromising the evidential integrity of testimony and distorting the fact-finding process. The broad response of the working group was to urge trial judges to adopt a more interventionist stance to prevent unnecessarily aggressive and inappropriate questioning. Alongside a recommendation that the Lord Chief Justice be invited to issue a Practice Direction in similar terms, the working group also proposed new restrictions on the use of sexual history evidence and extended prohibitions on cross-examination

---

[2] Davis, G., Hoyano, L., Keenan, C., Maitland, L. and Morgan, R., *An Assessment of the Admissibility and Sufficiency of Evidence in Child Abuse Prosecutions* (1999, London: Home Office).

in person and the use of intermediaries. These 'remedies' adhere to an accommodation approach in that they presuppose a continued commitment to the principle of party control over evidence testing. The narrow translator function ascribed to intermediaries means that this holds true for this special measure notwithstanding the degree of presentational control that cross-examiners must inevitably relinquish when questions and responses are explained.

The working group essentially failed to look beyond standard witness- and offence-specific explanations for the treatment of vulnerable witnesses during cross-examination. Above all, it failed to place cross-examination within the wider context of an adversarial process in which advocates are committed to a concept of trial advocacy that eschews responsibility for third parties and trial judges are forced to tread a judicial tightrope whenever they intervene to prevent improper questioning. When the systemic factors shaping cross-examination are given due recognition, the inadequacy of official responses so far is apparent. Many of the tactics and devices used by lawyers to embarrass, confuse, intimidate, and thereby discredit witnesses simply fall outside the scope of the YJCEA. The neglected question which ultimately needs to be tackled is whether cross-examination is an appropriate mechanism for testing the veracity of vulnerable witnesses. So unreserved is the commitment to cross-examination that no serious consideration has so far been given to the possibility of alternative methods of evidence testing. Until such a re-examination takes place there can be no meaningful integration of a witness perspective within the criminal process.

Overall, the paradigmatic adversarial trial offers limited scope for the improved treatment of vulnerable and intimidated witnesses. An accommodation approach must be eschewed in favour of a fundamental re-assessment of key features of the adversarial trial process. The ultimate test of the government's declared commitment to meeting the needs and interests of victims of crime and of witnesses more generally will be a preparedness to move beyond the straitjacket of established trial procedure in the search for solutions. In the wake of The YJCEA such a radical overhaul remains an indeterminate prospect.

Bibliography

Adler, Z., *Rape on Trial* (1987, London: Routledge and Kegan Paul)
—— 'The Relevance of Sexual History Evidence in Rape: Problems of Subjective Interpretation' [1985] *Criminal Law Review* 769
—— 'Rape: The Intention of Parliament and the Practice of the Courts' (1982) *Modern Law Review* 664
Ainsworth, P., *Psychology, Law and Eyewitness Testimony* (1998, Chichester: Wiley)
Allan, J., 'The Working and Rationale of the Hearsay Rule and the Implications of Modern Psychological Knowledge' (1991) 44 *Current Legal Problems* 217
Alschuler, A., 'How to win the trial of the century: The ethics of Lord Brougham and the O. J. Simpson defense team' (1998) 29 *McGeorge Law Review* 291
Aolain, F. N., 'Radical Rules: The Effects of Evidential and Procedural Rules on the Regulation of Sexual Violence in War' (1997) 60 *Albany Law Review* 892
Archbold, *Pleadings, Evidence and Practice in Criminal Cases* (1997, London: Sweet and Maxwell)
Ash, M., 'On Witnesses: A Radical Critique of Criminal Court Procedures' (1972) 48 *Notre Dame Lawyer* 159
Ashworth, A., 'Victims' Rights, Defendants' Rights and Criminal Procedure' in (eds.) Crawford, A. and Goodey, J., *Integrating a Victim Perspective within Criminal Justice* (2000, Hants: Ashgate) 185
—— '(2) Article 6 and the fairness of trials' [1999] *Criminal Law Review* 261
—— and Pattenden, R., 'Reliability, Hearsay Evidence and the English Criminal Trial' (1986) 102 *Law Quarterly Review* 292
Association of Chief Officers of Probation, *Probation Services and the Victims of Crime* (1997, London: Association of Chief Officers of Probation)
Atkinson, J. and Drew, P., *Order in Court* (1979, London: Macmillan)
Australian Law Reform Commission, *Report 84, Seen and heard: Priority for children in the legal process* (1997, Sydney: Australian Law Reform Commission)
Baird, V., *Rape in Court* (1999, London: Society of Labour Lawyers)
Bandalli, S., 'Abolition of the Presumption of Doli Incapax and the Criminalisation of Children' (1998) 37(2) *Howard Journal* 114
Barrett, E., 'The Adversary System and the Ethics of Advocacy' (1962) 37 *Notre Dame Lawyer* 481
Bates, P., 'The Youth Justice and Criminal Evidence Act: The evidence of children and vulnerable adults' (1999) 11(3) *Child and Family Law Quarterly*, 289
Batterman-Faunce, J. M. and Goodman, G., 'Effects of context on the accuracy and suggestibility of child witnesses' in (eds.) Goodman, G. and Bottoms, B., *Child Victims, Child Witnesses* (1993, New York: Guilford Press) 322
Beckett, J., 'The true value of the confrontation clause: A study of child sexual abuse trials' (1994) 82 *Georgetown Law Journal* 1605
Beerling, H. W. R., 'An Outline of Dutch Criminal Procedure' (1976) 5 *Anglo American Law Review* 50
Beijer, A. and Van Hoorn, A. M., 'Report on anonymous witnesses in the Netherlands' in (ed.) Hondius, E. M., *Report on the Fifteenth International Congress of Comparative Law* (1998, Antwerp, Groningen: Intersentia Rechtswetenschappen)

Beijer, A., Cobley, C. and Klip, A., 'Witness Evidence: Article 6 of the European Convention on Human Rights and the Principle of Open Justice' in (eds.) Harding, C., Fennell, P., Jörg, N. and Swart, B., *Criminal Justice in Europe: A Comparative Study*, (1995, Oxford: Clarendon Press) 299

Bennett, W. L. and Feldman, M., *Reconstructing Reality in the Courtroom* (1981, New Brunswick: Rutgers University Press)

Berger, V., 'Man's Trial, Women's Tribulation: Rape Cases in the Courtroom' [1977] 1 *Columbia Law Review* 11

Birch, D., 'A Better Deal for Vulnerable Witnesses?' [2000] *Criminal Law Review* 231

―― 'Children's Evidence' [1992] *Criminal Law Review* 262

―― and Leng, R., *Blackstone's Guide to the Youth Justice and Criminal Evidence Act 1999* (2000, London: Blackstone Press) 29

Blake, M. and Ashworth, A., 'Some Ethical Issues in Prosecuting and Defending Criminal Cases' [1998] *Criminal Law Review* 16

Blumenthal, J., 'A wipe of the hands, a lick of the lips: The validity of demeanour evidence in assessing witness credibility' (1993) 72 *Nebraska Law Review* 1157

Bottoms, B. and Goodman, G., (eds.) *International Perspectives on Child Abuse and Children's Testimony: Psychological Research and the Law* (1996, California: Sage)

Brants, C. and Field, S., 'Discretion and Accountability in Prosecution: A Comparative Perspective on Keeping Crime out of Court' in (eds.) Harding, C., Fennell, P., Jörg, N. and Swart, B., *Criminal Justice in Europe: A Comparative Study* (1995, Oxford: Clarendon Press)

Brennan, M., 'The discourse of denial: Cross-examining child victim witnesses' (1995) 23 *Journal of Pragmatics* 71

―― 'The Battle for Credibility: Themes in the Cross-examination of Child Victim Witnesses' (1994) 7(19) *International Journal for the Semiotics of Law* 51

―― and Brennan, R. E., *Strange Language: Child Victims under Cross-examination* (1988, Wagga Wagga, NSW: Riverina Murray Institute of Higher Education)

Brereton, D., 'How Different are Rape Trials? A Comparison of the Cross-examination of Complainants in Rape and Assault Trials' (1997) 37 *British Journal of Criminology* 242

Brienen, M. and Hoegen, E., *Victims of crime in 22 European criminal justice systems: The implementation of Recommendation (85) 11 of the Council of Europe on the position of the victim in the framework of criminal law and procedure* (2000, Nijmegen: Wolf Legal Productions)

Bronitt, S., 'The rules of recent complaint: Rape myths and the legal construction of the "reasonable" rape victim' in (ed.) Easteal, P., *Balancing the Scales: Rape, Law Reform and Australian Culture* (1998, Sydney: Federation Press) 41

―― and McSherry, B., 'The Use and Abuse of Counseling Records in Sexual Assault Trials: Reconstructing the "Rape Shield"?' (1997) 8(2) *Criminal Law Forum* 259

Brown, B., Burman, M. and Jamieson, L., *Sex Crimes on Trial: The Use of Sexual Evidence in Scottish Courts* (1993, Edinburgh: Edinburgh University Press)

Bull, R., 'Interviewing Children in Legal Contexts' in (eds.) Bull, R. and Carson, D., *Handbook of Psychology in Legal Contexts* (1995, Chichester: Wiley) 242

―― 'Interviewing People with Communicative Disabilities' in (eds.) Bull, R. and Carson, D., *Handbook of Psychology in Legal Contexts* (1995, Chichester: Wiley) 247

—— and Davies, G., 'The effect of child witness research on legislation in Great Britain' in (eds.) Bottoms, B. and Goodman, G., *International Perspectives on Child Abuse and Children's Testimony: Psychological Research and the Law* (1996, California: Sage) 96

Burgess, A. W. and Holmstrom, L., 'Rape trauma syndrome' (1974) 131 *American Journal of Psychiatry* 981

Cairns, D., *Advocacy and the Making of the Adversarial Criminal Trial 1800–1865* (1998, Oxford: Oxford University Press)

Carson, D., 'Regulating the examination of children' (1995) 4(1) *Expert Evidence* 2

Carter, C. A., Bottoms, B. L. and Levine, M., 'Linguistic and Socio-emotional Influences on the Accuracy of Children's Reports' (1996) 20(3) *Law and Human Behaviour* 350

Cashmore, J. and De Haas, N., *The Use of Closed Circuit Television for Child Witnesses in the ACT: A Report for the Australian Law Reform Committee and the Australian Capital Territorial Magistrates Court* (1992, Sydney: Australian Law Reform Commission)

Cavandino, P., 'Goodbye doli, must we leave you?' (1997) 9(2) *Child and Family Law Quarterly* 165

—— 'Children who kill: A European perspective' (1996) *New Law Journal* 1325

Chambers, G. and Millar, A., 'Proving Sexual Assault: Prosecuting the Offender or Persecuting the Victim?' in (eds.) Carlen, P. and Worral, A., *Gender, Crime and Justice* (1987, Milton Keynes: Open University Press)

Chandler, J. and Lait, D., 'An Analysis of the Treatment of Children as Witnesses in the Crown Court' in Victim Support, *Children in Court* (1996, London: Victim Support)

Chase, O., 'Legal Process and National Culture' (1997) 5 *Cardozo Journal of International and Comparative Law* 1

Cheney, D., Dickson, L., Fitzpatrick, J. and Uglow, S., *Criminal Justice and the Human Rights Act 1998* (1999, Bristol: Jordans)

Childline, *Going to court: Child witnesses in their own words* (1996, London: Childline)

Chinkin, C., 'Amicus Curiae Brief on Protective Measures for Victims and Witnesses' (1996) 7(1) *Criminal Law Forum* 179

Choo, A., *Hearsay and Confrontation in Criminal Trials* (1996, Oxford: Clarendon)

Chorus, J. M. J., Fokkema, D. C., Hondus, H. and Lisser, E., *An Introduction to Dutch Law for Foreign Lawyers* (1993, Kluwer: Law Tax Publications)

Christie, N., 'Conflicts as Property' (1977) 17 *British Journal of Criminology* 1

Clare, I. C. H. and Gudjonsson, G. H., 'Interrogative suggestibility, confabulation, and acquiescence in people with mild learning disabilities (mental handicap): Implications for reliability during police interrogations' (1993) 32 *British Journal of Clinical Psychology* 295

Costigan, R. and Thomas, P., 'Anonymous Witnesses' (2000) 51(2) *Northern Ireland Law Quarterly* 326

Criminal Law Revision Committee, *Eleventh Report Evidence* Cmnd. 4991 (1972, London: HMSO)

Crown Prosecution Service, *The Inspectorate's Report on Cases Involving Child Abuse* (1998, London: Crown Prosecution Service Inspectorate)

Damaska, M., 'The uncertain fate of evidentiary transplants: Anglo-American and continental experiments' (1997) 45 *American Journal of Comparative Law* 839

—— *Evidence Law Adrift* (1997, New Haven: Yale University Press)

—— 'Evidentiary Barriers to Conviction and Two Models of Criminal Procedure: A Comparative Study' (1973) 121 *University of Pennsylvania Law Review* 551

Danet, B., 'Language in the Legal Process' (1980) 14 *Law and Society Review* 514

—— and Bogoch, B., 'Fixed Fight or Free for All? An Empirical Study of Combativeness in the Adversary System of Justice' (1980) 7 *British Journal of Law and Society* 36

Davelaar van Tongeren, V., 'Verkrachting: Strafrechter, wat moet je ermee?' in (eds.) Davelaar van Tongeren, V. and Keijzeren, N., *Strafrecht in Perspectief* (1980, Arnhem: Gouda Quint)

Davies, E., Henderson, E. and Seymour, F. W., 'In the interests of justice? The cross-examination of child complainants of sexual abuse in criminal proceedings' (1997) 4(2) *Psychiatry, Psychology and the Law* 217

Davies, G. M. and Noon, E., *An Evaluation of the Live Link for Child Witnesses* (1991, London: Home Office)

Davies, G., 'The impact of television on the presentation and reception of children's testimony' (1999) 22 (3–4) *International Journal of Law and Psychiatry* 241

—— and Westcott, H., 'Videotechnology and the child witness' in (eds.) Dent, H. and Flin, R., *Children as Witnesses* (1992, Chichester: Wiley) 211

—— and Westcott, H., *Interviewing Child Witness under the Memorandum of Good Practice: A Research Review* Police Research Series Paper 115 (1999, London: Home Office)

—— Wilson, C., Mitchell, R. A. and Milsom, J., *Videotaping Children's Evidence: An Evaluation* (1995, London: Home Office)

Davies, L., 'The investigation of organised abuse: Considering alternatives' in (eds.) Westcott, H. and Jones, J., *Perspectives on the Memorandum, Policy, Practice and Research in Investigative Interviewing* (1997, Aldershot: Arena) 109

Davis, G., Hoyano, L., Keenan, C., Maitland, L. and Morgan, R., *An Assessment of the Admissibility and Sufficiency of Evidence in Child Abuse Prosecutions* (1999, London: Home Office)

Dennis, I., *The Law of Evidence* (1999, London: Sweet & Maxwell)

—— 'Criminal Procedure: The Advancement of International Standards' in (eds.) Nijboer, J. F. and Reijntjes, J. M., *Proceedings of the first World Conference on New Trends in Criminal Investigation and Evidence*, The Hague, 1–5 December 1995, World Conference on New Trends in Criminal Investigation and Evidence (1997, Netherlands: Koninklijke Vermande) 523

Dent, H., 'An experimental study of the effectiveness of different techniques of questioning mentally handicapped witnesses' (1986) 25 *British Journal of Clinical Psychology* 13

—— and Newton, S., 'The conflict between clinical and evidential interviewing in child sexual abuse' (1994) 1 *Psychology, Crime and Law* 181

—— and Flin, R., *Children as Witnesses* (1992, Chichester: Wiley)

Department for Women (NSW), *Heroines of Fortitude: The Experiences of Women in Court as Victims of Sexual Assault* (1996, Sydney: Department for Women)

DePaulo, B. M., Stone, J. I. and Lassiter, G. D., 'Deceiving and Detecting Deceit' in (ed.) Schlenker, B. R., *The Self and Social Life* (1985, New York: McGraw-Hill)

Devlin, P., *The Judge* (1979, Oxford: Oxford University Press)

Doak, J., 'Confrontation in the courtroom: Shielding vulnerable witnesses from the adversarial showdown' (2000) 5(3) *Journal of Civil Liberties* 296

Doan, L ., 'The Art of Trial Advocacy for Prosecutors' (1999) 33 *Prosecutor* 34

Doomen, J., *Heb Je Soms Aanleiding Gegeven, Handeleiding voor Slachtoffers van Verkrachting bij de Confrontie met Politie en Justitie* (1978, Amsterdam: Feministische Uitgeverij Sara).

Du Cann, R., *The Art of the Advocate* (1993, London: Penguin)

Dublin Rape Crisis Centre, *The Legal Process and Victims of Rape* (1998, Dublin: Dublin Rape Crisis Centre)

Durston, G., 'Cross-examination of rape complainants: Ongoing tensions between conflicting priorities in the criminal justice system' (1998) 62 *Journal of Criminal Law* 91

Eades, D., *Language in Evidence* (1995, Sydney: University of New South Wales Press)

Easton, S., 'The use of sexual history in rape trials' in (eds.) Childs, M. and Ellison, L., *Feminist Perspectives on Evidence* (2000, London: Cavendish) 167

Ebbinghaus, H., *Memory: A Contribution to Experimental Psychology* (1913, New York: Teachers College, Columbia University)

Edelman, R., 'Non Verbal Behaviour and Deception' in (eds.) Canter, D. and Alison, L., *Interviewing and Deception* (1999 Aldershot: Ashgate) 162

Edwards, H. T., 'Comments on Mirjan Damaska's of evidentiary transplants' (1997) 45 *American Journal of Comparative Law* 853

Edwards, S., *Female Sexuality and the Law* (1981, Oxford: Martin Robertson)

Egglestone, R., *Evidence, Proof and Probability* (1978, London: Weidenfeld and Nicolson)

—— 'What is Wrong with the Adversary System?' (1975) 49 *Australian Law Journal* 428

Ekman, P., *Telling Lies: Clues to Deception in the Marketplace, Marriage and Politics* (1986, New York: W.W. Norton)

—— and Friesen, W. V., 'Non-verbal Leakage and Clues to Deception' (1969) 32 *Psychiatry* 88

Elliott, D. W., 'Rape Complainants' Sexual Experience with Third Parties' [1984] *Criminal Law Review* 13

Elliott, R., 'Vulnerable and intimidated witnesses: A review of the literature' in Home Office, *Speaking Up For Justice* (1998, London: Home Office) 113

Ellison, L., 'The Protection of Vulnerable Witnesses in Court: An Anglo-Dutch Comparison' (1999) 3 *International Journal of Evidence and Proof* 29

—— 'Cross-examination in Rape Trials' [1998] *Criminal Law Review* 605

Ericson, K., Perlman, N. and Isaacs, B., 'Witness competency, communication issues and people with developmental disabilities' (1994) 22 *Developmental Disabilities Bulletin* 101

Estrich, S., *Real Rape* (1987, London: Harvard University Press)

European Forum for Victim Services, *Statement of Victims' Rights in the Process of Criminal Justice* (1996, London: European Forum)

Evans, K., *Golden Rules of Advocacy* (1993, London: Blackstone)

Fenwick, H., 'Procedural "Rights" of Victims of Crime: Public or Private Ordering of the Criminal Justice Process?' (1997) 60 *Modern Law Review* 317

—— 'Rights of Victims in the Criminal Justice System: Rhetoric or Reality?' [1995] *Criminal Law Review* 843

Field, H. S. and Bienen, L. B., *Jurors and Rape* (1980, Lexington, Mass.: Lexington Books)

Field, S., Alldridge, P. and Jörg, N., 'Prosecutors, Examining Judges and the Control of Police Investigations' in (eds.), Harding, C., Fennell, P., Jörg, N. and Swart, B., *Criminal Justice in Europe: A Comparative Study* (1995, Oxford: Clarendon Press)

Fife-Shaw, C., 'The influence of witness appearance and demeanour on witness credibility: A theoretical framework' (1995) 35(2) *Medicine, Science and Law* 107

Fionda, J., *Public Prosecutors and Discretion: A Comparative Study* (1995, Oxford:
Clarendon Press)

Fitzgerald, K., 'Problems of Prosecution and Adjudication of Rape and Other Sexual
Assaults under International Law' (1997) 8 *European Journal of International Law*
638

Flin, R., 'Hearing and Testing Children's Evidence' in (eds.) Goodman, G. and Bottoms,
B., *Child Witnesses, Child Victims* (1993, New York: Guilford Press) 279

—— H., Davies, G. and Tarrant, A., *The child witness: Final report to the Scottish
Home and Health Department* (1988, Aberdeen: Robert Gordon's Institute)

—— Bull, R., Boon, J. and Knox, A., 'Child Witnesses in Scottish Criminal Trials' (1993)
2 *International Review of Victimology* 319

Frank, J., *Courts on Trial: Myth and Reality in American Justice* (1963, Antheneum:
Massachusetts)

Frankel, M., 'The Search for Truth: An Umpireal View' (1975) 123 *University of
Pennsylvania Law Review* 1024

Freedman, M., *Lawyers' Ethics in an Adversary System* (1975, Indianapolis: Bobbs
Merrill)

Friedman, R., 'Thoughts from across the water on hearsay and confrontation' [1998]
Criminal Law Review 697

—— 'Confrontation Rights of Criminal Defendants' in (eds.) Nijboer, J. F. and Reijntjes,
J. M., *Proceedings of the First World Conference on New Trends in Criminal Investi-
gation and Evidence, The Hague, 1–5 December 1995* (1997, Netherlands: Koninklijke
Vermande) 534

Fyfe, N. and McKay, H., 'Desperately seeking safety: Witnesses' experiences of intimidation, protection and relocation' (2000) 40 *British Journal of Criminology* 675

Galvin, H., 'Shielding Rape Victims in the State and Federal Courts' (1986) 70 *Minnesota
Law Review* 763

General Council of the Bar of England and Wales, *Code of Conduct of the Bar of
England and Wales* (1991, London: Bar Council)

Glidewell, I., *The Review of the Crown Prosecution Service: A report* (1998, London:
HMSO)

Gooderson, R., 'Previous Consistent Statements' (1968) 26 *Cambridge Law Journal*
64

Goodman, G. and Bottoms, B., *Child Victims, Child Witnesses* (1993, London: Guilford
Publications)

—— Quas, J., Bulkley, J. and Shapiro, C., 'Innovations for child witnesses: A national
survey' (1999) 5 *Psychology, Public Policy and Law* 255

—— Tobet, A., Batterman-Faunce, J., Orcutt, H., Thomas, S., Shapiro, C. and
Sachsenmaier, T., 'Face to face confrontation: Effects of closed circuit technology on
children's eyewitness testimony and jurors' decisions' (1998) 22 *Law and Human
Behaviour* 165

—— Taub, E., Jones, D., England, P., Port, L., Rudy, L. and Prado, L., *Testifying in
Criminal Court: Emotional Effects on Child Sexual Assault Victims* (1992, Chicago:
University of Chicago Press)

Goodman, G. V. and Helgeson, 'Child Sexual Assault: Children's Memory and the Law'
(1985) 40 *Miami Law Review* 181

Goodpaster, G., 'On the Theory of American Adversary Criminal Trial' (1987) 78 *Journal of Criminal Law and Criminology* 120

Graham, M., 'Indicia of Reliability and Face to Face Confrontation: Emerging Issues in Child Sexual Abuse Prosecutions' (1985) 40 *University of Miami Law Review* 19

Greenstock, J. and Pipe, M., 'Interviewing children about past events: The influence of peer support and misleading questions' (1996) 20(1) *Child Abuse and Neglect* 69

Groenhuijsen, M, S., *Conflicts of Victims Interests and Offenders Rights in the Criminal Justice System: A European Perspective* (1994, paper presented at 8th International Symposium on Victimology, Adelaide, Australia, August)

—— 'Artikel 6 EVRM en de dagelijkse rechtspraktijk Inleiding en perspectief' cited in Henket, M., 'European Human Rights and the Pragmatics of Criminal Adjudication: The Case of Cardot v France' (1992) 15 *International Journal for the Semiotics of Law* 249

Gudjonsson, G., 'The vulnerabilities of mentally disordered witnesses' (1995) 35(2) *Medicine, Science and Law* 101

Gudjonsson, G. H., 'Testimony from persons with mental disorder' in (eds.) Heaton-Armstrong, A., Shepherd, E. and Wolchover, D., *Analysing Witness Testimony* (1999, London: Blackstone) 70

Gupta, A., 'Black Children and the Memorandum' in (eds.) Westcott, H. and Jones, J., *Perspectives on the Memorandum, Policy, Practice and Research in Investigative Interviewing* (1997, Aldershot: Arena) 81

Haines, P., 'Restraining the overly zealous advocate: Time for judicial intervention' (1990) 65 *Indiana Law Journal* 445

Hamilton Thielmeyer, L., 'Beyond Maryland v Craig: Can and should adult rape victims be permitted to testify by closed circuit television?' (1992) 67 *Indiana Law Journal* 797

Harnon, E., 'Children's Evidence in the Israeli Criminal Justice System with Special Emphasis on Sexual Offences' in (eds.) Spencer, J. R., Nicholson, G., Flin, R. and Bull, R., *Children's Evidence in Legal Proceedings: An International Perspective* (1989) 81

—— 'Examination of Children in Sexual Offences: The Israeli Law and Practice' [1988] *Criminal Law Review* 269

Harris J. and Grace, S., *A question of evidence? Investigating and prosecuting rape in the 1990s* HORS 196 (1999, London: HMSO)

Heenan, M. and McKelvie, H., *Evaluation of the Crimes (Rape) Act 1991* (1997, Melbourne: Department of Justice)

Henket, M., 'European Human Rights and the Pragmatics of Criminal Adjudication: The Case of Cardot v France' (1992) 15 *International Journal for the Semiotics of Law* 249

HEUNI (Helsinki United Nations Institute) *Changing Victim Policy: The United Nations Declaration and Recent Developments in Europe* (1989, Helsinki: HEUNI)

Hill, P. and Hill, S., 'Videotaping children's testimony: an empirical view' (1987) 85 *Michigan Law Review* 809

Ho, L., 'A Theory of Hearsay' (1999) 19(3) *Oxford Journal of Legal Studies* 403

Holthuis, H., 'The Role of the Public Prosecutor in the Netherlands' in NACRO, *International Comparisons in Criminal Justice The London Seminars* (1993, London: NACRO) 17

Home Office, *A Review of the Victim's Charter* (2001, London: Home Office)

—— *Provision of Therapy for Child Witnesses Prior to a Criminal Trial: Practical Guidance* (2001 London: Home Office)

Home Office, *Achieving Best Evidence in Criminal Proceedings: Guidance for Vulnerable or Intimidated Witnesses, Including Children* (2000, London: Home Office)

—— *Promoting Public Confidence in the Criminal Justice System* (2000, London: Home Office)

—— *Victim and Witness Intimidation: Findings from the British Crime Survey* (2000, London: Home Office)

—— *Setting the Boundaries: Reforming the Law on Sex Offences* (2000, London: Home Office)

—— *Action For Justice: Implementing the Speaking Up for Justice Report* (1999, London: Home Office)

—— *Explanatory Notes to the Youth Justice and Criminal Evidence Act* (1999, London: Home Office)

—— *Speaking Up For Justice: Report of the Interdepartmental Working Group on the Treatment of Vulnerable or Intimidated Witnesses in the Criminal Justice System* (1998, London: Home Office)

—— *The Victim's Charter: A Statement of the Service Standards for Victims of Crime* (1996, London: Home Office)

—— *Royal Commission on Criminal Justice Report* (1993, London: HMSO)

—— *Memorandum of Good Practice on Video Recorded Interviews with Child Witnesses for Criminal Proceedings* (1992, London: Home Office)

—— *Courts Charter* (1992, London: Home Office)

—— *Victim's Charter: A Statement of the Rights of Victims of Crime* (1990, London: Home Office)

—— *Pigot Committee: Report of the Advisory Group on Video Evidence* (1989, London: Home Office)

Hoyano, L. C. H., 'Variations on a theme by Pigot: Special measures directions for child witnesses' [2000] *Criminal Law Review* 250

Hulsman L. H. C. and Nijboer, J. F., 'Criminal Justice System' in (eds.) Chorus, J. M. J., Fokkema, D. C., Hondus, H. and Lisser, E., *An Introduction to Dutch Law for Foreign Lawyers* (1993, Kluwer: Law Tax Publications) 348

Hyam, M., *Advocacy Skills* (1999, London: Blackstone)

Jackson, J., 'Playing the Culture Card in Resisting Cross-Jurisdictional Transplants' (1997) 5 *Cardozo Journal of International and Comparative Law* 51

—— 'Judicial Responsibility in Criminal Proceedings' (1996) 49(2) *Current Legal Problems* 59

—— and Doran, S., *Judge Without Jury: Diplock Trials in the Adversary System* (1995, Oxford: Clarendon Press)

Jackson, J. D., 'Law's Truth, Lay Truth and Lawyers' Truth: The Representation of Evidence in Adversary Trials' (1992) 3 *Law and Critique* 31

—— 'Two Methods of Proof in Criminal Procedure' (1988) 51 *Modern Law Review* 549

—— *Law, Fact and Narrative Coherence* (1988, Liverpool: Deborah Charles)

Jeffreys, S. and Radford, J., 'Contributory Negligence or Being a Woman? The Car Rapist Case' in (eds.) Scraton, P. and Gordon, P., *Causes for Concern* (1984, London: Penguin)

Jörg, N., Field, S. and Brants, C., 'Are Inquisitorial and Adversarial Systems Converging?' in (eds.) Harding, C., Fennel, P., Jörg, N. and Swart, B., *Criminal Justice in Europe: A Comparative Study* (1995, Oxford: Clarendon Press) 43

Joutsen, M., 'Research on Victims and Criminal Policy in Europe' in (ed.) Hood, R., *Crime and Criminal Policy in Europe: Proceedings of a European Colloquium* (1989, Oxford: Centre for Criminological Research, University of Oxford) 50

—— Shapland, J., 'Changing Victim Policy: The United Nations Victim Declaration and Recent Developments in Europe' in HEUNI, *Changing Victim Policy: the United Nations Victim Declaration and Recent Developments in Europe* (1989, Helsinki: HEUNI)

Justice, *Victims in Criminal Justice, Report of the Committee on the Role of the Victim in Criminal Justice* (1998, London: Justice)

Kalven, H. and Zeisel, H., *The American Jury* (1966, Boston: Little, Brown)

Kebbell, M. and Johnson, D., 'Lawyers' Questioning: The Effects of Confusing Questions on Witness Confidence and Accuracy' (2000) 24(6) *Law and Human Behaviour* 629

—— and Hatton, C., 'People with retardation as witnesses in court: A review' (1999) 37(3) *Mental Retardation* 179

Keenan, C., Davis, G., Hoyano, L. and Maitland, L., 'Interviewing Alleged Abused Children with a View to Criminal Prosecution' [1999] *Criminal Law Review* 863

Kennedy, H., *Eve was Framed* (1992, London: Chatto & Windus)

Kerper, J., 'The Art and Ethics of Direct Examination' (1998) 22 *American Journal of Trial Advocacy* 377

Kibble, N., 'The sexual history provisions: Charting a course between inflexible legislative rules and wholly untrammelled judicial discretion?' [2000] *Criminal Law Review* 274

King, M., 'Use of video in child abuse trials' (1988) 1(5) *The Psychologist* 167

Kinports, K., 'Evidence Engendered' [1991] 2 *University of Illinois Law Review* 413

Koffman, L., *Crime Surveys and Victims of Crime* (1996, Cardiff: University of Wales Press)

Kohnken, G., 'The evaluation of statement credibility: Social judgment and expert diagnostic approaches' in (eds.) Spencer, J. R., Nicolson, G., Flin, R. and Bull, R., *Children's Evidence in Legal Proceedings: An International Perspective* (1990, Cambridge: Cambridge Law Faculty)

Konradi, A., '"I Don't Have to be Afraid of You": Rape Survivors' Emotion Management in Court' (1999) 22(1) *Symbolic Interaction* 45

Kranat, V. and Westcott, H., 'Under fire: Lawyers questioning children in criminal courts' (1994) 3(1) *Expert Evidence* 16

La Free, G., Reskin, B. F. and Vischer, C, A., 'Jurors' Responses to Victims' Behaviour and Legal Issues in Sexual Assault Trials' (1985) 32 *Social Problems*, cited in Ward, C. A., *Attitudes Towards Rape* (1995, London: Sage) 103

Lakatos, A., 'Evaluating the Rules of Procedure and Evidence for the International Tribunal in the Former Yugoslavia: Balancing Witnesses' Needs Against Defendants' Rights' (1995) 46 *Hastings Law Journal* 909

Landsman, S., 'Rise of the Contentious Spirit: Adversary Procedure in Eighteenth Century England' (1990) 75 *Cornell Law Review* 497

—— 'From Gilbert to Bentham: The Reconceptualisation of the Evidence Theory' (1989) 36 *Wayne Law Review* 1149

—— *The Adversary System: A Description and Defense* (1984, Washington, DC: American Enterprise Institute for Public Policy Research)

Law Commission for England and Wales, *Evidence in Criminal Proceedings: Hearsay and Related Topics* Consultation Paper No. 138 (1995, London: HMSO)

Law Commission for England and Wales, *Criminal law: Corroboration of evidence in criminal trials* (1991, London: HMSO)

Law Reform Commission NSW, *Report 80 People with an Intellectual Disability and the Criminal Justice System* (1996, Sydney: Law Reform Commission NSW)

Law Reform Commission of Western Australia, *Review of the Criminal and Civil Justice System Final Report* (1999, Perth: Law Reform Commission of Western Australia)

—— *Evidence of Children and Other Vulnerable Witnesses* (1991, Perth: Law Reform Commission of Western Australia)

Lees, S., *Carnal Knowledge: Rape on Trial* (1996, London: Hamish Hamilton)

—— 'Judicial Rape' (1993) 16 *Women's Studies International Forum* 26

Leigh, L. H. and Hall Williams, J. E., *The Management of the Prosecution Process in Denmark, Sweden and the Netherlands* (1981, Leamington Spa: James Hall)

Lensing, H. and Rayar, L., 'Notes on Criminal Procedure in the Netherlands' [1992] *Criminal Law Review* 623

Leuw, E., 'De Behandlung van Verkrachtinszaken voor de Rechtbank' (1985) *Tijdschrift voor Criminologie* 212

Levy, E., *Examination of Witnesses in Criminal Cases* (1991, Canada: Thompson Professional Publishing) 203

Lipovsky, J., 'The impact of court on children: Research findings and practical recommendations' (1994) 9(2) *Journal of Interpersonal Violence* 238

Loftus, E., *Eyewitness Testimony* (1979, Cambridge, Mass: Harvard University Press)

Louw, D. and Olivier, P., 'Listening to Children in South Africa' in (eds.) Bottoms, B. and Goodman, G., *International Perspectives on Child Abuse and Children's Testimony* (1996, London: Sage) 180

Luban, D., 'Partisanship, Betrayal and Autonomy in the Lawyer–Client Relationship: A Reply to Stephen Ellman' (1990) 90 *Columbia Law Review* 1004

—— *Lawyers and Justice: An Ethical Study* (1988, Princeton: Princeton University Press)

—— 'The Adversary System Excuse' in (ed.) Luban, D., *The Good Lawyer* (1983, Totowa, New Jersey: Rowman and Allanheld) 83

—— *Lawyers and Justice: An Ethical Study* (1988, Princeton: Princeton University Press)

Lubet, S., 'Persuasion at Trial' (1997) 21 *American Journal of Trial Advocacy* 325

Lurigio, A. J., 'Are all Victims Alike? The Adverse, Generalised and Differential Impact of Crime (1987) 33(4) *Crime and Delinquency* 452

Mack, K., '"You should scrutinise her evidence with great care": Corroboration of women's testimony about sexual assault' in (ed.) Easteal, P., *Balancing the Scales: Rape, Law Reform and Australian Culture* (1998, Sydney: Federation Press) 59

—— 'Continuing Barriers to Women's Credibility: A Feminist Perspective on the Proof Process' (1993) 4 *Criminal Law Forum* 327

Mackarel, M., Raitt, F. and Moody, S., *Briefing paper on legal issues and witness protection in criminal cases* (2001, Edinburgh: Scottish Executive Central Research Unit)

MacKay, R. and Colman, A., 'Equivocal Rulings on Expert Psychological and Psychiatric Evidence: Turning a Muddle into a Nonsense' [1996] *Criminal Law Review* 88

—— 'Excluding Expert Evidence: A tale of ordinary folk and common experience' [1991] *Criminal Law Review* 800

Macpherson, W., *The Stephen Lawrence Inquiry: Report of an inquiry* (1999, London: HMSO)

Maguire, M. and Bennett, T., *Burglary in a Dwelling* (1982, London: Heinemann) 125

Maley, Y. and Fahey, R., 'Presenting the Evidence: Constructions of Reality in Court' (1991) 4(10) *International Journal for the Semiotics of Law* 3

Marchant, R. and Page M., 'The Memorandum and disabled children' in (eds.) Westcott, H. and Jones, J., *Perspectives on the Memorandum, Policy, Practice and Research in Investigative Interviewing* (1997, Aldershot: Arena) 67

Martin, S. and Thomson, D., 'Videotapes and Multiple Interviews: The Effects on the Child Witness' (1994) 1(2) *Psychiatry, Psychology and Law* 119

Massaro, T., 'The Dignity Value of Face to Face Confrontations' (1988) 40 *University of Florida Law Review* 863

Matoesian, G., *Reproducing Rape* (1993, Cambridge: Polity Press)

Mawby. R. and Walklate, S., *Critical Victimology* (1994, London: Sage)

Maynard, W., *Witness Intimidation: Strategies for Prevention* (1994, London: Home Office Police Research Group Crime Detection and Prevention)

McBarnet, D., 'Victim in the Witness Box: Confronting Victimology's Stereotype' (1983) 7 *Contemporary Crises* 293

McColgan, A., *Women under the Law* (2000, Essex: Longman)

—— 'Common Law and the Relevance of Sexual History Evidence' (1996) 16 *Oxford Journal of Legal Studies*, 275

McEwan, J., 'In defence of vulnerable witnesses: The Youth Justice and Criminal Evidence Act 1999' (2000) 4 *International Journal of Evidence and Proof* 29

—— *Evidence and the Adversarial Process* (1998, Oxford: Hart)

—— 'Documentary Hearsay Evidence: Refuge for the Vulnerable Witness?' [1989] *Criminal Law Review* 642

McGough, L., *Child Witnesses: Fragile Voices in the American Legal System* (1994, New Haven: Yale University Press)

McNamera, P., 'Cross Examination of the Complainant in a Trial for Rape' (1981) 5 *Criminal Law Journal* 25

Mencap, *Barriers to Justice: A Mencap study into how the criminal justice system treats people with learning disabilities* (1997, London: Mencap)

Mendelsohn, B., 'The Origin of the Doctrine of Victimology' in (ed.) Rock, P., *Victimology* (1994, Aldershot: Dartmouth) 4

Mewett, A. W., 'Credibility of Witnesses' (1995) 37 *Criminal Law Quarterly* 37

Miers, D., 'The Responsibilities and Rights of Victims of Crime' (1992) 55 *Modern Law Review* 482

Mikkelson, H., 'Towards a Redefinition of the Role of the Court Interpreter' (1998) 3(1) *Interpreting* 21

Miller, G. R. and Stiff, J. B., 'Applied issues in studying deceptive communication' in (ed.) Feldman, R. S., *Applications of Non-Verbal Behavioral Theories and Research* (1992, Hillsdale, New Jersey: Erlbaum)

Miller, M. and Mauet, T., 'The Psychology of Jury Persuasion' (1999) 22 *American Journal of Trial Advocacy* 549

Milne, R. and Bull, R., *Investigative Interviewing Psychology and Practice* (1999, Chichester: Wiley)

Mirlees-Black, C., Budd, T., Partridge, S. and Mayhew, P., *The 1998 British Crime Survey England and Wales* (1998, London: Home Office)

Montoya, J., 'On truth and shielding in child abuse trials' (1992) 43 *Hastings Law Review* 1259

Morgan, E. M., *Some Problems of Proof Under the Anglo-American System of Litigation* (1975 Westport, Conn.: Greenwood Press)

Morgan, J. and Zedner, L., *Child Victims, Crime, Impact and Criminal Justice* (1992, Oxford: Clarendon Press)

—— and Plotnikoff, J., 'Children as victims of crime: Procedure in court' in (eds.) Spencer, J., Nicolson, G., Flin, R. and Bull, R., *Children's Evidence in Legal Proceedings: An International Perspective* (1990, Cambridge: Cambridge Law Faculty) 191.

—— Willem Winkel, F. and Williams, K. S., 'Protection of and Compensation for Victims of Crime' in (eds.) Harding, C., Fennell, P., Jörg, N. and Swart, B., *Criminal Justice in Europe: A Comparative Study* (1995, Oxford: Clarendon Press)

Morris, R., 'The gum syndrome: Predicaments in court interpreting' (1999) 6(1) *Forensic Linguistics* 8

—— 'The Interlingual Interpreter: Cypher or Intelligent Participant?' (1993) 6(18) *International Journal for the Semiotics of Law* 291

Morrison, J. and Leith, P., *The Barrister's World and the Nature of Law* (1992, Milton Keynes: Open University Press)

Mortimer, A. and Shepherd, E., 'The Frailty of Children's Testimony' in (eds.) Heaton-Armstrong, A., Shepherd, E. and Wolchover, D., *Analysing Witness Testimony* (1999, London: Blackstone) 46

Munkman, J. H., *The Techniques of Advocacy* (1986, London: Sweet and Maxwell)

Murphy, P., 'Previous Consistent and Inconsistent Statements: A Proposal to Make Life Easier for Juries' [1985] *Criminal Law Review* 270

Murray, K., *Live television link: An evaluation of its use by child witnesses in Scottish criminal trials* (1995, Edinburgh: Scottish Office)

Myers, J., 'A decade of international reform to accommodate child witnesses' in (eds.) Bottoms, B. and Goodman, G., (eds.) *International Perspectives on Child Abuse and Children's Testimony: Psychological Research and the Law* (1996, California: Sage) 221

—— Saywitz, K. and Goodman, G., 'Psychological research on children as witnesses: Practical implications for forensic interviews and courtroom testimony' (1996) 28 *Pacific Law Journal* 3

NACRO, *International Comparisons in Criminal Justice: The London Seminars* (1993, London: NACRO)

Napley, D., *The Technique of Persuasion* (1970, London: Sweet & Maxwell)

New Zealand Law Commission, *Evidence Report 55 Volume 1: Reform of the Law* (1999, Wellington: New Zealand Law Commission) 460

—— *The Evidence of Children and other Vulnerable Witnesses* (1996, Wellington: New Zealand Law Commission)

Nijboer, J. F., 'Protection of Victims in Rape and Sexual Abuse Cases in the Netherlands' in (ed.) Nijboer, J. F., *Proof and Criminal Justice Systems Comparative Essays* (1995, Frankfurt: Peter Lang) 99

—— 'Common Law Tradition in Evidence Scholarship Observed from a Continental Perspective' (1993) 41 *American Journal of Comparative Law* 299

—— 'The Law of Evidence in Criminal Cases (The Netherlands)' in (ed.) Nijboer, J. F., *Forensic Expertise and the Law of Evidence* (1992, Amsterdam: Elsevier) 63

—— 'The Requirement of a Fair Process and the Law of Evidence in Dutch Criminal Proceedings' in (ed.) Nijboer, J. F., *Forensic Expertise* (1992, Amsterdam: Elsevier)

Nilsen, E., 'Criminal defense lawyer's reliance on bias and prejudice' (1994) 8 *Georgetown Journal of Legal Ethics* 1

Norris, J. and Edward, M., 'Myths, Hidden Facts and Common Sense: Expert Opinion Evidence and the Assessment of Credibility' (1995) 38 *Criminal Law Quarterly* 73

O'Barr, W. M., *Language, power and strategy in the courtroom* (1982, New York: Academic Press)

O'Grady C., *Child Witnesses and Jury Trials: An Evaluation of the Use of Closed Circuit Television and Removable Screens in Western Australia* (1996, Perth: Western Australia Ministry of Justice)

O'Sullivan, M., Ekman, P. and Freisen, W. V., 'The effect of behavioral comparison in detecting deception' (1988) 12 *Journal of Non-verbal Behavior* 203

Office of Women's Policy, Department of Equity and Fair Trading (Qld) *Report of the Taskforce on Women and the Criminal Code* (2000, Brisbane: Office of Women's Policy)

Orenstein, A., '"My God!": A Feminist Critique of the Excited Utterance Exception to the Hearsay Rule' (1997) 85 *California Law Review* 159

Osborne, C., 'Hearsay and the Court of Human Rights' [1993] *Criminal Law Review* 255

Osner, N., Quinn, A. and Crown, G., *Criminal Justice Systems in Other Jurisdictions* (1993, London: HMSO)

Pannick, D., *Advocates* (1992, Oxford: Oxford University Press)

Papke, D. R., *Narrative and Legal Discourse: A Reader in Storytelling and Law* (1991, Liverpool: Deborah Charles)

Pattenden, R., 'The Character of Victims and Third Parties in Criminal Proceedings Other than Rape Trials' [1986] *Criminal Law Review* 367

Pattullo, P., *Judging Women* (1983, London: NCCL)

Penders, L., 'Guidelines for Police and Prosecutors: An interest of victims; a matter of justice' in *First European Conference of Victim Support Workers: Guidelines for Victim Support in Europe* (1989, Utrecht: The Netherlands)

Perlman, N., Ericson, K., Esses, V and Isaacs, B., 'The Developmentally Handicapped Witness: Competence as a Function of Question Format' (1994) 18(2) *Law and Human Behaviour* 186

Perry, N. W., McAuliff, B. D., Tam, P., Claycomb, L., Dostal, C. and Flanagan, C., 'When Lawyers Question Children Is Justice Served?' (1995) 19 *Law and Human Behaviour* 609

Peters, D., 'The influence of stress and arousal on the child witness' in (ed.) Doris, J., *The Suggestibility of Children's Recollections: Implications for Eyewitness Testimony* (1991, Washington: American Psychological Association) 60

Peterson, C., Dowden, C. and Tobin, J., 'Interviewing preschoolers: Comparisons of yes/no and wh- questions' (1999) 23(5) *Law and Human Behaviour* 539

Pinard, M., 'Limitations on judicial activism in criminal trials' (2000) 33 *Connecticut Law Review* 243

Pizzi, W., 'Crime victims in German courtrooms: A comparative perspective on American problems' (1996) 32 *Stanford Journal of International Law* 37

Plotnikoff, J. and Woolfson, R., *Prosecuting Child Abuse: An Evaluation of the Government's Speedy Progress Policy* (1995, London: Blackstone)

Pointing, M. and Maguire, M., 'The Rediscovery of the Crime Victim' in (eds.) Maguire, M. and Pointing, M., *Victims of Crime: A New Deal?* (1988, Milton Keynes: Open University Press)

Pollard, C., 'Victims and the Criminal Justice System: A New Vision' [2000] *Criminal Law Review* 5

Practice Direction by the Lord Chief Justice of England and Wales, Trial of Children and Young Persons in the Crown Court (February, 2000)

Queensland Children's Commission, *Response to Queensland Law Reform Commission Discussion Paper WP No. 53 (1998) The Receipt of Evidence By Queenslands Courts: The Evidence of Children* (1999, Brisbane: Queensland Children's Commission)

Queensland Law Reform Commission, *The Receipt of Evidence by Queensland Courts: The Evidence of Children*, Report No. 55 Part 1 (2000, Brisbane: Queensland Law Reform Commission)

Raine, J. W. and Smith, R. E., *The Victim/Witness in Court Project: Report of the Research Programme* (1991, London: Victim Support)

Raitt, F., 'Gender Bias in the Hearsay Rule' in (eds.) Childs, M., Ellison, L., *Feminist Perspectives on Evidence* (2000, London: Cavendish) 59

—— and Zeedyk, S., *The Implicit Relation of Psychology and Law, Women and Syndrome Evidence* (2000, London: Routledge)

Re, L., 'Oral v. written evidence: the myth of the "impressive witness"' (1983) 57 *Australian Law Journal* 679

Recommendation No. R (97) 13 on Intimidation of Witnesses and the Rights of the Defence

Recommendation (87) 21 on Assistance to Victims and Prevention of Victimisation

Recommendation No. R (85) 11 on the Position of the Victim in the Framework of Criminal Law and Procedure

Reiz, J., 'Why we probably cannot adopt the German advantage in civil procedure' (1990) 75 *Iowa Law Review* 987

Resick, P., 'Psychological Effects of Victimization: Implications for the Criminal Justice System (1987) 33(4) *Crime and Delinquency* 468

Rock, P., 'Acknowledging victims' needs and rights' (1999) 35 *Criminal Justice Matters* 4

—— *Victimology* (1994, Aldershot: Dartmouth)

—— *The Social World of the English Crown Court* (1993, Oxford: Clarendon Press)

—— 'Witnesses and Space in a Crown Court' (1991) 31 *British Journal of Criminology* 268

—— *Helping Victims of Crime* (1990, Oxford: Clarendon Press)

Ross, D., Hopkins, S., Hanson, E., Lindsay, R., Hazen, K. and Eslinger, T., 'The impact of protective shields and videotape testimony on conviction rates in a simulated trial of child sexual abuse' (1994) 18(5) *Law and Human Behavior* 553

Rossett, A., 'Trial and Discretion in Dutch Criminal Justice' (1972) 19 *UCLA Law Review* 353

Roth, M. D., 'Laissez faire videoconferencing: Remote witness testimony and adversarial truth' (2000) 48 *UCLA Law Review* 185

Rumney, P., 'Male Rape in the Courtroom: Issues and Concerns [2001] *Criminal Law Review* 205

Saltzburg, S., 'The unnecessarily expanding role of the American trial judge' (1978) 64 *Virginia Law Review* 1

Sanders, A., Creaton, J., Bird, S. and Weber, L., *Victims with Learning Disabilities Negotiating the Criminal Justice System* (1997, Oxford: Centre for Criminological Research, University of Oxford)

Sanders, A., Creaton, J., Bird, S. and Weber, L., *Witnesses with Learning Disabilities*, Home Office Research Findings 44 (1996, London: HMSO)

Saywitz, K., 'Children's Conceptions of the Legal System: "Court is a Place to Play Basketball"' in (eds.) Ceci, S. J., Ross, D. F. and Toglia, M. P., *Perspectives on Children's Testimony* (1989, New York: Springer Verlag)

—— and Nathanson, R., 'Children's testimony and their perception of stress in and out of the courtroom' (1993) 17 *Child Abuse and Neglect* 613

—— Synder, L. and Nathanson, R., 'Facilitating the communicative competence of the child witness' (1999) 3(1) *Applied Developmental Science* 58

Scallen, E., 'Constitutional Dimensions of Hearsay Reform: Toward a Three Dimensional Confrontation Clause' (1992) 76 *Minnesota Law Review* 623

Schepple, K. L., 'Just the Facts, Ma'am: Sexualised Violence, Evidentiary Habits, and the Revision of Truths' (1992) 37 *New York School Law Review* 123

Scottish Executive, *Redressing the Balance* (2000, Edinburgh: Scottish Executive)

Scottish Office, *Towards a Just Conclusion: Vulnerable and Intimidated Witnesses in Scottish Criminal and Civil Cases* (1998, Edinburgh: Scottish Office)

Sedley, Lord Justice *Freedom, Law and Justice* The Hamlyn Lectures; 50th series (1999, London: Sweet & Maxwell)

Shapland, J. and Cohen, D., 'Facilities for Victims: The Role of the Police and the Courts' [1987] *Criminal Law Review* 28

—— Willmore, J. and Duff, P., *Victims in the Criminal Justice System* (1985, Aldershot: Gower)

Sherman, A., 'Sympathy for The Devil: Examining a Defendant's Right to Confront before the International War Crimes Tribunal' (1996) 10 *Emory International Law Review* 833

Sherr, A., *Legal Practice Handbook: Advocacy* (1993, London: Blackstone)

Siegel, C. K., Budd, E. C., Spanhel, C. L. and Schroenrock, C. J., 'Asking questions of retarded persons: A comparison of yes-no and either/or formats' (1981) *Applied Research in Mental Retardation* 347

Simon, W., 'The ethics of criminal defense' (1993) 91 *Michigan Law Review* 1703

Smith, L. J. F., *Concerns About Rape*, Home Office Research Study No. 106 (1989, London: HMSO)

South African Law Commission, *The Protection of the Child Witness Project 71* (1991, Pretoria: South African Law Commission)

Spencer, J., 'Hearsay Reform: A Bridge Not Far Enough' [1996] *Criminal Law Review* 29, 33

—— 'Orality and the Evidence of Absent Witnesses' [1994] *Criminal Law Review* 628

Spencer, J. R., 'The Memorandum: An international perspective' in (eds.) Westcott, H. and Jones, J., *Perspectives on the Memorandum: Policy, Practice and Research in Investigative Interviewing* (1997, Aldershot: Arena) 105

—— 'Reforming the law on children's evidence in England: The Pigot Committee and after' in (eds.) Dent, H. and Flin, R., *Children as Witnesses* (1992, Chichester: Wiley) 113

—— 'Children's Evidence and the Criminal Justice Act: A Lost Opportunity' (1991) November *Magistrate* 182

—— and Flin, R., *Evidence of Children: The Law and the Psychology* (1993, London: Blackstone)

Spencer, J. R., Nicholson G., Flin, R. and Bull, R., *Children's Evidence in Legal Proceedings: An International Perspective* (1990, Cambridge: Selwyn College)

Stanchi, K., 'The Paradox of the Fresh Complaint Rule' (1996) 37 *Boston College Law Review* 441

Stephenson, G., *The Psychology of Criminal Justice* (1992, Oxford: Blackwell)

Sternberg, K., Lamb, M. and Hershkowitz, I., 'Child Sexual Abuse Investigations in Israel: Evaluating Innovative Practices' in (eds.) Bottoms, B. and Goodman, G., *International Perspectives on Child Abuse and Children's Testimony* (1996, London: Sage) 7

Stolwijk, S. A. M., 'Wachten op Cardot' (1991) 21 *Delikt en Delinkwent* 109

Stone, M., *Cross-Examination in Criminal Trials* (1995, London: Butterworths)

—— 'Instant Lie Detection? Demeanour and Credibility in Criminal Trials' [1991] *Criminal Law Review* 821

—— *The Proof of Facts in Criminal Trials* (1984, Edinburgh: Green)

Stuart, H. V., 'Towards a Civilised Law Against Sexual Violence'(1990, unpublished paper)

Suni, E., 'Who stole the cookie from the cookie jar? The law and ethics of shifting blame in criminal cases' (2000) 68 *Fordham Law Review* 1643

Swart, A. H. J., 'The Netherlands' in (ed.) Van Den Wyngaert, C., *Criminal Procedure Systems in the European Community* (1993, London: Butterworths)

Swart, B. and Young, J., 'The European Convention on Human Rights and Criminal Justice in the Netherlands and the United Kingdom' in (eds.) Harding, C., Fennell, P., Jörg, N. and Swart, B., *Criminal Justice in Europe: A Comparative Study* (1995, Oxford: Clarendon Press) 71

Swim, J., Borgida, E. and McCoy, K., 'Videotaped versus in court witness testimony: Does protecting the child witness jeopardize due process?' (1993) 23 *Journal of Applied Social Psychology* 603

Tak, P., *Criminal Justice Systems in Europe: The Netherlands* (1993, Kluwer: HEUNI)

Tapper, C., *Cross and Tapper on Evidence* 9th edn. (1999, London: Butterworths)

Taslitz, A., *Rape and the Culture of the Courtroom* (1999, New York University Press)

—— 'Patriarchal Stories: Cultural Rape Narratives in the Courtroom' (1996) 5 *Southern California Review of Law and Women's Studies* 387

Temkin, J., 'Prosecuting and defending rape: Perspectives from the Bar' (2000) 27(2) *Journal of Law and Society* 219.

—— 'Disability, Child Abuse and Criminal Justice' [1994] *Modern Law Review* 402

—— 'Sexual History Evidence: The Ravishment of Section 2' [1993] *Criminal Law Review* 3

—— *Rape and the Legal Process* (1987, London: Sweet and Maxwell)

Thornburg, E., 'Metaphors Matter: How Images of Battle, Sports and Sex Shape the Adversary System' (1995) 10 *Wisconsin Women's Law Journal* 13

Torrey, M., 'When Will We Be Believed? Rape Myths and the Idea of a Fair Trial in Rape Prosecutions' (1991) 24 *University of California, Davis Law Review* 1013

Tully, B. and Cahill, D., *Police interviewing of the mentally handicapped: An experimental study* (1984, London: The Police Federation)

Turbak, N., 'Effective Direct Examination' (1998) 34 *Trial* 68

United Nations, *Handbook On Justice For Victims: On the use and application of the United Nations Declaration of Basic Principles of Justice for Victims of Crime and Abuse of Power* (1999, New York: United Nations ODCCP)

United Nations, *Declaration of Basic Principles of Justice for Victims of Crime and Abuse of Power* (1985)

—— *United Nations Standard Minimum Rules for the Administration of Juvenile Justice* ('The Beijing Rules'), UN GA Res. 40/33 1985

Van de Bunt, H. G., 'Officieren van Justitie: verslag van een participerend observatieonderzoek' cited in Field, S., Alldridge, P. and Jörg, N., 'Prosecutors, Examining Judges and the Control of Police Investigations' in (eds.), Harding, C., Fennell, P., Jörg, N. and Swart, B., *Criminal Justice in Europe: A Comparative Study* (1995, Oxford: Clarendon Press) 236

Van der Merwe, S., 'Cross-examination of the (Sexually Abused) Child Witness in a Constitutionalized Adversarial Trial System: Is the South African Intermediary the Solution?' in (eds.) Nijboer, J. F. and Reijntjes, J. M., *Proceedings of the first World Conference on New Trends in Criminal Investigation and Evidence*, The Hague, 1–5 December 1995, World Conference on New Trends in Criminal Investigation and Evidence (1997, Netherlands: Koninklijke Vermande) 240

Van Dijk, P. and Van Hoof, G. J. H., *Theory and Practice of the European Convention on Human Rights* 3rd edn. (1998, The Hague: Kluwer Law International)

Van Driem, G., 'Waarom Slachtoffers van Seksueel Geweld het Strafproces Moeten Mijden' in (ed.) Soetenhorst de Savorin Lohman, J., *Slachtoffers van misdrijven ontwikkelingen in hulpververlening recht en beleid* (1989, Arnhem: Gouda Quint)

Van Kessel, G., 'Adversary Excesses in the American Criminal Trial' (1992) 67 *Notre Dame Law Review* 403

Victim Support, *Women, Rape and the Criminal Justice System* (1996, London: Victim Support)

—— *The Rights of Victims of Crime: A Policy Paper* (1995, London: Victim Support)

Vogelman, L., 'The big black man syndrome: The Rodney King trial and the use of racial stereotypes in the courtroom' (1993) 20 *Fordham Urban Law Journal* 571

Vogler, R., 'Learning from the Inquisitors' (1994) June *Legal Executive* 29

VOICE, *Competent to tell the truth* (1998, Derby: Voice UK)

Von Hentig, H., *The Criminal and his Victim* (1948, New Haven, Conn.: Yale University Press)

Wade, A., Lawson, A. and Aldridge, J., 'Stories in Court' (1998) 10(2) *Child and Family Law Quarterly* 179

Walker, A. G., *Handbook on Questioning Children: A Linguistic Perspective* (1994, Washington: American Bar Association)

—— 'Questioning Young Children in Court: A Linguistic Case Study' (1993) 17 *Law and Human Behaviour* 59

Walker, L., *The Battered Woman* (1979, New York: Harper & Row)

Weinreb, L. L., *The Denial of Justice* (1977, London: Free Press)

Wellborn, O. G., 'Demeanour' (1991) 76 *Cornell Law Review* 1075

Wellman, F. L., *The Art of Cross-examination* 4th edn. (1997, New York: Simon and Shuster)

Wemmers, J. M., *Victims in the Criminal Justice System* (1996, Amsterdam: Kluger Publications)

Westcott, H., 'Children's experiences of being examined and cross-examined: The opportunity to be heard?' (1995) 4(1) *Expert Evidence* 13

—— Davies, G. and Clifford, B., 'The credibility of child witnesses seen on closed circuit television' (1991) 15(1) *Adoption and Fostering* 14

Westcott, H., Davies, G. and Spencer, J., 'Protecting the child witness: Hearsay techniques and other innovations' (1999) 5 *Psychology, Public Policy and Law* 282

Whitney, L. and Cook, A., *The Use of Closed Circuit Television in New Zealand Courts: The First Six Trials* (1990, Wellington: Department of Justice)

Wigmore, J. H., *A Treatise on the Anglo-American System of Evidence in Trials Common Law* 3rd edn. (1940, Boston: Little, Brown) vol. 5

—— *Evidence* (1976, Boston, Mass.: Chadbourn revision) vol. 4, 298

Wrottesley, F. J., *The Examination of Witnesses in Court* (1931, London: Sweet and Maxwell) 64

Yaroshefsky, E., 'Balancing Victim's Rights and Vigorous Advocacy for the Defendant' (1989) *Annual Survey of American Law* 152

Yuille, J. and Daylen, J., 'The Impact of Traumatic Events on Eyewitness Memory' in (eds.) Thompson, C., Herrmann, D., Read, J., Bruce, D., Payne, D. and Toglia, M., *Eyewitness Memory* (1998, Mahwah, New Jersey: Lawrence Erlbaum Associates) 155

Zedner, L., 'Victims' in (eds.) Maguire, M., Morgan, R. and Reiner, R., *The Oxford Handbook of Criminology* 2nd edn. (1997, Oxford: Oxford University Press) 577

Zuckerman, A. A. S., *Principles of Criminal Evidence* (1989, Oxford: Clarendon Press)

INDEX